CRISES IN TIME

First published in 2024 by
Sean Kingston Publishing
www.seankingston.co.uk
Canon Pyon

British Library Cataloguing in Publication Data
A catalogue record for this book is available from the British Library.
The moral rights of the editor and authors have been asserted.

Paperback ISBN 978-1-912385-59-1

Ebook DOI 10.26581/B.CROO01

Crises in Time

Ethnographic Horizons in
Amazonia and Melanesia

EDITED BY

TONY CROOK AND MARILYN STRATHERN

SK publishing

Sean Kingston Publishing
www.seankingston.co.uk
Canon Pyon

PREFACE

Crises in time

TONY CROOK[1]

Time has been central to anthropology's depiction of crises, including its own. Anthropologists and the discipline of anthropology are unavoidably implicated in multiple crises in their own times and of their own making. Generations of scholars have trained in epochs defined by 'endless methodological debates [and] contests of perspective' constituting various 'turns' in a wider disciplinary crisis – so much so that with hindsight Kapferer suggests that 'Crisis is sociocultural anthropology's mode of disciplinary reproduction.' (2018:1). However, Clifford's original diagnosis also poses an important alternative thought experiment: 'What would it require, for example, consistently to associate the inventive, resilient, enormously varied societies of Melanesia with the cultural *future* of the planet?' (1986:115, original emphasis). As the following chapters attest, Clifford could of course also have said Amazonia.

A preface is conventionally a forward-looking support to the reader that anticipates the future by framing what follows; but at the same time, it rehearses the past, with a backwards look at the volume's origins, written in retrospect, after the event. The moment affords its own ethnographic horizon, a position which differs from others preceding and following it in a research-and-writing project. The present volume and the wider 'Ethnographic Horizons' project are motivated by the consequences of, and responses to, diverse conceptual bases informing descriptions, analyses and interventions, and open up questions as to what figures as a 'crisis' and how notions of 'time' are interlinked. Of course, such conceptualizations are polyphonic and instructive – as our ethnographic examples from Amazonia, Melanesia, and one from North America, discuss. For example, the causes, 'responsibilizations' and consequences of crises entail particular commitments to time (Crook and Strathern 2021). *Crises in Time*

[1]   This work, produced under the auspices of the Ethnographic Horizons project at the Centre for Pacific Studies, University of St Andrews, was supported by the International Balzan Foundation.

includes ethnographic examples and analyses that problematize these terms, which serve the volume as catalysts and provocations to question the bases for conceptual equivalence or co-dependent linkages.

Ideas of time and ideas of crisis might appear as naturally bound up, implicating each other as mutually necessary for their definition. As a consequence, understanding time as linear would carry the possibility of time running out. Coming to a critical point or even to the end of time would constitute a crisis. Equally, responding to crises in this reckoning carries an urgency to act in time. Problematizing such connections is an indicative reminder of a particular ethnographic horizon – in which taken for granted connections are seen to lose force. It is surely telling that multiple contemporary crises are experienced hand in hand with disturbances to a naturalness of understandings of time. That ideas of time are in crisis, so to speak, provides impetus for the book's contributions. Going beyond the question of how diverse ideas of time might characterize different ideas of crisis begs the question of alternatives – whether belying primacy or refusing necessity – to such interlinkages.

Strathern's Introduction to this volume sets out an approach to the ethnographic horizon as a vantage point, and elaborates how an ethnographer's own temporal horizon may not be the best position from which to approach narratives of crises and of time. The method here involves nothing more complex or elusive than straightforward borrowing from examples of relational logics and of particular social, aesthetic and temporal commitments. *Crises in Time* acknowledges that an ethnographer's own temporal figuration and horizon necessarily afford a specific and partial view, and explores this as a productive vantage point on problems motivating present thinking: problems such as 'crises' and 'time', as described and analysed in this volume, for example.

References

Clifford, J. 1986. 'On ethnographic allegory'. In J. Clifford and G. Marcus (eds), *Writing Culture: The Poetics and Politics of Ethnography*, pp. 98–121. Berkeley: University of California Press.

Crook, T. and Strathern, M. 2021. 'The attribution of responsibility and modes of crisis response', , Association of Social Anthropologists Conference 2021, St Andrews and online: www.theasa.org/conferences/asa2021/panels#9953 (accessed 20 May 2023).

Kapferer, B. 2018. 'Anthropology at risk', *Anthropology Today* 34(6):1–2.

Acknowledgements

Crises in Time is a collective work arising from the 'Time and the ethnographic horizon in moments of crisis' research project, which was funded by the International Balzan Foundation as part of the 2018 Balzan Prize in Social Anthropology awarded to Marilyn Strathern. Hosted by the Centre for Pacific Studies in the Department of Social Anthropology at the University of St Andrews, this venture has contributed to St Andrews' regional expertise in South America and the Pacific, and thematic interests in time and temporality. For a research project running between 2019 and 2022, the Covid-19 pandemic provided an all-too-real first-hand comparative example of shared crisis – and involved in particular the reconfiguration of the geographically distant participants, each living in their home countries, whose research focuses on Amazonia and Melanesia and who comprise this volume's authors. Whilst St Andrews and the Centro Incontri Umani in Ascona, Switzerland, served as occasional gathering points, the distributed research format came into its own through enlivened virtual connections. This extended the project's reach and maintained our presence in one another's horizons – and thus enacted theoretical concerns in unexpectedly important and productive ways. *Crises in Time* stands as an acknowledgement of the International Balzan Foundation's support, especially for our four early career researchers, whose chapters form the core of this volume, accompanied by contributions from the two editors and from the two project advisors.

We are very grateful to both Aparecida Vilaça and Andrew Moutu for their encouragement and advice along the way; in the context of this volume, that extends to Vilaça for providing her own perspective on the endeavour, and to Moutu for allowing us to reproduce a dialogue that came out of the depths of Covid-19. Christina Toren and Françoise Barbira Freedman have been stimulating commentators. The Balzan Foundation has also been supporting the doctoral research of Gregory Bablis (National Museum and Art Gallery, Port Moresby, supervised by Adam Reed at St Andrews University), who enlivened our collective discussion during his pre-fieldwork year.

St Andrews University was proactive in its support of the original project ('Time and the ethnographic horizon in moments of crisis') and generous in its facilitations of the various research trajectories involved. This would not have happened without the enthusiasm of the Principal, Professor Dame Sally Mapstone, and the goodwill of the Vice-Principal for Research, Professor Derek Woollins. The Director of the Centre for Pacific Studies undertook the bulk of the administrative work involved. The project was repeatedly hosted by the Centro Incontri Umani in Ascona, where we especially thank the Director, Angela Hobart, for her hospitality.

Finally, our gratitude is due to those involved in the anonymous review process, and the helpful suggestions that came out of it, and especially to Sean Kingston, and the long vision he had of the potential of this volume.

Tony Crook, St Andrews
Marilyn Strathern, Cambridge

CONTENTS

1

Relocations of time

An introduction

Marilyn Strathern[1]

✳

Bureaucracy in Papua New Guinea, cash credits in Indigenous central Brazil, prophetic movements in the Amazon, military confrontations on Bougainville Island: these are not the subjects that immediately come to mind when social anthropologists bring together Amazonia and Melanesia. That is partly because of anthropology's traditional narratives, with their own sense of time's flow, recalling the formation of those categories (Melanesia, Amazonia) in former analytical ambitions that no longer have currency. This is just one of the senses of time addressed in this book, but by no means the only one.

The starting point of the research from which the book came may be briefly stated. One might think that the more the world changes, the more remote previous epochs become. Anthropologists are, after all, acutely aware that their ethnographic studies engage specific temporal horizons. The kind of present time in which ethnographers carry out their observations helps create an 'ethnographic horizon' bound to recede into the past. The process simply seems the work of time, leaving the horizon's integrity as a record of the then present intact. Yet, in retrospect, the ethnographer's particular present has not necessarily furnished the most appropriate tools for understanding contemporary social life 'of the time'. This becomes not just a matter of evolving analytical interests but also of changing circumstances in the ethnographer's wider universe. What was apparently past can come to make sense in a way that refuses be held at arm's length. Perhaps, indeed, one

1   This work, produced under the auspices of the Ethnographic Horizons project at the Centre for Pacific Studies, University of St Andrews, was supported by the International Balzan Foundation.

should expect slippages between the epoch of the researcher and of what is being researched. Likely at any juncture, the expectation is sharpened when the present seems to point inexorably to disruption. These days, perceptions of societal and environmental calamity – along with new uncertainties and doubtful futures – engender an acute sensibility towards times thought of as in crisis. Time out of joint may even appear as a crisis in time itself, as others have remarked (Bear 2020:ix; Rowlands 2022:44). There is at once nothing new about such perceptions of present times and everything new – insofar as they do indeed inform 'the present'. This is the context in which these chapters were written. Yet there is so much 'crisis' packed into today's present, one wonders how the concept could ever invite fresh understandings of a moment pervaded by a sense of times awry.

These essays hold the promise of a response; it lies in the way they situate crises 'in' relation to time. What follows sketches some of the thinking behind the essays and some of the thinking they have generated. My remarks are in the manner of an interpretation, which also invites the distinct chapters to speak for themselves.

The time of the anthropologist

In her 2021 Firth Lecture Aparecida Vilaça reminds us that more than fifty years ago Lévi-Strauss compared the actions of viruses, which compel other beings to reproduce them, and colonialism's method of imposition. 'Virus' jumps off the page: Lévi-Strauss' words could not have read then as they do now.[2] No one has been untouched by the Covid-19 coronavirus, and there are many senses in which today's anthropologists find that, like everyone else's, their horizons have shifted. To be conscious of the time of the anthropologist is one way in which to appreciate multiplicity in temporal orderings.[3] Thus Fabian's once radical evocation of coevalness, the 'sharing of present Time' (1983:32; and see 2010), which insisted on the temporal parity of Indigenous societies with the rest of the world (against their so often being dismissed as belonging in a traditional past), can nowadays be criticized for not tackling the hegemonic assumption that everyone's present is the same (e.g. Otto 2016; Rifkin 2017). People sharing the same present may be living at different times, and anthropologists write readily of multiple

---

2   Even though the 'pandemic imaginary' has a long history (Lynteris 2020).

3   As Stavrianakis (2019:4) has observed of himself and his interlocutors, the 'historical space in which my own inquiry moves begins in a present, a present in which both I, as subject conducting the inquiry, and those people with whom I sought to engage … are in motion.'

temporalities.[4] Melanesian debates over the now indiginized term 'custom' have highlighted the inappropriate temporal register implied by translating it back into English as 'tradition'. In fact, it is the English language that introduces a reference to time where one might prefer to acknowledge a more general metaphysical force inseparable from continuous change (Hirsch 2021:20, apropos the Melanesian Fuyuge),[5] or, with Fausto and Heckenberger (2007:5) on Amazonia, the capacity for constant transformation.

Note how the anthropologist's sense of time shifts. Rifkin's (2017:30) 'temporal frames of reference' are deliberately pluralized in order to talk (in the context of settler North America) about both Native and non-native trajectories, and thereby hold them together without implying notions of time shared in the same present. The impetus to recognize coevalness or contemporaneity across societies thus reappears again,[6] but through Rifkin opening up another horizon of time, now one of 'discrepant temporalities' or 'interlocking epochs' affecting one another.[7] His is a call to action. Time, ethnographically understood, is henceforth to be a register of productive differentiation. The issue is how far we wish to take this.

Fausto and Heckenberger start with a familiar location for the anthropologist's time, often evoked in tandem with evolving assumptions and paradigms within the discipline (see Foster *et al.* 1979:330; Howell and Talle 2012:15, noting Colson 1984). In fact they take transformations in anthropological models as liable to a suspicious presentism, especially when it can be shown how the models align with global political or economic trends.

---

4   A thorough discussion of the notion of temporality is found in Ringel (2016). He argues that the concept of 'multiple temporality' conflates understanding the character of 'culturally' discrete objects or epochs with the phenomenon of co-existing hetereogeneity in temporal relations; for the latter he prefers to talk of 'temporal multiplicity' (see also Rifkin 2017:16).

5   Hirsch (2021:214) later cites Gow's (2001:309) 'transformations of transformations' in this context. On the ironic 'forgetting' of 'custom', see Demian 2021.

6   That is, Fabian's argument about restoring dignity to accounts of Indigenous peoples, by stressing the historical reality of their co-existence with colonizers and others, is turned around to demand the dignity of treating people's frames of reference (that which renders anything coeval) on their own terms. Rifkin (2017:31) makes it clear that the problem was with the way the earlier formulation came to be interpreted as a seeming endorsement of a universal chronology.

7   Thus, in the era of US treaties with Native peoples, the non-natives' frame of reference was oriented around settler anticipations of civilization, whereas Native frames of reference focused on land long in their trust being sustained in face of encroachment (Rifkin 2017:77–8, 95). My rendering is not altogether fair to Rifkin, who also tries to overcome the antinomy by advocating the political recognition of 'temporal sovereignty' (ibid.:179).

Accusing new theoretical moves of being fashionable is of course always in the critic's arsenal.[8] However, their point is that the constant 'acceleration of our reflexive consciousness' has an untoward effect; it pulls anthropologists 'out of time', making them 'incapable of defining [their] own dynamic intellectual tradition' (Fausto and Heckenberger 2007:3). One might indeed put it that anthropologists are invariably out of time in some respect, whether in relation to their discipline or to their object of study. Writing of the Malaysian Chewong, whose cosmology had so inspired her, Howell (2012:159) years later found herself turning to older anthropological debates in which she had hardly participated. The savage deforestation of Chewong lands had subsequently focused her interests on hunting and gathering practices, and literature that had once passed her by became urgently present.

The possibility of being thrown out of time looms large when the time of the anthropologist entails a future of mass extinction – imagining, for example, the next pandemic as its harbinger. Lynteris (2020:1) takes this as one of the many 'mythical variations of the end of the world' delineated by Danowski and Viveiros de Castro (2017), to whom time is already in a differentiating mode. For an almost inconceivable horizon of termination is to be found in present-day settler South America. We are asked to contort the sense of a horizon ahead by imagining extinction in the past. The ends of the world with their scenarios of catastrophe cannot ignore the Spanish conquest, and for the people of the Americas the end of the world has already happened. The desire for a future, Danowski and Viveiros de Castro observe, may instead be activated as a matter of going back to being Indigenous again. That 'being Indigenous' will animate its own temporal orderings. Thus we hear of Amazonian people who hold radically alternative versions of their being and becoming (Vilaça 2007:172, 2016), just as the alternating generations, moieties and sibling pairs (elder–younger brother) of the Melanesian Iatmul, as Andrew Moutu (2013) describes them, forever juxtapose one temporal state with its other.

Imagining there are scales and degrees of termination may work as an ameliorative gesture for Euro-American climate-watchers. How much can one salvage? How much time do we have left? It is the other side of a progressive or evolutionary sense of forward-moving futures. However, the transformations of epochs in the worlds of Amazonians and Melanesians often imply a form of reversibility – to echo Corsín Jiménez and Willerslev's (2007) remarks on

---

8   Needless to say, one does need to be critical of present persuasions. It is likely to be 'our most cherished cultural notions, those that positively define our contemporary subjective experience, such as historical consciousness and individual agency' that get projected onto the subjects of study (Fausto and Heckenberger 2007:4).

Siberia – in a repetitive alternation of viewpoints, even while (as I shortly claim in a Melanesian case) people's social horizons are being freshly reconfigured.[9] The capacity in question is that of becoming something else, of flourishing where before one did not, of being a dead rather than a living kinsperson: transformation is often abrupt, cataclysmic. Such worlds are of course constantly transforming themselves too[10] – as is underlined in the following chapters – through ways Euro-Americans tend to describe in temporal terms as a matter of history. It might be interesting to historicize a particular moment from a Euro-American perspective.

The power of Lévi-Strauss's conjunction, viral colonization, lay in a comparison of reproductive processes.[11] Colonization was borne in on me in Papua New Guinea in 2015, as I had never really apprehended it in 1964–5 or over the years leading to independence (1975). If I suddenly found myself shaken by the impact of enforced development in a new way, it was not through new comparative or analytic tools, but because my own time horizon had altered. The changing circumstances of the anthropologist's world ignited an earlier epoch, as though the time of colonization had been waiting for me to catch up. Pacific islanders have endlessly been told they are remote and vulnerable, attributes not so much an invention of the present climate emergency as long-standing colonial tropes (Crook and Rudiak-Gould 2018:15). Perhaps we can re-perceive that trope of vulnerability. Climate emergency was the agent, and in being overwhelmed by it, momentarily I felt nothing short of 'colonized'; it knocked me into another re-perception.

Briefly, the whole country was in the middle of an unusually intense El Niño phase.[12] Offshore islands are habituated to drought; but this is hardly the case, to this extent at least, in the Highlands, where Hagen people saw mountain streams dry up and foliage wilt. The vision of shrivelling plants was an epiphany: something I had known for fifty years was now seen again. This was the vulnerability of the crops people cultivated. Their practices of regeneration allowed no seed stage; you needed tubers, corms or stems to create tubers, corms or stems. Suddenly, recalling Howell's turnabout, the whole of the former Highlands' subsistence base took on new significance

---

9   One may be one's ancestor (Moutu 2013:145; Rumsey 2000) without repeating the particularity of that person's relationships.

10   I follow the inflection given by Hirsch (2021:11): the Papua New Guinean Fuyuge 'understand the changes brought by missionaries and government as processes they themselves initiated in the ancestral past'.

11   Not overlooking the role that viruses played in premonitions of Tupi extinction seen from the eyes of a sixteenth century observer (Werbner 2016:51).

12   These are recurrent events; 2015–16 was prolonged and severe (see Jorgensen 2016).

because it was 2015, with its horizon stretching only to irreversible climate change. My delayed reaction to the vegetal basis of Hagen livelihood threw me into an ethnographic present, as though ancient cultivation practices had also been waiting for me (the world I was in) to catch up.

This has driven me to re-describe the Hagen world of 1964–5, with an altered appreciation of the propagation of plants and people.[13] One living being is generated from another, as though indissolubly combined. Yet it is only through the severing and partitioning of material that a new plant springs up in the place of the old. Gardeners cut their plants, just as people separate persons from one another and re-combine their vital capacities in new conjunctions to produce future generations. Partition is crucial; the creation of the new parent plant (the fragment of material to be replanted) from the previous child (in the case of taro and yam, the growing tuber or corm dug up to be eaten) is where, in social life, persons must divide themselves (by gender, clan, generation, moiety) in order to reproduce. The vitality of the one is exhausted in the flourishing of the other. With an Amazonian inflection, we could emphasize the alternating states of being: parents are transformed into the children they generate and children are transformed into generative parents, each replacement affording new horizons of relationships.[14] 'Replacement' – a Melanesian notion[15] – might suggest timeless repetition. In truth, there almost seems too much temporality in the recurrent re-creation of horizon-creating events.[16]

'Steady states ruptured by catastrophic events that restructure the world and result in new steady states' (Scaglion 1999:212): thus did an ethnographer of the yam-growing Abelam in lowland Papua New Guinea depict an episodic view of history.[17] People see the past divided into distinct epochs: the time of

---

13   Strathern 2017, 2019a, 2019b, 2021. Plants and their cultivation hold a place in these accounts rather similar to the 'objects and artefacts' that inform Fortis and Küchler's (2021:2, 10) analysis of visual systems.

14   Apropos plants, this is dramatically enacted in the way people search for new varieties to be planted alongside one another, and open up fresh soil to change the plant's growing conditions.

15   For example, Scaglion 1999:221–2; Stasch 2009:147.

16   In the (Euro-American) natural world, time forever flows, bringing new circumstances about. Existential questions follow from this: how to deal with change (answer: people respond and adapt). A Melanesian view, per contra, might point to the way people alter the time they are in through their new practices, thereby effecting change just as they effect life and death. Change is not the existential 'problem' it is for those who take time as a flowing continuity; for an Amazonian comment, see Vilaça 2016:241.

17   The tenor of Abelam life is differentiated into a growing season and a ceremonial season, there being numerous variants across Amazonia and Melanesia of such

the ancestors, the time of the Australians, the time of independence. When change happens it is cataclysmic, 'all at once'. Yet such epochs may also appear as scaled-up versions of everyday acts. People make dramatic ruptures out of marriage, initiation, becoming an ancestor. It follows that, as action is always needed to keep 'life' in circulation, regeneration is not automatic. The same year, Iteanu (1999) was making similar observations for the taro-growing Orokaiva. Everything is uncertain, and one cannot depend on things to grow by themselves or recur unaided.[18] As is routinely true for the way children mature or plants flourish, growth has to be effected through acts of personal attention. Concomitantly, people see signs of persons' actions everywhere. So, in this register, which itself recurs over and again in accounts of Melanesian sociality, is something of a crisis being made of everyday occurrences? The apparent paradox gives one pause.

Whether the re-perception was an epiphany or my own little ethnographic crisis, in it lay the genesis of the present endeavour that has brought together different generations of Melanesianists and Amazonianists. They have something rather interesting to say about the concept of crisis. Indeed, the variations in temporal register encountered here make one wonder about the extent to which the concept of crisis does or does not remain a constant. As we shall see, the concept pushes us more strongly than that: it emerges as a lens through which certain articulations of time may be differentiated from one another, not forgetting what I have been calling the time of the anthropologist.

Putting time and crisis together

Over the decade before the pandemic, 'time' had become a feature of anthropological thoughts on ethnographic practice (e.g. Dalsgaard and Nielsen 2016; Kirtsoglou and Simpson 2020; Melhuus, Mitchell and Wulff 2010; Ringel 2019; Rollason 2014). Such musings engage scholars who have experienced all kinds of time-depths to their studies. The opportunity for the present writer to see beyond her 1964–5 horizon, as it vividly became present in 2015, has offered itself in the work of those whose essays make up this collection. Crook and Vilaça, along with Moutu who joined our conversations, were of the generation who had undertaken their first fieldwork against the background

---

temporal oscillations, whether understood as co-existent alternations or each as producing new horizons for further action. See Ballard 2018 for a reappraisal of the episodic among other modes of Pacific temporalities.

18   The generic and often repeated nature of this assumption is, if anything, underlined by Goldman's (1993) demonstration for the Papua New Guinean Huli that, when it comes to personal accountability, it is possible to imagine 'unaided' accidents.

of anthropology learnt in the 1990s, while Amaral, Kenema, Guimarães and Santos da Costa were trained some two decades later.

Rendered thus, the anthropologist's time has a linearity to it, as indeed has my depiction of the events that took place in Hagen. Waiting for time to catch up is a very linear way of expressing the predicament that – in addressing the scope of historical accounting – the twentieth-century historian Koselleck (2022)[19] perceives in terms of an inevitable disjunction between actions and conceptualizations, experience and speech. These may change at different tempos. The disjunction is made vividly apparent in Ferme's (2018) evocation of belatedness. She writes of the painful process of recalling, eventually, being a witness to a spectacle during fieldwork in Sierra Leone, the unburying of a trauma that leads her to the phenomenon of belatedness (after Caruth 1996) in the processing of violent events. She was subjected to an excess of vision, 'the bursting into view of an aspect of experience that cannot be assimilated in the present' (Ferme 2018:40). She talks too of the disjunctive or discordant temporalities of enslavement and colonialism, and then of the unprecedented disruptions people suffered during the 1991–2002 civil war. For her, Ferme (2018:24) is explicit, it only became possible to write about the civil war after the fact because, among other things, she was dealing with 'events that were virtually forgotten within short-time spans'.

This seems to me a particularly powerful provocation to the notion of the ethnographic present. Writing in the time of one's fieldwork is an axiom that ethnographer-anthropologists take to heart. Whenever it takes place (mostly on analysis and reflection), problems of ethnographic fidelity often seem to revolve around adequacy of recall or record. Yet no amount of attention to the processes of memory and interlocution can deal with this issue cutting at right angles (Viveiros de Castro 2015:195) to the ethnographic moment: the fact that the present that the ethnographer inhabited was not necessarily an all-seeing vantage point from which to record what was happening. Indeed, perhaps one can put alongside the inconceivability (the not-knowing) of extinction, the state of not-knowing into which Ferme was propelled. However, this was not the only sense of time that made the war palpable. The war was brought back for everyone as an ongoing presence in the Mende story of a child refugee who died a decade later because, when a new farm was being burned, he did not have the knowledge or the reflexes of one who had grown up amid such everyday tasks. Through the Mende chief with oversight of the incident, people collectively concluded that it was the war that was the cause of the fatality.

---

19 I take liberties here, as from the point of view of his own interests Koselleck himself (2002:23) would argue that there never can be a 'catch up'.

The delayed harm of war can bear the structure of trauma, like that of the violence Ferme witnessed.[20] Here is what we might conceive as a forking of ways, a temporal divergence, between the ethnographer's moment of witnessing (which continued forward in unalterable form) and the moment of recall (dormant until activated in another context). Insofar as what unfolds belatedly becomes recoverable long after, as she observes, then the initial witnessing does 'not lead to cumulative knowledge of the event' (2018:39). Her observation offers us a pertinent contrast to the concept of crisis. Ideas of crisis seem to specifically summon the co-occurrence of divergent possibilities, where life hangs in the balance or directionality becomes evidently disruptable, and may even be articulated as a superfluity of events. Far from the lapse of time that interests Ferme, futures are imagined as imminent, almost as though they were gathering up accumulations of knowledge too numerous to lead to predictable outcomes. Bryant and Knight (2019:43) emphasize the present-ness (of the present) that crisis brings to the fore. What framings of time, then, do such imaginings elicit? Putting the question this way suggests we might ask of the concept of crisis what exactly it tells us about time.

I do not wish to imply that this was our motivating question. To the contrary, it is (among others) a question our research led us to. The original rubric, as Tony Crook's Preface lays out, put crisis alongside time for the very good reason of their frequent juxtaposition in the Euro-American vernacular, also informative, of course, of much anthropological exposition. What might putting them together once more, this time deliberately, generate? A thoroughly globalized concept, crisis straddles innumerable locations of academic and popular discourse, even while its analytic utility is frequently subject to scrutiny. Crisis thus gathers to itself all manner of deployments (Moutu 2020), its very ubiquity a sign of superfluity. Used originally for life-or-death decision-making (and see Koselleck 2002:237), it implies a forking of destinies according to what is about to happen, a temporal pressing of the future on the present. Ethnographically interesting, then, is how anthropologists and their interlocutors summon crisis as a concept. Here the four core chapters of this

---

20 Ferme's own commentary concerns the advantage of slow observation, the lapses of time that can only take place at their own tempo. The phenomenon of divergent futures is well known from Munn's (1990) account of the Melanesian Gawa; see, for example, Nielson's (2014:168) deployment of her argument. Kenema (Chapter 3) talks of Bougainvilleans being careful of the potential in any solution (of a problem) to set in train events that go off in unexpected directions. Similar as this orientation might seem to a sense of crisis (the bifurcation of a present moment), Bougainvilleans seem rather to be taking care of the future as they do of the past.

volume provide considerable insight. I pick out certain features from them for the purposes of debate; these are also noted at each chapter head.

The core chapters: an interpretation

Simon Kenema (Chapter 3) addresses civil war in Papua New Guinea (PNG). He locates an explicit narrative of crisis, called just that in the national media, the 'Bougainville Crisis'. The PNG state imagined a forking of future possibilities as a forking of people, insofar as opposing sides would concretize those differences into winners and losers, positions repeated when a referendum seemed the solution to fighting.[21] Disruptive as the Nagovisi of southern Bougainville found it all, their concern was for a future with quite different contours: the destiny of that interpenetration of persons with one another understood as a plane of kinship. This evoked not what a state might see, an absence of conflict, but to the contrary, a nexus of anticipations where conflict – like anything else in daily affairs – is dealt with according to the 'relational density' of people's lives. Civil war threatened the extinction of such lives.[22]

It is a rather different interpenetration of persons that the Apanjekra clients in central Brazil, presented by Bruno Guimarães (Chapter 4), wish to extract from their relations with the patron bosses on whose management capacities they depend.[23] Guimarães demonstrates just how the former's pressing claims to interpersonal engagement create a crisis for the bosses, given the choices the latter are forced into through these claims all the while they are having to secure their own livelihood, investments in time and calculations of timing being part of it. The very system itself is regarded by its critics as creating other kinds of crises. But if their Apanjekra clients do not

---

21 See Bryant and Knight (2019:46–7) on the crisis of the post-conflict Cyprus referendum, or Greenhouse (2019:79) on the split in Trump's United States of America, when voting the other way would make one into a different kind of person.

22 Extinction is not too dramatic a term for the obliteration of the life that seemed under threat. One may add that the war's conflicts were far from the (pro)creative processes of division and partition, such as moiety relations, that in Nagovisi inhered in the 'immanentist plane' (my phrase) of kinship. Kenema depicts the war as introducing an alien temporal logic.

23 With the previous account in mind, one may note Guimarães' description of Apanjekra assumptions that if interactions cease, the debt (the relation they hold in place) fades into nothing.

seem to be chronically in the cleft of such dilemmas, this leads to a query.[24] What kind of crisis-ridden time are the bosses and their critics caught up in?

Perhaps the very recognition of crisis is something of a diagnostic of the temporality in question. If the notion of crisis as the co-occurrence of divergent possibilities seems particularly germane to the historicizing view of the Papua New Guinea state or to the economic rationale of a Brazilian middleman, then pondering on such horizons may bring one to an apprehension of the kind of time being invoked. We can give it a name.

Building on numerous predecessors who have taken time as their subject, Hodges (2014) offers a particularly apt if not surprising name. He analyses, after Arendt, what he calls 'processual time' as a configuration specific to modern organizations (of knowledge, of capitalist expansion, of governmental regimes). A cousin to linear time, it involves a 'spatialized, riverine "flow" or "flux" through which processes unfold' towards future goals (2014:34–5). In the English vernacular, this entails the common-sense perception of time's flow. It is also the time of much social science, the flux that enables the study of social life as process, as though time existed the same for all actors, whose acts are thus perceived in terms of its (time's) ever-forward organizational effects. Discerning processual effects, by drawing on the organizational enablement of time's flow, seems as apt for the forward thinking of a state or army hoping to turn events into a particular direction as it does for the strategic decision-making that must weigh up likely economic outcomes.

There is, moreover, a(n external) vantage point from which social science can conceive and analyse processual time. Hodges crystallizes the insights of many thinkers and writers into the (contrasting) notion of temporal immanence.[25] Here time is nothing other than an emergent property of events. It is a differential multiplicity 'concerned with the creation of epochal moments' (2014:47), which – rather than providing any transcendent measurement through the connections of distinct moments – points instead to the temporalizing potential of any reality in the making.[26] A model of processual time is inadequate for conceiving the actualization of events that

---

24 Although, as Apanjekra accounts attest, there had been a choice that was epochally foundational: they are now living the time brought into existence when they chose a bow over a gun.

25 This is the sense in which I refer to immanence in this chapter. The clarification is necessary insofar as I have elsewhere adopted from Alan Strathern (2019) the concept of immanentism as definitive of certain cosmologies while also an element of all.

26 Providing another description in the same volume, Nielson (2014:168) traces, as did Hodges (2008), the genealogy of such thinking through Bergson and Deleuze, Deleuze himself drawing on Bateson (and see Jensen and Rödje 2010:18–22).

can only be 'immanent in time' (Hodges 2014:46). An example comes from the failure of a French seed-development company, the future of which was taken over by a new genetic interpretation of how to control plant processes in order to promote the production of biocapital. The processual aims of greater efficiency and instrumentality, based on GM modification, blotted out the rationale of the original breeding practices, which had valorized what might emerge from experiments in hybridization. Not subordinated to procedure in the same way, those (aborted) emergent futures had relied on the potential of what remained immanent.[27] Before reflecting on such temporal immanence in relation to our two chapters, it is necessary to complete the quartet.

That crises figure in specific narratives and not others is precisely what Virgínia Amaral presses home for the Amazonian Ingarikó (Chapter 2). This is in the light of a body of teachings, known as Areruya, which make it evident that it is white people (*brancos*) who have most to fear from particular future catastrophes, and whose lives visibly enact the crises that Ingarikó attribute not to present times but to that of their former prophets. They do not regard themselves as party to such apprehensions. Rather, an Ingarikó future could almost be an enactment of an expansive present (see below), a plane of possibilities that – in English one might say 'within which' – is also where people live. Being conscious of her own historicizing point of view allows the ethnographer to ponder on Amerindianist theorizing on points of view as such.

With Priscila Santos da Costa (Chapter 5), we encounter within one and the same body of teachings – that of the Unity Team, a Papua New Guinean reformist movement battling against what they saw as the corruption of the national parliament – both processual time and a counter to it. On the one hand, Santos da Costa emphasizes the linearity of their historical narrative and the identification of repeated crises precipitating triumphant moments of power. On the other hand, rather than being simultaneously oriented towards a future yet to arrive, the Unity Team understood themselves as living in an expansive present. This meant that they were already able to realize a capacity or power for propelling action and could point to signs of its presence. Indeed, the power immanent in their present condition was made evident on the occasion of the Bible presentation with which da Costa's account begins.

These four chapters summon a notion of crisis articulated by or attributed to specific contexts. Whether crisis is associated with certain types of political commentary, the preoccupations of entrepreneurs, the habits of whites or

---

27 Had the development succeeded, the end result would have been a species of plant that was challenging to control, 'whose genomic and reproductive identity was resistant to commodification' (Hodges 2014:38).

with a long-term view of changing fortunes, it seems to elicit an acute sense of Hodge's processual time. In this conceptualization, time moves ever forward. That said, each chapter also indicates quite other temporal understandings, and we return to Hodges' counter description of actualizations that can only be immanent in time. Yet staying with the shorthand, 'immanent in time' would imply that time continues flowing, which is not Hodges' intention. He advocates a conception of social life as existing not within a flow of time but as 'generated in an immanent field' (of events in the making) (2014:47). Here time is anything but 'forward or backward', as Greenhouse (2019:73) observes, and agency is not in time but is (makes) time. Stripping away the veneer of linear time, she argues, reveals time as a kinetic energy produced in the heat of contest or commitment, whose index – far from (processual) sequence or output – is the energy it gives or takes. Engagement thus removes any distance between one moment and another. Might we wish to locate some counterpart to such agency or energy in our chapters? Might it be implied in the way in which people sustain kinship ties, or augment patron-client bonds, or pursue adherence to teachings, or, indeed, cultivate the present capacity that reformists find in themselves?

Relocations (with a Melanesian bias)

It would be helpful, in pursuit of this last point, to refine certain processual understandings with respect to time's flow. Insofar as such flow brings with it a notion of forward motion, an anticipated sequence of events can also be interrupted. What presents itself as cessation or rupture of movement (movement in those actions and inclinations people see as otherwise carrying on) is perhaps apprehended as a forking of ways – as a crisis – insofar as something will carry on forwards even if it is not the trajectory one thought one was on. That something is 'time', and the kind of time that crisis makes.

By way of concrete examples, Bryant and Knight (2019:43) deal with 'vernacular' (Euro-American) times of crisis precisely in the sense of diverted flow, 'moments when anticipation, and therefore the alleviation of anxiety, are not possible', yet where the future is being made in the present instant ('right now'). While time continues to flow into the future, there is radical uncertainty as to the path it will take. A natural or autonomous flow of events has suddenly failed, and crises recur as uncertainty about the future recurs. We are shown a moment when this takes shape:

> sitting at my desk, I have no more sense of a 'now' than I have of a 'here'.
> [...] But I may become aware of both in moments of what we call crisis,

moments when contingency comes into play and interrupts my intentional
relation to the world.

(ibid.:46)

When focus shifts to interruption, as in a recent disquisitions on rupture
(Holbraad, Kapferer and Sauma 2019),[28] breaks may be imagined (after
Weber) in a crisis-like fashion, as a critical cut or switch-point that instigates
a fundamental change of direction. The effect may be positive or negative,
but time's continuing movement seems to remain inexorable.[29] That said,
the editors' own intention is to let the concept of rupture multiply through
diverse ethnographic fields and in turn 'rupture' presumptions about linearity.
So what about those catastrophic shifts to which Scaglion referred (above)?
Here my interpretation takes a specifically Melanesian turn. I recall the people
of Hagen and their congeners, for whom the staging of breaks and divisions
probes the (immanent) condition of the world, and does so through prodding
people into action. If such breaks are ruptures, rather than being crisis-like
they point to the kind of cataclysmic transformations that, as Hodges's epochal
moments suggest, on myriad scales precipitates the present as another epoch
(Hirsch 2021: 27).

Division between generations can have such an epochal effect, as when
the one seems to spring up in the place of the other. Describing old age in
Orokaiva, Iteanu (1999) notes that men and women do not grow old through
and because of 'time', but because of what people do (in terms, say, of their
relations with all kinds entities). Orokaiva thus regard bodily growth and
decay as a consequence not of duration, or the lapse of time in this sense,
but of people's deliberate actions. If prodding people into action is a mode of
enquiry into the state of the world – to put it in English – then this is not quite
the action that Koselleck (above) saw in counterpoint to conceptualization;
perhaps it lies rather closer to Greenhouse's (2019:87) notion of agency found
not 'in' time but as time, at once waxing and waning, 'indeterminate and
potentiating heat'. If one were to transpose (equivocate) these abstractions
into Melanesian, a shorthand for the immanence of time in the actualization

---

28   Holbraad, Kapferer and Sauma (2019:15) themselves dismiss 'crisis' as too freighted
     a framework for delineating contemporary upheavals, locating its constituting
     force in the '"grand narrative" of modern historical reckoning … [where it] has
     become a prominent ingredient of ideological formations of contemporary
     capitalism'. They prefer, given their ethnographic purposes, the concept of
     'rupture' for its lighter baggage.

29   Thus Hodges (2014:40) characterizes one processual vision of contemporary
     history as 'adjacent intervals in the "flow of time" [...] divided by major ruptures'.

of events might be rather phrased as the actualization of actions immanent in – or as an immanent field of – 'persons'. Persons include metapersons, visible and invisible, and events (time) in this sense would be immanent in persons' actions.

This is where we can locate something analogous to the energy of agency. The analytical advantage of such a formulation is the social dynamic that it inscribes. Consider the temporal dimensions of episodic regeneration, as was observed briefly apropos Melanesian plant cultivation. Implied in the growth and decay of bodies of all kinds is the cosmological necessity (Moutu 2013) to constantly bring phenomena into being. My understanding of the actions implicated in this necessity is that, over lesser or greater intervals, only fresh action will sustain the status quo. This is because any 'one' act exhausts itself in its effects. Taking action has consequences and it is only when these consequences later come to light that the quality or character of the action – what it actually was, what happened – is revealed; this is in turn because the original act is 'consumed' thereby, just as the growing plant consumes its generative parent in its flourishing. That is why one has to do things again. A previous act is not 'over' because time has passed (so it goes into a kind of 'past') but because it was transformed into what it created. What it created endures in that relation between cause and effect. To have further future effect, the creation must be re-caused. Every action is thus in this sense a singularity, a 'new' event, every event a fresh constellation of relations. One is reminded of those Apanjekra who did something not anticipated at the point of acquiring avian breeding stock; their new action, we might suppose, was to eat the birds now to hand.

It is striking how Scott (2007) delineates a phenomenon that only comes into being with people. However, he is talking not about events but about places. We know elsewhere from Melanesia something of the attraction of places, and the way they are bound up with temporal notions of increase and decrease (for example, Crook 2007; Goldman and Ballard 1998; Jolly 1994; Leach 2003; Mitchell and Bolton 2021). Scott's own account of primordial times in Arosi (Solomon Islands) includes the unforgettable image of not-places or proto-places 'still unformed by human agency' (2007:201) waiting to come into view, as a Euro-American might say. He refers to de Coppet's (1985) remark of Malaita that locality cannot be conceived of without persons, in this case, ancestors. More generally, we might say that Melanesian places are where persons are. One might extrapolate that it is persons' intra- and inter-actions – agency implied, relations implied – that differentiate places. Places as well as events are seemingly immanent in and thus manifested by people's actions.

Without laying too much emphasis on a single instance with its own notable characteristics, it is interesting how Mesoamericanists Rodríguez and López (2019) are moved to take up the notion of 'event-based', 'intersectional time' as it has been surmised (after Wagner) for ancient Mayan temporal systems.[30] Like the movements of a weaver that cross weft threads with warp, for today's Chol Mayans an intersection of ceremonial and agricultural calendars pinpoints a simultaneous repetition and progression of events. What is interesting is that the authors resort to a spatial (locational) model by way of exposition: this is 'the pattern followed in the planting of a cornfield' (ibid.:175). Two rows of plantings (up/down and left/right) form pathways meeting at intersections, corners or 'places' (my term), we may say, where the completion of one activity leads to the next. In the more general terms of which Danowski and Viveiros de Castro (2017:121) write, Amerindian people's desire for a future activated in terms of their being Indigenous again is not inappropriately bound up with the places where they live, even if somewhat inappropriately requiring them to demonstrate 'historical continuity' of land occupation. In old Melanesia transformational possibilities were implied, across the generations, in the notion of people returning to the actions of their forebears as creative moments for the present. Concomitantly, they were open as to what the consequences of people's previous acts at this or that place (and the actions they did not take) might turn out to be. I speculate as to whether or not some of present-day Brazilian people's 'ceaseless rebecoming-indigenous' (ibid.:122) has the transformational effects of – temporal, locational – re-enactment too.

We are now in a position to consider certain connotations of the locational image of horizon. Habituated as it is in the Newtonian universe of everyday Euro-American parlance, it also finds a place in descriptions inspired by Amerindian and Pacific realities. Yet it belongs, like the time anthropologists find themselves in, to the anthropologist's vernacular discourse. As a concept, 'horizon' marks a conceptual limit to the transpositions or equivocations by which it makes some sense in English to describe diverse (Melanesian/ Amazonian) events or places as when / where persons are at. At right angles indeed to such a supposition, the principal agent of an (otherwise generally unpopulated) horizon is the viewer in the foreground.

---

30 Discussions of time as event has been used, Rodríguez and López (2019:165–6) argue, by anthropologists wishing to escape the linear/cyclical dichotomy in models of time.

Whose horizon?

Today's narratives of anthropogenic climate change may well entail assumptions that have long been standard ontological premises for many peoples. What to some seems an entanglement of nature and culture is no surprise to those who never made that distinction, or who in any case see evidence of persons' (human, living or otherwise) activity everywhere. These observations, taken from Crook and Rudiak-Gould's (2018) engagement with studies across the Pacific, accompany a wry comment about climate change being adopted as a catch-all for all kinds of calamities, while simultaneously underscoring uncertainty as a persistent existential condition. So the concept (climate change) has already become swept up in Pacific people's ongoing endeavours, excuses[31] or concerns about futures and livelihoods, and this fuels a present sense of emergency. The temporal registers here include observers' appeals to centuries-deep time, as Amaral herself makes for the Amazonian formation of Areruya.[32] If a crisis such as climate change bursts on the world as a signature of present calamities, what about all the observers' ontological premises? Where have their time horizons been? The question is asked with some urgency by Irvine (2020:171): 'Consciousness of catastrophe as our mark in deep time demands that human societies expand their time horizons, just as the burgeoning sense of crisis threaten to close them.'

When it entails a human subject at a particular location, a horizon envisions a processual perspective on the world and the kinds of coordinates implied. It is as spatial as it is temporal, a sense that perhaps informs Robbins' (2008) references to spatial hierarchies in Urapmin (PNG) and the idea of the Christian heaven as a distinct place, 'over the horizon' in both time and location. Such an axis is one of several readings of horizon that find theoretical address in an appraisal of Siikala's work in the Pacific (Kaartinen and Sather 2008). There, first, horizon refers to the limits of the observer's point of view; and, when the observer is an ethnographer, to limitations of cultural awareness. Second, horizon evokes what is discernible beyond it: lying at a distance from the immediate perceptual field is a potential domain projected from a background of familiar experience. Insofar as this reading

---

31   Thus Newell (2018:104) suggests reference to climate change can be 'a convenient way for people to side-step personal, traditional, "ordinary" environmental responsibility'; see Salmond (2018:157), to the contrary, on such discourse as a 'weapon of the weak'. For a view on the way in which Pacific Islanders might see themselves as 'contributors to our own demise', see Hereniko (2014:234).

32   Who is or is not an observer is a matter for equivocation not expounded here; thus, there seems a sense in which members of the Unity Team, as explicated by Santos da Costa, are also their own observers, with their explorations of a kind of deep time.

implies transcending a subject's situated position, it recalls Rollason's (2014) description of a projection into a future seen from what would come about.[33] Josephides (2014:43) draws attention to Euro-American articulations of a 'horizon of knowledge' that beckons towards the unknown, and suggests we might see such a beckoning in the bid of a Kewa (PNG) woman, Lari, to escape the confines of her current existence. A sense of opening up or out captures just such a transcendent image when Gefou-Madianou (2010:160) talks of 'open horizons'. A third inflection of horizon, observe Kaartinen and Sather (2008:9), draws upon Siikala's investment in society as a conceptual world, and the possibility of objects of attention – such as a Bible or a cash allowance – inviting the realization of (newly conceived) horizons of their own. Perhaps we can add a fourth and, with Santos da Costa's expansive present or Kenema's eternal kinship in mind, think of the plateau-like character that horizon may also evoke in an observer familiar with geophysical coordinates.

Just as any articulation of the concept of crisis depends on (elicits) a particular configuration of time, namely time conceived in flow or flux, the horizon may also be defined (in English) as that part of the earth's surface that would be visible if no irregularities were in the way. The preceding expanse is what gives it a perceptible rim; conversely, the image of an outer ever-receding, unattainable rim draws attention to the expanse before it – hence also horizon's connotations of a range. Such an image of horizon may for all intents and purposes figure a plane of immanence.[34] When the boundary become indeterminately remote, the foregrounded expanse emerges as plateau-like, something resonant of a continuous intensity. Thus, Guimarães observes that insofar as the image of horizon does not entail specific notions of past or future, it allows the narrator to focus on the actors' temporalizing moves.

This does not mean that the narrator's world of processual coordinates is relinquished, nor the kinds of actions made possible when places stay still and time is thought to move. Indeed, posing the issue of the time of the anthropologist-ethnographer drew on the concept of an ethnographic horizon, and its effects on what is perceived 'at the time'. Such a processual apprehension may offer significant descriptive interventions. This is made

---

33   A future anterior ('the perspective of that which will have been' [Frederiksen 2020:159]).

34   Hodges (2014:44) suggests that all 'that exists of timespace resides and differentiates "within" the living present ... [which, quoting Deleuze and Guattari] might be conceptualized ... as a "plane of immanence"'. It is hardly necessary to add that one such 'piece of immanence' (Deleuze and Guattari 2004:175) is imaged or figured as a plateau without beginning or end.

explicit in Petryna's (2017:246–7) evidently processual vision of 'horizoning', which is conceived as a tool for intervention; by this she means 'a particular kind of intellectual labour that reconfigures possibilities for knowledge and action'. In the inability to act before everything that is known about the motors of climate change, alongside everything as yet unknown, Petryna argues that a willed orientation to horizon-scanning may circumvent some of the foreclosures encouraged by globally current epistemological and technical practices and their predictions.[35] Her argument recalls the plea from Irvine (above), who specifically observes that 'time horizons drawn close to the present obscure the material conditions of human existence.' (2020:173). Her interventionist tool (horizoning) invites adaptation to any branch of knowledge-making where the ratio of what is grasped and what falls out of one's grasp shifts all the time and thus, for the knowledge-maker, shifts over time.

It is just such a horizoning that Crook's Al Gore (Chapter 6) sets in train, and this serves as a nice conclusion. Through diverse genres of intervention, this latter-day prophet mobilized different perceptions of time summoned by the multidimensional crisis of climate change. In the context of this volume, Crook's ethnographic account in fact thickens the ways in which time may be grasped as (processual) flow. Paying attention to the different modalities of Gore's thinking, he depicts some of the creative possibilities that the notion of time's movement generates. An interesting comment on the linear imagination emerges: non-linearity is somehow our – the world's – future. It is almost as though time were still moving, still flowing, despite its no longer linear direction. But, then, the chapter reminds us of Latour's (2005) comment on synchronic interaction: aligning the 'time' things occupy has long lost its ordering force.

Last words

Being in the future of the previous disciplinary crises, as adumbrated in the Preface, allows one to remark on how times have shifted the questions. A question that emerges from this book is to ask precisely in what respects the future poses problems for the present. If we have identified the notion of crisis as spinning from the pressure of an inevitable future on already existent circumstances, we have also encountered futures that slip below the horizon of present activity or that become perceptible the moment they are realizable,

---

35   At the point at which data fails, when predictions from past or present become misleading, horizoning work invites 'the construction of appropriate scaling rules and cultivating "equipment" for modeling, managing, and facing a complex future that is right at hand' (Petryna 2017:263).

as when (new-old) futures emerge with seeming abruptness from the past. Otherwise phrased, how may one give weight to the processual imagination while also being attentive to the futures of people who do not rely on being borne by currents of 'time' to get there? Here the concept of crisis has emerged as something of a differentiating diagnostic.

One might or might not wish to argue that an apprehension of crisis elicits an emphasis on time's (usually forward) flow. But, taken together, these essays map out some of the kinds of terrain where it seems appropriate – or otherwise – to give the concept analytical prominence, and thus identify the temporality it entails. Diverse details in the expositions show how people imagine, accommodate, remain oblivious to, resist or shift between registers of relations that may be processually denoted as 'different kinds of' time (as in spacetime). Spacetime is supposedly the same for all beings, so the notion allows no direct translation into those situations where it is persons (including meta-persons) who are the instruments of differentiation, and where events/places appear with persons coming into existence or presence in this or that distinctive manner.

This can be expressed in terms of a general issue in anthropological understanding aired by Robbins (2003, 2007) twenty years ago. What is it about modern Euro-American temporalities that interpret abrupt transitions as untoward or exotic, and thus with unsettling effects? Are ideas about the flow of time so taken for granted that continuity appears to be the very opposite of change, and juxtaposing the two produces a kind of frisson? In the processual view, steady states imply lack of change rather than a horizon for the next change. Lack of change has of course been a powerful default mode in colonial thinking about the peoples who inhabited old Amazonia and old Melanesia. Yet, whereas those who are living processual time may imagine existing only through incessant (onward) novelty for themselves, it is also possible to be continuously innovative[36] while oriented towards a future that has brought into being again (replicated) what has already been. In the latter mode, the new may lie less in the character of an act – which may be quite routine – than in what it opens up to fresh enactments of relations.

---

36 Apropos the ethos of constant transformation in Amazonia noted at the outset, it is of the Pacific that Rollason (2014:1–2, after Crook 2007) remarks, 'social lives are inherently innovative in that they continuously fabricate new constellations of social relations'. Thus, Fuyuge have all kinds of ideas about how to interpret the present state of their relationships, and what it means 'to act in a timely manner given the current horizons in which people conduct their lives' (Hirsch 2021:32).

Acknowledgements

Apart from many interchanges with colleagues on this endeavour, I am most grateful for particular bibliographic pointers from Chris Ballard, Justin Shaffner and an anonymous reviewer.

References

Ballard, C. 2018. 'Afterword: Pacific futurities'. In W. Andrerson, M. Johnson and B. Brookes (eds), *Pacific Futures: Past and Present*, pp. 280–93. Honolulu: University of Hawaii Press.

Bear, L. 2020. 'Chronocracy and its anthropological alternatives'. In E. Kirtsoglou and B. Simpson (eds), *The Time of Anthropology: Studies of Contemporary Chronopolitics*, pp. ix–xvi. London: Routledge.

Bryant, R. and Knight, D. M. 2019. *The Anthropology of the Future*. Cambridge: Cambridge University Press.

Caruth, C. 1996. *Unclaimed Experience: Trauma, Narrative, and History*. Baltimore: Johns Hopkins University Press.

Colson, E. 1984. 'The reordering of experience: anthropological involvement with time', *Journal of Anthropological Research* 40(1):1–13.

Corsín Jiménez, A. and Willerslev, R. 2007. '"An anthropological concept of the concept": reversibility among the Siberian Yukaghirs', *JRAI* (NS) 13(3):527–44.

Crook, T. 2007. *Exchanging Skin: Anthropological Knowledge, Secrecy and Bolivip, Papua New Guinea*. Oxford: Oxford University Press for The British Academy.

Crook, T. and Rudiak-Gould, P. 2018. 'Introduction: Pacific climate cultures'. In *Pacific Climate Cultures: Living Climate Change in Oceania*, pp. 1–20. Warsaw/Berlin: De Gruyter.

Dalsgaard, S. and Nielsen, M. 2016. 'Introduction: time and the field'. In S. Dalsgaard and M. Nielson (eds), *Time and the Field*, pp. 1–19. Oxford: Berghahn Books.

Danowski, D. and Viveiros de Castro, E. 2017. *The Ends of the World* (trans. R Nunes). Cambridge: Polity Press.

De Coppet, D. 1985. '... Land owns people'. In R.H. Barnes, D. de Coppet and R.J. Parkin, *Contexts and levels: Anthropological Essays on Hierarchy*, pp. 78–90. Oxford: Anthropological Society.

Deleuze, G. and Guattari, F. 2004 [1980]. *A Thousand Plateaus: Capitalism and Schizophrenia* (trans. B. Massumi). London: Continuum, The Athlone Press Ltd.

Demian, M. 2021. *In Memory of Times to Come: Ironies of History in Southeastern Papua New Guinea*. Oxford: Berghahn Books.

Fabian, J. 1983. *Time and the Other: How Anthropology Makes its Subject.* New York: Columbia University Press.

——— 2010. 'Ethnography and memory'. In M. Melhuus, J.P. Mitchell and H. Wulff (eds), *Ethnographic Practice in the Present*, pp. 16–27. New York: Berghahn Books.

Fausto, C. and Heckenberger, M. 2007. 'Introduction: history and the history of the "Indians"'. In C. Fausto and M. Heckenberger (eds), *Time and Memory in Indigenous Amazonia: Anthropological Perspectives*, pp. 1–43. Gainesville: University Press of Florida.

Ferme, M. 2018. *Out of War: Violence, Trauma, and the Political Imagination in Sierra Leone.* Oakland: University of California Press.

Fortis, P. and Küchler, S. 2021. 'Introduction'. In *Time and its Object: A Perspective from Amerindian and Melanesian Societies on the Temporality of Images*, pp.1–20. London: Routledge.

Foster, G., Scudder, T., Colson, E. and Kemper, R. 1979. 'Conclusion: the long-term study in perspective'. In G. Foster, T. Scudder, E. Colson and R. Kemper (eds), *Long Term Field Research in Social Anthropology*, pp. 323–48. New York: Academic Press.

Frederiksen, M.D. 2020. 'Now is not: future anteriority and Georgian in Russia'. In M. Flaherty, L. Meinert and A.L. Dalsgård (eds), *Time Work: Studies of Temporal Agency*, pp. 158–72. New York: Berghahn.

Gefou-Madianou, D. 2010. 'Ethnography in motion: shifting fields on an airport ground'. In M. Melhuus, J.P. Mitchell and H. Wulff (eds), *Ethnographic Practice in the Present*, pp.152–68. New York: Berghahn Books.

Goldman, L.R. 1993. *The Culture of Coincidence: Accident and Absolute Liability in Huli.* Oxford: Clarendon Press.

Goldman, L.R. and Ballard C. (eds) 1998. *Fluid Ontologies: Myth, Ritual and Philosophy in the Highlands of Papua New Guinea.* Westport, CT: Bergin and Garvey.

Gow, P. 2001. *An Amazonian Myth and its History.* Oxford: Oxford University Press.

Greenhouse, C. 2019. 'Times like the present: political rupture and the heat of the moment'. In M. Holbraad, B. Kapferer and J. Sauma (eds), *Ruptures: Anthropologies of Discontinuity in Times of Turmoil*, pp. 70–92. London: UCL Press.

Hereniko, V. 2014. 'The human face of climate change: notes from Rotuma and Tuvalu'. In W. Rollason (ed.), *Pacific Futures: Projects, Politics and Interests*, pp. 226–35. Oxford: Berghahn Books.

Hirsch, E. 2021. *Ancestral Presence: Cosmology and Historical Experience in the Papua Highlands.* New York: Berghahn Books.

Hodges, M. 2008. 'Rethinking time's arrow: Bergson, Deleuze and the anthropology of time', *Anthropological Theory* 8(4):399–429.

———— 2014. 'Immanent anthropology: a comparative study of "process" in contemporary France'. In L. Bear (ed.), 'Doubt, conflict, mediation: the anthropology of modern time',. *Journal of the Royal Anthropological Institute* (NS) S1:33–51.

Holbraad, M., Kapferer, B. and Sauma, J. (eds) 2019. *Ruptures: Anthropologies of Discontinuity in Times of Turmoil*, London: UCL Press.

Howell, S. 2012. 'Cumulative understandings: experiences from the study of two Southeast Asian societies'. In S. Howell and A. Talle (eds), *Returns to the Field: Multitemporal Research and Contemporary Anthropology*, pp. 153–79. Bloomington: Indiana University Press.

Howell, S. and Talle, A. 2012. 'Introduction'. In S. Howell and A. Talle (eds), *Returns to the Field: Multitemporal Research and Contemporary Anthropology*, pp. 1–22. Bloomington: Indiana University Press.

Irvine, R. 2020. *The Anthropology of Deep Time: Geological Temporality and Social Life*. Cambridge: Cambridge University Press.

Iteanu, A. 1999. 'Synchronisations among the Orokaiva', *Social Anthropology* 7(3):265–78.

Jolly, M. 1994. *Women of the Place: 'Kastom', Colonialism and Gender in Vanuatu*. Chur, Switzerland: Harwood Academic Publishers.

Jensen, C.B. and Rödje, K. 2010. 'Introduction'. In C.B. Jensen and K. Rödje (eds), *Deleuzian Intersections: Science, Technology, Anthropology*, pp. 1–35. Oxford: Berghahn Books.

Jorgensen, D. 2016. 'The garden and beyond: the dry season, the Ok Tedi shutdown, and the footprint of the 2015 El Niño drought', *Oceania*, 86(1):25–39.

Josephides, L. 2014. 'Imagining the future: an existential and practical activity'. In W. Rollason (ed.), *Pacific Futures: Projects, Politics and Interests*, pp. 28–47. Oxford: Berghahn Books.

Kaartinen, T. and Sather, C. (eds) 2008. *Beyond the Horizon: Essays on Myth, History, Travel and Society* (Studia Fennica 2). Helsinki: Finnish Literature Society.

Kirtsoglou, E. and Simpson, B. (eds) 2020. *The Time of Anthropology: Studies of Contemporary Chronopolitics*. London: Routledge.

Koselleck, R. 2002. *The Practice of Conceptual History: Timing History, Spacing Concepts* (trans. T.S. Presner *et al.*). Stanford: Stanford University Press.

Latour, B. 2005. *Reassembling the Social: An Introduction to Actor-Network-Theory*. Oxford: Oxford University Press.

Leach, J. 2003. *Creative Land: Place and Procreation on the Rai Coast of Papua New Guinea*. Oxford: Berghahn Books.

Lynteris, C. 2020. *Human Extinction and the Pandemic Imaginary*. Abingdon, Oxon: Routledge.

Melhuus, M., Mitchell, J.P. and Wulff, H. (eds) 2010. *Ethnographic Practice in the Present*. New York: Berghahn Books.

Mitchell, J. and Bolton, L. (eds) 2021. 'Aesthetic satisfaction and the art of gardens', *Anthropological Forum* (Special Issue) 31(4):339–51.

Moutu, A. 2013. *Names are Thicker than Blood: Kinship and Ownership amongst the Iatmul.* Oxford: Oxford University Press for The British Academy.

——— 2020. 'Time in moments of crisis', paper presented in 'Time and the Ethnographic Horizons in Moments of Crisis', Museum Seminar Series, PNG National Museum and Art Gallery, Port Moresby.

Munn, N. 1990. 'Constructing regional worlds in experience: kula exchange, witchcraft and Gawan local events', *Man* (n.s.) 25(1):1 - 17.

Newell, J. 2019. 'Weathering climate change in Samoa: resources for resilience'. In T. Crook, and P. Rudiak-Gould (eds), *Pacific Climate Cultures: Living Climate Change in Oceania*, pp. 88–105. Warsaw/Berlin: De Gruyter.

Nielsen, M. 2014. 'A wedge of time: futures in the present and presents without futures in Maputo, Mozambique'. In L. Bear (ed.), 'Doubt, conflict, mediation: the anthropology of modern time', *Journal of the Royal Anthropological Institute* (NS) S1:166–82.

Otto, T. 2017. 'Times of the other: The temporalities of ethnographic fieldwork'. In S. Dalsgaard and M. Nielsen (eds), *Time and the Field,* pp. 64–79. Oxford: Berghahn Books.

Petryna, A. 2017. 'Horizoning'. In J. Biehl and P. Locke (eds), *Unfinished: The Anthropology of Becoming*, pp. 243–66. Durham, NC: Duke University Press.

Rifkin, M. 2017. *Beyond Settler Time: Temporal Sovereignty and Indigenous Self-determination.* Durham, NC: Duke University Press.

Ringel, F. 2016. 'Beyond temporality: notes on the anthropology of time from a shrinking field site', *Anthropological Theory* 16(4):390–412.

——— 2019. *Back to the Postindustrial Future: An Ethnography of Germany's Fastest-shrinking City.* Oxford: Berghahn Books.

Robbins, J. 2003. 'On the paradoxes of global Pentecostalism and the perils of continuity thinking', *Religion* 33(3):221–31.

——— 2007. 'Continuity thinking and the problem of Christian culture: belief, time, and the anthropology of Christianity', *Current Anthropology* 48(1):5–38.

——— 2008. 'The future is a foreign country: time, space and hierarchy among the Urapmin on Papua New Guinea'. In T. Kaartinen and C. Sather (eds), *Beyond the Horizon: Essays on Myth, History, Travel and Society: In Honour of Jukka Siikala* (Studia Fennica 2), pp. 23–36. Helsinki: Finnish Literature Society.

Rodríguez, L. and López, S. 2019. 'The crossroads of time'. In P. Pitarch and J. Kelly (eds), *The Culture of Invention in the Americas: Anthropological Experiments with Roy Wagner*, pp. 159–85. Canon Pyon (UK): Sean Kingston Publishing.

Rollason, W. (ed.) 2014. *Pacific Futures: Projects, Politics and Interests*. Oxford: Berghahn Books.

Rowlands, M. 2022. 'Time and permanence: in the epoch of the anachronic'. In D.N. Gellner and D.P. Martinez (eds), *Re-creating Anthropology: Sociality, Matter and the Imagination*, pp. 45–56. London: Routledge.

Rumsey, A. 2000. 'Agency, personhood and the "I" of discourse in the Pacific and beyond', *JRAI* 6(1):101–15.

Salmond, A. 2018. 'Think like a fish: Pacific philosophies and climate change'. In T. Crook and P. Rudiak-Gould, (eds), *Pacific Climate Cultures: Living Climate Change in Oceania*, pp. 155–9. Warsaw/Berlin: De Gruyter.

Scaglion, R. 1999. 'Yam cycles and timeless time in Melanesia', *Ethnology* 38(3):211–25.

Scott, M.W. 2007. *The Severed Snake: Matrilineages, Making place, and a Melanesian Christianity in Southeast Solomon Islands*, Durham: Carolina Academic Press.

Stasch, R. 2009. *Society of Others: Kinship and Mourning in a West Papuan Place*. Berkeley: University of California Press.

Stavrianakis, A. 2019. *Leaving: A Narrative of Assisted Suicide*. Oakland, CA: University of California Press.

Strathern, A.L. 2019. *Unearthly Powers: Religious and Political Change in World History*. Cambridge: Cambridge University Press.

Strathern, M. 2017. 'Gathered fields: a tale about rhizomes', *ANUAC* 6(2):271–92.

——— 2019a. 'A clash of ontologies? Time, law and science in Papua New Guinea', *HAU, Journal of Ethnographic Theory* 9(1):58–74.

——— 2019b 'Generating plants and people'. In G. Cometti, P. Le Roux, T. Manicon and N. Martin (eds), *Au Seuil de la Forêt: Hommage a Philippe Descola, l'Anthropologue de la Nature*, pp. 1019–27. Paris: Tautem.

——— 2021. 'Regeneração vegetativa: um ensaio sobre relações de gênero [Vegetative regeneration: an essay on gender relations, trans. B. N. Guimarães]', *Mana* 27(1):1–31.

Vilaça, A. 2007. 'Cultural change as body metamorphosis', in Fausto, C. and Heckenberger, M. (eds), *Time and Memory in Indigenous Amazonia: Anthropological Perspectives*, pp.169-193. Gainesville: University Press of Florida.

——— 2016. *Praying and Preying: Christianity in Indigenous Amazonia*. Oakland: University of California Press.

——— 2021. 'Viruses, human-animal relations and response-ability in Indigenous Amazonia', Raymond Firth Memorial Lecture, ASA conference, 'Responsibility', St Andrews.

Viveiros de Castro, E. 2015. *The Relative Native: Essays on Indigenous Conceptual Worlds*. Chicago: HAU Books.

Werbner, P. 2016. 'Between *Tristes Tropiques* and cultural creativity: modern times and the vanishing primitive'. In B. Kapferer and D. Theodossopolous (eds), *Against Exoticism: Toward the Transcendence of Relativism and Universalism in Anthropology*, pp. 44–64. New York: Berghahn Books.

2

Time and crisis in the Areruya religion

Virgínia Amaral[1]

In the Areruya teachings of the Amazonian Ingarikó, crisis figures in certain specific narratives of temporality but not in others. From an Ingarikó point of view, their own future appears as the enactment of a plane of possibilities that have already been laid there. As far as the destinies of particular persons are concerned – themselves and others such as the ethnographer herself – these teachings point to the way in which a perception of certain future catastrophes, and of any crises they might produce in the present, belongs to those who are called *brancos* or whites. Ingarikó are not touched by such crises. Thus, taking the ethnographer's historicizing point of view, it is as though what has slipped below the horizon here is the colonial origin of what Ingarikó regard simply as an Indigenous religion. So, too, the old prophets' future cataclysms recede from people's immediate present. As the reader learns, all that remains are traces of moments that induce an outside observer to apply the concept of crisis to them. This chapter provocatively proceeds to put a discussion of cataclysm and rupture into the context of Amerindianist theorizing on points of view as such, and speculates on futures from which an ethnographer might in turn look back. To this end, it also engages directly with the notion of horizon.

1   This work was produced under the auspices of the Ethnographic Horizons project at the Centre for Pacific Studies, University of St Andrews, and was supported by the International Balzan Foundation.

❋

A crisis at home sets the scene for this chapter, not because it anticipates the subjects to follow, but because, crucially, it puts in place the time of the anthropologist and the related emergence of a catastrophic horizon. The notion of horizon used here relates to the possibility of knowing what is beyond the immediate field of perception. Fieldwork among the Amazonian Ingarikó people made evident the contrast between my new catastrophic horizon and the fact that my hosts no longer fear the cataclysmic end of their world, as predicted in the past by their old prophets, who saw themselves inhabiting a world in crisis. Furthermore, ethnography revealed that the Ingarikó have also transformed their ancestors' understanding about the determining role of colonization in that crisis. This chapter discusses these resignifications with a temporal focus, suggesting that the Ingarikó and other Amazonian peoples seek to use time to their advantage. I argue that such strategic use of time occurs through bodily practices conceived as capable of maintaining or transforming certain states of affairs.

The last two decades have seen the proliferation of scientific research identifying an ecological crisis at a planetary scale, the main agent of which is humanity. However, there are diverging views regarding the concept of Anthropocene and the pertinence of referring to human action as a geological force capable of outstripping the agencies of other beings, when it comes to environmental transformations and disasters of the present era (e.g. Chakrabarty 2008; Crutzen 2002; Crutzen and Stoermer 2000; Haraway 2015; Latour 2018; Lewis and Maslin 2015; Swanson, Bubandt and Tsing 2015; Tsing 2015). There are those who protest against blaming such disasters on the whole of the human species, given that such collective responsibility would minimize the role played by those at the apex of the capitalist hierarchy, who are, in the majority of cases, the greatest emitters of gases resulting from the burning of fossil fuels. It would be unfair (they say) to extend this responsibility to non-capitalist peoples, whose lifestyles have nowhere near the same level of socio-environmental impact (Haraway 2015; Malm 2018; Moore 2015). There is rather more consensus when it comes to the recognition that human determination of certain dynamics, previously seen as pertaining to the realm of the natural sciences, requires an understanding that these are socio-cultural phenomena. This realization chimes with the perspective of many peoples about current ecological degradation, an understanding informed by cosmologies that establish a moral and political continuity between human relations and interactions with a variety of familiar beings and elements (Crook and Rudiak-Gould 2018; Efi 2018; Kopenawa and Albert 2013; Krenak 2020). Anthropologists have also observed that environmental catastrophes predicted by scientists from capitalist countries are not seen with surprise by those Indigenous interlocutors who cultivate a cataclysmic eschatology, and have experienced the end of the world through their fateful encounter with colonialism.[2]

In an article that considers distinct forms of historicity, Gellner (1971) suggests that the 'horizon' of a people relates to how they imagine their own history from its very beginning (cosmogony) up until the foretold end (eschatology). Set apart from familiar reality, the horizon, as a supposed harder-to-reach zone, comes to be intriguing in an evocative manner. So-called modern and naturalistic societies would lack a horizon because they would not take supernatural and eschatological cosmogonies seriously. In other words, for them, 'What is on the horizon is known to be similar in type to the ordinary stuff of daily life.' (ibid.:161).

Part of this definition resonates with more recent anthropological works discussing conceptions of the horizon as a spatiotemporal metaphor that stands for the possibility of knowing what is beyond the immediate field of perception, including that of ethnographic work itself (Bryant and Knight 2019:35-6; Kaartinen and Sather 2008:9). These conceptualizations will be helpful for subsequent reflections. The other part is of limited use, because it associates cosmogony and eschatology with the 'supernatural'. That said, it is helpful insofar as it enables us to realize, conversely, that the Anthropocene and other theories about climate change seem to have opened up a new eschatological horizon to the scientific community.[3]

A field without crisis

This was my own horizon when I first went to the region inhabited by the Ingarikó Amazonian people in 2014. Warnings about planetary ecological degradation by scientists was a source of concern, as was the Brazilian scenario of that period, which saw the intensification of predatory economic activities – both legal and illegal, public and private – over regions of the Amazon forest and on land occupied by 'traditional peoples', including Indigenous land. This time also saw an increase in attacks targeted at these populations. The federal

2   For case studies in the lowlands of South America, see the pioneering work by Albert 1993; also Danowski and Viveiros de Castro 2017; Pierri 2013.

3   I am aware that the scientific community has diverse conceptions about the end of the world, as observed by Danowski and Viveiros de Castro (2017:22): 'These fluctuations or equivocations do not detract from the salience and potency of the idea of "the end of the world". Rather, they diffract and multiply them in a variety of ends and of worlds which nonetheless all seem to express the same historical intuition: it has been disclosed to us that things are changing fast and not for the good of human life "as we know it".

government then, markedly different from the one that took over in 2018, with devastating impact on Indigenous populations, was at least committed to the goals established through international environmental agreements. Contemporary news was still shocking: far less land was given official approval for Indigenous use than by previous governments; deforestation rates in the Brazilian Amazon were up after almost a decade of reductions; violence against the Guarani Kaiowá Indigenous people by farmers and their allies persisted in Mato Grosso do Sul, as did high suicide rates amongst Indigenous young people; the construction of the Belo Monte hydroelectric dam, promoted by the federal government despite wide-ranging opposition, was bringing chaos to Altamira, a city at the heart of the Amazon forest;[4] and the invasion of the Yanomami Indigenous land by gold prospectors (out of control at the time of writing) had already begun to increase.[5]

I was therefore surprised by my own realization that in the north of the state of Roraima, not too far from the Yanomami, the Ingarikó were living relatively well – an impression that persisted during the four years of my fieldwork amongst them, despite the fact that Brazilian and world circumstances were getting worse. Obviously there were problems: they were facing hardships related to public health and educational initiatives tailored for Indigenous peoples, and stocks of fish and game were decreasing in their region. However, the Ingarikó did not have their territory invaded by land squatters, gold prospectors or timber merchants; they were neither threatened by farmers nor any other governmental enterprise; the population had more than doubled over the previous two decades; unlike other Amerindians, their youngsters were not affected by outbreaks of suicide and tended to remain in the locality, which protected them from a life on the margins in urban centres;[6] and, Ingarikó men and women were able to dedicate a good part of their time doing what they prized the most – having gatherings with plenty of *kaasiri* (a fermented drink made with manioc), while animatedly exchanging comic anecdotes.

---

4   People feared eviction and the fragmentation of Indigenous and river
    communities inhabiting the region of the Xingu river, as did in fact happen.

5   Each of these processes is easily verifiable, as they have all been well documented.
    See, for example: cop23.unfccc.int/news/presidents-of-us-and-brazil-commit-
    to-successful-paris-outcome and www.aljazeera.com/features/2012/1/20/dam-it-
    brazils-belo-monte-stirs-controversy (both accessed 5 February 2023).

6   There are plenty of ethnographic examples of young Amerindians who move to
    urban environments to supposedly conclude their studies. Boyer 2012 suggested a
    correlation between this phenomenon and the high suicide rates amongst young
    people in Mesoamerica. See Aráuz and Aparicio 2015 for further reflections on
    Indigenous suicide in South America.

The residual cataclysmology of the Areruya

I had another surprise when I came across an apocalyptic message transmitted in the Ingarikó's weekly religious rituals.[7] Similar to the Akawaio and the Patamona, the Ingarikó self-identify as Kapon – a term that can be translated as 'human being', 'humanity' or 'person'. These people inhabit the tri-border region between Brazil-Guyana-Venezuela, in northern Amazonia, and have as neighbouring peoples the Pemon, also known as Makuxi, Taurepan, Arekuna and Kamarakoto. Amongst the Kapon and the Pemon, only a few practise the Areruya religion. Some Indigenous people and anthropologists prefer to name the religion Aleluia or Hallelujah, the Portuguese and English translations used in Brazil and Guyana. I have opted for 'Areruya', a version that matches the pronunciation of the majority of the population and the spelling of those Ingarikó who have become literate. The religious ceremonies are always comprised of prayers, chants and a collective circular dance in longhouses called *soosi* (from the English 'church'). They happen weekly, as well as on festive dates such as Christmas and New Year's Eve, and were documented by the German ethnologist Koch-Grünberg (1981:74, 112) in 1911, when he visited villages of the Taurepan, Makuxi and Wapixana peoples. According to the Jesuit Cary-Elwes, as early as 1917 the Akawaio people already recognized Areruya as their religion, and it was officially recognized by the Guyana Council of Churches in 1977 (Bridges 1985:101–7; Butt Colson 1998:79–81; Goodrich 2003:70, 73).

Religious leaders say that their old prophets would dream of the Christian god, who transmitted his wisdom to them and warned them of the cataclysm that would destroy the Earth, an event that would be presaged by the appearance of Jesus Christ. Up to this day, religious hymns, prayers and sermons announce the eruption of *parau*, an incandescent water that shall burn the entirety of earthly matter, including all human beings. Jesus will save those who are most committed to the ethics and practice of the Indigenous religion, who by then will have been bodily transformed into divine beings able to live in celestial heaven without dying. The Ingarikó do not have a great deal of information about heaven, but they say that it is a place permanently lit, clean and free from suffering and death. By contrast, they consider the Earth to be *ëri* – an adjective that stands for wickedness, dirt and ugliness. What makes the Earth evil is death, disease, old age, hunger and the fighting that its inhabitants impose over one another. All of us, including animals and other terrestrial beings, are *makoi* (evil creatures or sinners). For that reason, Areruya predicts the destruction of this world.

---

7 Confirming what I had read in the ethnography by Abreu (2004), carried out amongst the Ingarikó in the 1990s.

However, most Ingarikó, including the most religious, doubt their own ability to access divine paradise without dying, declaring instead that their endeavour to practise religious principles must have as its ultimate goal to live well on Earth amongst one's relatives, in harmony, and with good and abundant food. This contemporary utopia seems to explain the social well-being I attributed to them. As for the predicted cataclysm, they do not believe in its imminence. Some would suggest that it is a metaphor for the degradation that all of us, as terrestrial beings, are experiencing, regardless of the fact that it is being caused by non-Indigenous lifestyles rooted in the accumulation of money and goods at the expense of human and inter-species relations of generosity and respect. For that very reason, it is the so-called *brancos*, or whites, who are subject to the environmental wars and catastrophes that the Ingarikó see on television when they go to the nearest towns.[8] They understand that, for the time being, they have been relatively spared from such crises, but that this does not mean that one will never affect them.

Their anthropological critique resonates with one made by another Indigenous people of South America, the Guarani-Mbya, according to an ethnography by Pierri (2013). Like the Ingarikó, the Mbya conceive of the divine celestial paradise as ontologically superior to the terrestrial dimension, the degeneration of which is mostly attributed to the whites' capitalist way of life. They do not doubt the advent of the cataclysm predicted by their shamans, but their understanding is that they will be spared. The cataclysm will bring an end to the whites' existence but not to Earth. In conversation with those both theorizing and criticizing the Anthropocene, the Mbya would be likely to say that the whites will be the only victims of their own geological force. The Ingarikó also refuse to share with whites the ideal world they aspire to for themselves; the difference is that they locate this ideal in the celestial dimension, and aim at achieving it spiritually, after death, and regardless of any cataclysm.

Thanks to ethnographic work previously carried out amongst the Kapon and the Pemon, I had already heard about Areruya's eschatology, even before I had met any Ingarikó people (Abreu 2004; Andrello 1993; Butt

---

8   The Ingarikó generally refer to non-Indigenous Brazilians as *karaiwa*, in contrast to other foreigners whom they and their ancestors had contact with over the centuries: *mekoro*, black people; *sipanio* (of Spanish origin), to refer to people from Venezuela; and *paranakîrî*, people with very light-coloured skin who often speak English. These categories are adjusted according to context in such a way that any non-Indigenous person may be referred to as *karaiwa*. As for the Portuguese term *brancos* ('whites'), the Ingarikó use it to refer to anyone they would call *karaiwa*, in other words, any non-Indigenous person including people with darker skin who would not normally be considered 'white' in Brazil.

1960; Butt Colson 1998). The novelty that fieldwork revealed to me was the resignification of the cataclysm. Another intriguing finding was the Ingarikó confirmation of the   exclusively Indigenous origin of their religion, linked neither to colonization nor to missionary endeavours. Both findings unveiled a new 'ethnographic horizon' to me, insofar as they prompted me to reflect on the mechanisms through which they construct their originating past and their eschatology, challenging thereby my own temporal conceptions.

Precursory forms of prophetism

Reports from chroniclers suggest that the Areruya religion originated from Kapon and Pemon prophetic movements that emerged mostly in the nineteenth century, not long after the arrival of the English in Guyana. This was a period in which the native populations were decimated by epidemics and inter-ethnic wars, which had intensified in the previous century due to a larger number of Indigenous people being captured to supply the Dutch demand for slaves.[9] Exploitative relations also contributed to a complete change of traditional political networks amongst the native populations.

Many of the prophetic movements were led by shamans, who, after ephemeral and periodic exchanges with Christian missionaries, started to reproduce certain elements of Christian liturgy and encourage Indigenous followers to engage with it through intense ritual practice. In return, followers would be saved from an imminent cataclysm, would potentially gain a place in Christian paradise and, in some cases, would attain the goods of colonizers. In my view, the predicted cataclysm is the strongest evidence that the prophets and their followers saw themselves, at that time, as inhabiting a world in crisis.

This historical reconstitution of the forms of prophetism predating Areruya, made in collaboration with other anthropologists (drawing on primary sources), contrasts with the Ingarikó conception of the exclusively Indigenous origin of their religion. As Butt (1960) has already noted in her well-known article on the birth of this religion, several of Areruya's origin stories emphasize how the Indigenous pioneers received Areruya's words straight from God, whom they contacted directly, bypassing any missionary mediation. Some versions state that this contact was made through dreamlike spiritual journeys, a method typical of shamanism. It is therefore necessary

---

9   In the seventeenth and eighteenth centuries, commercial relations between native populations of western Guiana and Europeans coexisted with the traditional inter-ethnic wars that came to be motivated by ambition to control the goods included in the Indigenous exchange system, mainly by the Dutch. These, on the other hand, demanded slaves – a role that was imposed on captives imprisoned in those wars (Dreyfus 1993; Farage 1991; Whitehead 1990).

to emphasize that the Indigenous originality of the religion, claimed by the Ingarikó, owes much to the shamanic nature of several of the religious practices.

That said, many of these myths associate the emergence of the religion with colonization, even if they describe the phenomena as concurrent, rather than the former being directly influenced by the latter. They narrate how the religion was born from an encounter between its founding prophets and non-Indigenous religious people, although a doubt is cast on the authenticity of the knowledge held by the latter. In one Ingarikó account, the divine words are better taught by the Indigenous prophet Pîraikoman than by his white rival, Noah, who invented the biblical religions. In another account by the neighbouring Akawaio, British white missionaries refrained from showing their Indigenous pupils the path to heaven. When a pupil finds his way by his own skills, God tells him not to trust white people, who are murderers (Amaral 2019:122–7, 141–8).

Revenge through myth

Santos-Granero (2007) faced a similar ethnographic problem. This author speculates that in a pre-Colombian past the Yanesha of the Andean Piedmont incorporated liturgical elements from Inca and, later, from Catholic priests. They maintain the two ritual traditions in the present day without, however, acknowledging what had been appropriated. Considering that in both cases the unremembered appropriations presupposed relations of domination that were disadvantageous for the Yanesha, Santos-Granero suggests that such processes of forgetting should be seen as political strategies: 'By forgetting, the Yanesha disempower the others, to empower themselves.' (ibid.:62).

This argument may lead us to understand, by equivocation (*sensu* Viveiros de Castro 2004), that the manipulation of memory per se is a political strategy that is empowering.[10] Like Santos-Granero and other anthropologists who faced analogous ethnographic situations in the Amazon (Gow 2001; Hugh Jones 1988), the limitations of my own historical understandings lead me to

---

10 For example, we could speculate that the way the past is narrated can foster self-esteem or a collective sense of pride and motivate a particular political standing in relation to certain adversaries – colonizers, for instance – in order to change asymmetrical relations. As I shall argue, this way of reasoning is very different from Amerindian ways of conceiving the possibilities of transformation through continuous bodily practices. According to the latter's temporal conceptions, it would be useless to cultivate particular narratives about the past to generate future political results if the desired outcome is not already anticipated in contemporary practices.

suppose that a people such as the Yanesha have transformed a past marked by asymmetrical relations of enmity. I will, however, argue later that – according to certain Ingarikó and other Amazonian temporal conceptions – what makes the transformation of the past into a political strategy are its possible, but in a sense already existing, effects in the present and the future.

I shall initially consider two Amerindian studies on the social relevance of remembering and forgetting the enemy. One of them is an article on temporal conceptions of the ancient Tupinambá warrior people by Carneiro da Cunha and Viveiros de Castro (1985). According to the authors, the Tupinambá were interested not so much in the status of their dead peers as in the number of deaths among the enemies themselves, memory of whom triggered new reasons for revenge. The ritualization of the enemies' deaths enabled captors to appropriate enemy names for themselves, as well as guaranteeing the emergence of new warriors and the continuity of social life. Thus, revenge was a temporal axis for the Tupinambá, connecting the past and the future. Or rather, it connected previous deaths to those still to come.

The other is Taylor's study of Jivaro Amazonian peoples of the Ecuador–Peru border (1993). According to the article, they endeavoured to forget their dead, including great warriors who transformed themselves into *arutam* spirits capable of transmitting to future generations the principles of war as well as names for newborn children. The Jivaro, however, did not forget those of their own deceased whose heads had been hunted by enemies, an act that deprived living relatives of the means to perform the necessary mourning rites that were fundamental to the erasure of these deceased's memory and concomitantly to the general continuity of life. And it was precisely the impossibility of forgetting that motivated them to take revenge. However, unlike the Tupinambá, who reminisced about the circumstances of their peers' deaths and the accomplishments of their enemies, revenge was not a cog in a Jivaro historical machine bridging the past to a future of reparation.

While the Ingarikó have forgotten their white enemies, they cultivate the memory of the ancient prophets, from whom the religious philosophy and values that govern their social life were inherited. Incidentally, many of them adopted biblical names or names rooted in Christian cosmology, such as Noah, Abel, Kîraisi (from 'Christ'), Inserî (from 'angel') and Epîn (from 'heaven'). Thus, Ingarikó differ from both Jivaro and Tupinambá, neither of whom memorized the biography of their illustrious ancestors. Nevertheless, the exemplary trajectories of the precursors of the Indigenous Areruya religion are usually mythologized. It is also important to observe that these prophets are remembered as people with extraordinary powers, who contacted the Christian god in their own right. The rare narratives that mention their encounter with white people emphasize the superiority of Indigenous religious knowledge over the biblical one, and the fact that Areruya followers will have exclusive access to divine paradise as a *post mortem* destination. The Ingarikó and some of their Kapon and Pemon neighbours have not historicized their hostile relationship with white people, locating it instead in mythology, where their revenge is carried out. This process 'empowers' them to the detriment of their enemy. However, I argue that, from the perspective of these Indigenous peoples, the mythical inversion of the colonial asymmetry is a political strategy insofar as it aims at a self-transformation in the present and future. To understand it as such requires a consideration of its temporalizing mechanisms.

Reproductions and ruptures: two types of transformation

In their introduction to *Time and Memory in Indigenous Amazonia*, the editors make the following remark regarding the intellectual systems of the peoples inhabiting that region:

> the concepts of action and agency are linked to the problem of producing transformations in a world that is not seen as a product of social conventions. Agency here supposes the possibility of producing transformations in the order established by myth and not the substitution of one convention for another convention.
>
> (Fausto and Heckenberger 2007:13)

According to this line of reasoning, the temporal conceptions of these peoples would require desired transformations to take place in mythical time, the conventions of which would always be reproduced by the agents. Concomitantly, it would seem that the great political potentiality of the mythological reversal for Areruya followers would be found in the possibility, admitted by them, that this process may determine the transformation of the future. In other words, they would have transformed the agency of their mythical ancestors, because they understood that its updating would generate a different and desirable present and future, in which they would create their own relations with the Christian spirits and would seek revenge on the whites by reversing the asymmetries imposed upon them. It is thus apparent that nowadays the Ingarikó and others practising Areruya differ from the early Tupinambá, who 'historicized' their hostile relations by considering them to be past causes of future deaths. The latter probably proceeded with this reasoning – and this is key – because they did not intend to change what the memorialization of the enemies had in store for them: further wars and revenge.

However, Indigenous people from the Amazon and other lowland South American regions have at least one additional way of understanding their collective transformations. Many find themselves in a spatiotemporal context (a world and an era) that would have been preceded by other spatiotemporal contexts. Generally speaking, the first is the pre-speciation mythical time, when all terrestrial beings shared the same human subjectivity. The second era is often marked by speciation – in other words, differentiation between terrestrial beings according to their respective forms – and the separation of immortal inhabitants in the sky from those inhabiting the earth, whose fate would be marked by death and disease. Some ethnic groups see themselves as belonging to this second era. Others see it as an era that precedes a current one characterized by colonialist asymmetries and by the correlated need to deplete the earth, whose degeneration would be mainly due to the colonizers' lifestyle (Gow 1991; Pierri 2013:257–8; Santos-Granero 2007:48–51; Taylor 2007:154–7; Wright 2005:263–4).

In many of these cosmologies, transitions are triggered by cataclysms. This is the story told by older and more knowledgeable Ingarikó: the world has already been made extinct twice by floods. After the first deluge, caused by the bad behaviour of the mythological brothers Makunaimë and Siikë, terrestrial beings were differentiated among themselves as well as from celestial humanity. The second deluge, rooted in the biblical myth of Noah, gives rise to the current era of the Areruya religion, placing the achievement of celestial immortality on the horizon of terrestrial humanity. According to religious doctrine, the third deluge will make this achievement possible.

Anthropologists such as Santos-Granero (2007:48) and Taylor (2007:155–6) identified continuities or even a linear relationship between eras conceived, respectively, by the Yanesha and the Quechua-speaking neighbours of the Jivaro peoples of the upper Amazon. As noted by Taylor, it is possible that the latter developed a 'Westernized (or at least Andeanized)' linear register. By contrast, I call attention to the ruptures that separate the eras conceived by the Ingarikó, given that each of them presents its own ontological conditions which are radically distinct from the others. This follows Danowski and Viveiros de Castro's observation regarding the eschatology of Amerindian peoples, whose ontologies they consider as being perspectivist (*sensu* Viveiros de Castro 1998):

> What seems to be a constant in Indigenous mythologies concerning the
> end of the world is the unthinkability of a world without people, without
> a humankind of some sort, however different from ours – as a matter of
> fact, the humankinds of each cosmic era generally tend to be entirely alien
> to each other, like separate species. The destruction of the world is the

destruction of humankind and vice versa; the recreation of the world is the
recreation of some form of life, that is, of experience and perspective; and,
as we have seen, the form of every life is 'human.'

(Danowski and Viveiros de Castro 2017:75)

In an Amerindian perspectivist ontology, the 'world', as perceived by
each human group or species, is an attribute of the bodies of the members of
that group. Bodies are constructed through shared practices that make them
consubstantial, and, at the same time, differentiate them from other bodies,
or from other perspectives and their respective worlds. Thus, the authors
suggest, 'The destruction of the world is the destruction of humankind and
vice versa.' Following a perspectivist reasoning, to speak about the end of the
world is to speak about the end of a collective and permanently constructed
perspective; in other words, of a set of practices that makes up a community
of consubstantial bodies. It is through these lenses that I envisage a potential
sense of 'rupture' for an Amazonian people such as the Ingarikó. In other
words, it appears that they see each cataclysm as marking a rupture between
distinct perspectives constructed by them (the present one and a prospective
one) and by their ancestors (the post-speciation mythical time, which, as we
shall see, is not exactly a past one).[11]

Some works on the anthropology of time describe temporalities with
eras that are the result of ruptures (described as 'episodic') as different from
those with an evolutionist understanding, as seen in European traditions,
where collective transformation is seen to be the result of a linear and gradual
process. The episodic model conceives that a particular 'state of affairs' comes
into being through a singular disruptive episode (Gellner 1964:4–6; Munn
1992:12; Robbins 2007:11–12).

An original approach to the topic was given by Strathern (2021:39–41),
drawing on ethnographies about the growing of yams and other crops with
regenerative capacities in Melanesia. Strathern suggests that these agricultural
practices might inspire episodic notions of transformation. An example is
given by the people of Ambrym Island in Vanuatu (Rio 2007:114–15). They
metaphorized the life cycle of a tuber such as the yam in conformity with the
generational transitions of human dynamics of procreation and death. These
transitions were seen as ruptures: to grow yams, it was necessary to bury a
whole tuber, or part of it. The burial was conceived as death and the 'killed'
tuber as the 'father' of those which would originate from its regeneration.

---

11   It is worth remarking on the inexistence of well-defined and diverse perspectives
      during the pre-speciation mythical era, when the bodies of the collective groups
      had not yet reached their definitive forms.

Over time, it was necessary to prevent its rotting process from contaminating the offspring, which would have already been developing. The farmer would then dig up the remnants of the once generative tuber, separating it from its children. The division promoted a generational rupture. At the same time, it guaranteed regeneration. From then on, a piece of a new-generation tuber would be reburied, becoming the father of another offspring, even if this depended on its own death.

Analogically, from a procreative point of view, people from early Papua New Guinea saw a radical discontinuity between their time and that of their ancestors. What was recreated between one era and the next was the intergenerational rupture, which could activate the (re)generative potential in people.

> Their ancestors had lived in a present with its evident future potential, that is, today's people: the people alive now were the cuttings or offshoots of that previous potential, which they brought into their own present so they too could be regenerators of a new future.
>
> (Strathern 2021:41)[12]

Strathern also recognizes an episodic temporality in Melanesian prophetism. Prompted by the desire to transform power relations between Indigenous people and colonizers, prophets would recreate the very past where these asymmetrical relations were established (Strathern 2019:67). Thus, I contend, they could regenerate the capacities of their ancestors that determined the transformed past. Returning to the Ingarikó, I have suggested that their cataclysmology is a fine example of a particular Indigenous conception of collective transformations through ruptures, or more precisely, through changes in perspective. On the other hand, I have also argued that they cultivate a prophetism that transforms and mythifies a past, where colonialist asymmetry was rooted, so that they may regenerate it according to their interests. However, the Ingarikó do not conceive of this past as belonging to another era that predates the last deluge. There is no rupture separating it from the present. The conquest of Areruya by the mythic prophet Pîraikoman, which ensures a possible path towards divination for religious people (even if *post mortem*), continues to be a major event that defines the current era. As for the previous world of Makunaimë and Siikë, as we shall see, while a deluge did separate that era from the current one, the perspective maintained by that

---

12   See also Strathern (2019:69–70) for similar reflections drawing on other examples from Melanesia.

world's inhabitants remains as a dimension of the Ingarikó person, even if Areruya followers endeavour to differentiate themselves from it.

It is true that religious leaders announce the prospect of an incandescent cataclysm along with a correlated radical transformation of perspective, whereby religious people will become divine in heaven, and non-religious terrestrial beings will be fated to live in darkness. Such a conception of transformation through rupture relates to another one that redefines a past to be regenerated, albeit differently from the dynamics of separation and continuity between eras we saw in the episodic temporalities of Melanesia. This becomes more salient when we consider the two prospective horizons of religious Ingarikó: the conception of a cataclysmic transformation does not envisage a 'future' understood as the continuity of the contemporary world in the hereafter. The other conception has a 'future' and supposes that this future is already lived in the present.

In other words, Areruya followers anticipate the hereafter by continuing to perform certain ritual and everyday practices that will warrant a gradual and deferred divinization.[13] There is no contradiction between the two horizons in question and they can even complement each other. As the religion states, at the moment of the cataclysm, only those who went through a gradual transformation over the course of their lives will be able to assume a fully divine perspective and rise into heaven with Jesus Christ; in the worst-case scenario, devotees will burn on earth but will be able to save their spiritual being. In any case, we have already seen that the majority of Ingarikó people today, including the most religious ones, relativize the announced cataclysm and the possibility of moulding a body that is deserving of divine immortality. I also understand that both relativizations are signs that the Ingarikó do not long that much for a rupture from their current world.

Temporality of the field

Unlike what Vilaça (2015:216, 2016: 245–8) identified amongst the Wari' of south-west Amazonia and what Robbins (2004:297) saw with the Melanesian Urapmin, who became Christians a few decades ago, I did not witness, in the context of Areruya, confessional rites or any other practice that would foment the conception of an individualizing inner self. The same could not be said

---

13   Practising Areruya speak about stages in the transformation of a person and of a religious collective over one's life course and in terms of ethical and ritual commitment. At each stage, the subject will become closer to divinity. The following is a superficial characterization of these stages: *ekoneka* (to organize and prepare oneself); *epîrema* (to pray for oneself); *emaimupa* (to become endowed by the divine word); *esensima* (to transform oneself); and *emîsaka* (to rise to heaven).

regarding civil-service jobs, as held by teachers and Indigenous health agents, occupations that are highly coveted amongst Ingarikó youth. Nowadays, most of them are employed, involved in projects or in school education, all of which in their understanding can translate into sources of income. Older people go so far as to say that, unlike their experiences when they were young, this is now the time for school education. While those who secure such jobs tend to share their income with the closest members of their family, an asymmetry between waged and non-waged family groups is already apparent – a phenomenon that clashes with values that Robbins would describe as 'relationalist'. Furthermore, some have adopted an incipient meritocratic discourse, which values individual drive, in order to justify inequalities resulting from salaried work. Church leaders complain about the absence of students and their tutors at weekly ceremonies. In fact, it is not uncommon to hear from young teachers several justifications for not being present at any of them. Still, most youth resemble the rest of the population, as they observe at least some of the religious practices and share the religion's ethical principles.

It is then possible to make the following generalization: almost all Ingarikó are religious and perceive the conditions on earth as ontologically inferior to those in celestial heaven, where the Christian god and other deities dwell. The earth is home to Makoi, the Devil, a spirit who is a shape-shifter and can influence pernicious actions and thoughts. The term *makoi* also denotes evil and 'sin', a word used to characterize those who quarrel, perform witchcraft, kill, attack other people or behave in a morally reprehensible manner. Given that all beings inhabiting the earth frequently display flawed behaviour, they habitually share the perspective of Makoi. Thus, when the Ingarikó of today endeavour to transform their bodies in the image of divinity by practising Areruya's rites and ethics, they are differentiating themselves from their own *makoi* condition.

It has not always been like this. Early ethnographic descriptions of Kapon and Pemon cosmologies, the oral history of the Ingarikó, their mythology, their shamanic songs and ancient rites no longer in use – all reveal that in the past, their ancestors resembled other Amazonian peoples in conceiving of an anthropomorphic spiritual backdrop, shared by all types of being, against which they built their consubstantial bodies through certain practices. In this way they constituted a specific perspective that was distinct from the others.[14] In other words, they kept a set of habits that defined Kapon humanity: they

---

14   See Taylor (1996:207) and Vilaça (1992:34, 52–4, 2005:449–50, 457) for reflections on consubstantiality created in the process of Amazonian kinship production; and Viveiros de Castro (2015) for the association between this theme and Amerindian perspectivism.

grew crops, consumed fermented drinks, fished, made use of *taren* magical enunciations, healed themselves through shamanism and organized the now extinct *parisara* and *tukuik* feasts, while men hunted and warred against enemies and women were responsible for cooking.

This was the lifestyle of the mythological brothers Makunaimë and Siikë, in the era of speciation, a life style that contemporary Ingarikó deem *makoi* and from which they endeavour to distance themselves. However, their ancestors valued that way of life and, in non-ritual everyday life, would try to eclipse the spiritual component of each person that enabled the communication with other beings, as used to happen in the mythical era prior to speciation and the first flood.[15]

Over time, the perspective that was collectively constructed in one era would become the ontological realm from which the people of the following era would differentiate themselves, and this would happen once again. This does not mean that all practices that defined human perspective in a given era were completely abandoned in another. For example, working the land, hunting and consuming fermented drinks are to this day considered fundamental for the constitution of Kapon humanity and as in conformity with the principles of the Areruya religion, which endorses food abundance. Nor have contemporary Ingarikó abandoned the anthropomorphic spiritual realm of their ancestors, which is markedly present in their oneiric experiences of encounters with unknown people that show signs of being animal spirits. This realm also emerges when the Ingarikó seek the help of their only working shaman to intervene on their behalf with the spirits who are masters of particular game animals. The shaman can also be requested to heal patients whose bodies are being transformed after their spirits have been taken and turned into kin of animals' spirits, although this is increasingly rare. In fact, I see the continuation of shamanism as a sign that contemporary Ingarikó maintain certain ontological conceptions of their ancestors: given the threat of a transformation that would liken them to animals, they endeavour to preserve their Kapon perspective by strengthening human kinship bonds and habits. In other words, I suggest that while the Ingarikó, particularly the most religious ones, are striving to produce a divinized perspective in order to distance themselves from their habitual *makoi* condition, they maintain practices that their ancestors would recognize as defining the Kapon perspective. In any case,

---

15   See Viveiros de Castro (2007) regarding the time preceding specific differences. Amerindian mythology tells that, at that time, all beings communicated with each other more easily. They were equipped with a subjectivity similar to the human one and differed less from one another than from their own selves, being capable of continuous self-transformation.

their religiosity seems to lead them to a gradual ontological de-animalization, similar to that which Vilaça (2011, 2015, 2016:266–70) observed of the Wari'. The latter retain something of their traditional perspectivist notion of personhood, which is contradictory to the conception of the inner self that they have adopted throughout Christianity. However, they no longer see themselves as subjected to perspectival transformations via animal predation. Instead, they find themselves oscillating between the perspectives of God and the Devil, the latter being capable of subjecting them to the position of prey.

In a commentary on Vilaça's ethnographic material concerning the alternating ontological states of the Wari', Strathern (this volume, pp. 4–5) observes the capacity of both Amazonian and Melanesian people to live distinct temporalities.[16] This also appears to be the case for Ingarikó nowadays. They occasionally communicate with other beings, running the risk of letting themselves be captured in the ambit of spiritual virtuality (a generalized human condition of the beginning of times). They avoid being captured by reconfiguring their ancestors' perspective. However, because they became religious and started to see the perspective shaped by their ancestors as degenerate, they distance themselves from it by putting their divinized future into practice. Though this religious future no longer forms most people's horizon, it still gives rise to another possible future of schooling and monetization that is also anticipated, even if only by a younger fraction of the population.

The Ingarikó conception of the *makoi* dimension relates not only to themselves but to the earth as well, and is located in a specific spacetime, which also situates my 'field' in temporal terms. An ethnography that is strictly in the present tense would only make salient the contradiction between that conception and the social well-being that the Ingarikó aim to perpetuate. However, if our ethnographic focus is the future, we come to realize that while this conception prevailed over another (the human dimension of which was built under a permanent risk of animalization), it is giving way to a conception of personhood performed mainly by younger people. And we saw that this

---

16　This observation echoes an earlier text in which Strathern (2001) also analyses problems in Amazonia and in Melanesia, with both contexts shedding light on one another. When commenting on the Melanesian cases, Strathern interprets gender relations (same-sex and cross-sex) and their defining mechanisms (of continuity and division) as a metaphor for thinking about generational relations and related Indigenous conceptions about perpetuation or transformation of practices at a given time. One of the relevant insights of this exercise is that people who alternate between these distinct ontological states can live in the present as someone from the past or from the future.

notion indeed has elements of the modern 'individual', differing from that of the religious conception.

Now, if we examine the past of the Ingarikó through a historical lens, we can perceive the *makoi* condition that they attribute to themselves and to all other earthly beings as a trace of early prophetic narratives about the degeneration of life on earth – narratives that their ancestors elaborated both from colonial asymmetries imposed upon them and from the Christianity they appropriated. Their religious vocabulary is therefore made up of concepts such as *makoi* and *parau* (a cataclysm announced in religious songs and sermons), suggesting that although they do not see themselves as living a crisis in the present, at a certain moment their ancestors had apparently lived in a time of crisis.

Dalsgaard and Nielsen (2016:2) propose that we should imagine the ethnographer's 'field' as a temporal as well as a spatial concept. As suggested in the sub-heading of one of the previous sections, in the field where I lived alongside the Ingarikó, I did not see any indication that they saw their context as one of crisis. And I understand that this ethnographic horizon was drawn in contrast to my new eschatological horizon, influenced by studies on current climate change. Furthermore, I would not be surprised if I were to return to the Ingarikó region in a few decades from now and find the majority of the population striving to produce bodies of students, teachers, Indigenous health agents and other types of salaried worker. The divinization prophecy associated with a cataclysm would then be completely obsolete and would be abandoned or, more likely, radically re-signified – something that has already occurred with a number of concepts that make up the Areruya repertoire. '*Parau*', the incandescent cataclysmic water, would incorporate even more layers of semantic transformation, and the distance between the new meanings of the concept and the crisis that was once a related metaphor would increase.

In line with my own temporal conceptions, the realization of this hypothesis would only be viable if 'my crisis' – the contemporary planetary crisis mostly resulting from capitalism – did not affect them to the extent that they would also see themselves as being in crisis, leading them to re-appropriate the disruptive eschatological horizon of the past.

The fact that they relativize the religious cataclysm is also an example of a temporal determinations of the 'field', given that this relativization only drew my attention because at the time I met them I was myself facing a potentially cataclysmic future. It is noteworthy that they never relativized 'my crisis'. However, the Ingarikó understand that, for now, their religion ensures they are spared, while the non-Indigenous have reason to fear the end of the world that they have degenerated.

Acknowledgements

This chapter resumes some reflections presented at the 2021 conference of the Society for the Anthropology of Lowland South America. I am grateful to Laura Mentore and George Mentore, whose comments helped me refine my ideas. Between 2022 and 2023, it benefited from support from the National Council for Scientific and Technological Development (CNPq – Brazil). This work also benefited from dialogue with all members of the Balzan project on time and the ethnographic horizon. I am especially grateful for advice from Aparecida Vilaça and comments from Marilyn Strathern and Tony Crook. A preliminary version was translated from Portuguese into English by Luciana Lang, whom I thank.

References

Abreu, S.A. 2004. *Aleluia e o Banco de Luz*. Campinas: Centro de Memória Unicamp.

Albert, B. 1993. 'L'Or cannibale et la chute du ciel: une critique chamanique de l'économie politique de la nature (Yanomami, Brésil)', *L'Homme* 33(126–8):349–78.

Amaral, V. 2019. Os Ingarikó e a religião Areruya. PhD Thesis. Museu Nacional at Universidade Federal do Rio de Janeiro.

Andrello, G. 1993. Os Taurepáng: memória e profetismo do século XX. Masters thesis. Campinas: Universidade Estadual de Campinas.

Aráuz, L.C. and Aparicio, M. (eds) 2015. *Etnografías del Suicidio en América del Sur*. Quito: Editorial Universitaria Abya-Yala.

Boyer, I.N. 2012. 'Ach' kuxlejal: el nuevo vivir. Amor, carácter y voluntad en la modernidad tzotzil'. In P. Pitarch and G. Orobitg (eds), *Modernidades Indígenas*, pp. 279–317. Madrid: Iberoamericana Vervuert.

Bridges, J. 1985. *Rupununi Mission: The Story of Curthbert Cary-Elwes among the Indians of Guiana*. London: Jesuit Missions.

Bryant, R. and Knight, D.M. 2019. *The Anthropology of the Future*. Cambridge: Cambridge University Press.

Butt, A. 1960. 'The birth of a religion'. *The Journal of the Royal Anthropological Institute* (NS) 90(1):66–106.

Butt Colson, A. 1998. *Fr. Cary-Elwes S. J. and the Alleluia Indians*. Georgetown: University of Guyana.

Carneiro da Cunha, M. and Viveiros de Castro, E., 1985. 'Vingança e temporalidade: os Tupinambás', *Journal de la Societé des Américanistes* 71:191–208.

Chakrabarty, D. 2008. 'The climate of history: four theses', *Critical Inquiry* 35:197–222.

Crook, T. and Rudiak-Gould, P. 2018. 'Introduction: Pacific climate cultures'. In T. Crook and P. Rudiak-Gould (eds), *Pacific Climate Cultures: Living Climate Change in Oceania*, pp. 1–20. Warsaw/Berlin: De Gruyter.

Crutzen, P. and Stoermer, E.F. 2000. 'The Anthropocene', *IGBP Global Change Newsletter* 41:17–18.

Crutzen, P. 2002. 'Geology of mankind', *Nature* 415:23.

Dalsgaard, S. and Nielson, M. 2016. 'Introduction: time and the field'. In S. Dalsgaard and M. Nielson (eds), *Time and the Field*, pp. 1–19 Oxford: Berghahn Books.

Danowski, D. and Viveiros de Castro, E. 2017 [2014]. *The Ends of the World* (trans. R. Nunes). London: Polity Press.

Dreyfus, S. 1993. 'Os empreendimentos coloniais e os espaços políticos indígenas no interior da Guiana ocidental (entre o Orenoco e o Corentino) de 1613 a 1796'. In E. Viveiros de Castro and M. Carneiro da Cunha (eds), *Amazônia: Etnologia e História Indígena*. pp. 19-42. São Paulo: USP/Fapesp.

Efi, T.T.T. 2018. 'Prelude: climate change and the perspective of the fish'. In T. Crook and P. Rudiak-Gould (eds), *Pacific Climate Cultures: Living Climate Change in Oceania*, pp. ix–xiii. Berlin: De Gruyter.

Farage, N. 1991. *As muralhas dos sertões: os povos indígenas no Rio Branco e a colonização*. Rio de Janeiro: Paz e Terra/Anpocs.

Fausto, C. and Heckenberger, M. 2007. 'Introduction: Indigenous history and the history of the "Indians"'. In C. Fausto and M. Heckenberger (eds), *Time and Memory in Indigenous Amazonia: Anthropological Perspectives*, pp. 1–43. Gainesville, FL: University Press of Florida.

Gellner, E. 1964. *Thought and Change*. London: Weidenfeld and Nicolson.

——— 1971. 'Our current sense of history', *European Journal of Sociology* 12(2):159–79.

Goodrich, D. 2003. *Old-style Missionary: The Ministry of John Dorman, Priest in Guyana*. East Harling, Norfolk: Taverner Publications.

Gow, P. 1991. *Of Mixed Blood: Kinship and History in Peruvian Amazonia*. Oxford: Clarendon Press.

——— 2001. *An Amazonian Myth and its History*. Oxford: Oxford University Press.

Haraway, D. 2015. 'Anthropocene, Capitalocene, Plantationocene, Chthulucene: making kin', *Environmental Humanities* 6:159–65.

Hugh Jones, S. 1988. 'The gun and the bow: myths of the white man and Indians', *L'Homme* 28(106–7):138–55.

Kaartinen, T. and Sather, C. 2008. 'Introduction'. In C. Sather and T. Kaartinen (eds), *Beyond the Horizon: Essays on Myth, History, Travel and Society* (Studia Fennica 2), pp. 7–22. Helsinki: Finnish Literature Society. .

Koch-Grünberg, T. 1981 [1917]. *Del Roraima al Orinoco*. Tomo I. Caracas: Ernesto Armitano.

Kopenawa, D. and Albert, B. 2013 [2010]. *The Falling Sky: Words of a Yanomami Shaman*. Cambridge, MA: Harvard University Press.

Krenak, A. 2020 [2019]. *Ideas to Postpone the End of the World*. Toronto: House of Anansi.

Latour, B. 2018 [2017]. *Down to Earth: Politics in the New Climatic Regime.* Cambridge: Polity Press.

Lewis, S. and Maslin, M. 2015. 'Defining the Anthropocene', *Nature* 519:171–80.

Malm, A. 2018. 'The view from Dominica: Anthropocene or Capitalocene?', *The Unesco Courier* 2:23–5.

Moore, J. 2015. *Capitalism in the Web of Life: Ecology and the Accumulation of Capital.* London: Verso.

Munn, N. 1992. 'The cultural anthropology of time: A critical essay', *Annual Review of Anthropology* 21:93–123.

Pierri, D. 2013. O Perecível e o Imperecível: Lógica do Sensível e Corporalidade no Pensamento Guarani-mbya. Masters thesis. São Paulo: Universidade de São Paulo.

Rio, K. 2007. *The Power of Perspective: Social Ontology and Agency on Ambrym Island, Vanuatu.* Oxford: Berghahn Books.

Robbins, J. 2004. *Becoming Sinners: Christianity and Moral Torment in a Papua New Guinea Society.* Berkeley: University of California Press.

——— 2007. 'Continuity thinking and the problem of Christian culture: belief, time, and the Anthropology of Christianity', *Current Anthropology* 48(1):5–38.

Santos-Granero, F. 2007. 'Time is disease, suffering and oblivion: Yanesha historicity and the struggle against temporality'. In: C. Fausto and M. Heckenberger (orgs), *Time and Memory in Indigenous Amazonia: Anthropological Perspectives*, pp. 47–73. Gainesville, FL: University Press of Florida.

Strathern, M. 2001. 'Same-sex and cross-sex relations: some internal comparisons'. In T. Gregor and D. Tuzin (eds), *Gender in Amazonia and Melanesia: An Exploration of the Comparative Method*, pp. 221–44. Berkeley: University of California Press.

——— 2019. 'A clash of ontologies?: time, law and science in Papua New Guinea', *HAU, Journal of Ethnographic Theory* 9(1):58–74.

——— 2021. 'New and old worlds: a perspective from social anthropology', *European Review* 29(1):34–44.

Swanson, H. A., Bubandt, N. and Tsing, A. 2015. 'Less Than One But More Than Many: Anthropocene as Science Fic/on and Scholarship-in-the-Making'. *Environment and Society: Advances in Research* 6: 149–166

Taylor, A.-C. 1993. 'Remembering to forget: identity, mourning and memory among the Jivaro', *Man* (NS) 28(4):653–78.

——— 1996. 'The soul's body and its states: an Amazonian perspective of being human', *The Journal of the Royal Anthropological Institute* 2(2):201–15.

——— 2007. 'Sick of history: contrasting regimes of historicity'. In C. Fausto and M. Heckenberger (orgs) *Time and Memory in Indigenous Amazonia: Anthropological Perspectives*, pp. 133–68. University Press of Florida.

Tsing, A. 2015. *The Mushroom at the End of the World: On the Possibility of Life in Capitalist Ruins*. Princeton, NJ: Princeton University Press.

Vilaça, A. 1992. *Comendo Como Gente: Formas do Canibalismo Wari'*. Rio de Janeiro: Editora UFRJ/Anpocs.

——— 2011. 'Dividuality in Amazonia: God, the devil and the constitution of personhood in Wari' Christianity', *Journal of the Royal Anthropological Institute* (NS) 17(2):243–62.

——— 2015. 'Dividualism and individualism in Indigenous Christianity: a debate seen from Amazonia', *Hau: Journal of Ethnographic Theory* (5)1:197–225.

——— 2016. *Praying and Preying: Christianity in Indigenous Amazonia*. Berkeley: University of California Press.

Viveiros de Castro, E. 1998. 'Cosmological deixis and Amerindian perspectivism', *Journal of the Royal Anthropological Institute* (NS) 4(3):469–88.

——— 2004. 'Perspectival anthropology and the method of controlled equivocation', *Tipití: Journal of Society for Anthropology of Lowland South America* 2(1):3–22.

——— 2007. 'The crystal forest: notes on the ontology of Amazonian spirits', *Inner Asia* 9(2):153–72.

——— 2015. 'Along the spider thread: virtuality, actualization, and the kinship process in Amazonia'. In E. Viveiros de Castro, *The Relative Native*, pp. 97–138. Chicago: HAU Books.

Whitehead, N. 1990. 'The Snake Warriors – Sons of the Tiger's Teeth: a descriptive analysis of Carib warfare, ca. 1500–1820'. In J. Haas (ed.), *The Anthropology of War*. pp. 146–70. Cambridge: Cambridge University Press.

Wright, R. 2005. 'O tempo de Sophie'. In *História Indígena e do Indigenismo no alto Rio Negro*, pp. 203–69. São Paulo: Instituto Socioambiental.

3

The Bougainville Crisis

A Nagovisi perspective

SIMON KENEMA[1]

❋

In needing to give their lives a future, Nagovisi Bougainvilleans reacted to national conflict with a great sense of urgency. Yet the burden of the following account is that they applied notions of responsibility for the troubles in idioms at a considerable remove from the dominant public narrative. The latter narrative, the 'Bougainville Crisis', refers to a period that Nagovisi nowadays bracket off in public idiom as 'the time of crisis'. This was an artefact of the history of Bougainville's relations with the central Papua New Guinean state, reiterated in numerous political commentaries, popular and academic, in which a forking of ways into the future is manifested as a forking of people. In this view, people must be committed to one side or another, and opposed allegiances clarified, future action being imagined as concretizing those differences into winners and losers of a war or a referendum. Nagovisi people talk readily enough of troubles and disputes among themselves, and events erupt to call forth specific alignments, but it is against another backdrop altogether: the indissoluble interpenetration of persons with one another. This chapter explicates that founding vision of social life (*mono*), a 'relational density' understood as a plane of kinship. There are no alternatives. Its dissolution or disintegration would imply no less than kinship extinguished into oblivion.

---

1   This work was produced under the auspices of the Ethnographic Horizons project at the Centre for Pacific Studies, University of St Andrews, and was supported by the International Balzan Foundation.

❃

Introduction

As the war wore on, there was an explicit concern about who would bear the burden of repairing fragmented kinship relations. The unspoken answer felt terribly urgent to factions on all sides. The responsibility to end the fighting derived from combatants' realization that their opposing counterparts were close kin members, who, for whatever reason, had become sworn enemies. There was a palpable fear that – as war continued – the chasm of hostilities would erode kinship ties and memories. The overriding worry was that, with the remaining knowledge of kinship extinguished by the ravages of war, those born into a vacuum of alienation and detachment from historical kinship connections would find themselves eternally estranged, that is become non-kin to people they should share kinship bonds with. When people talk about the time of crisis (1989–97) and the contemporary peace, they often allude to the way the thread of kinship played a significant role in overcoming the horrors of war, allowing fragmented communities and families to repair familial relations. I use the idiom of kinship here in the associational and expansive sense of relatedness (Carsten 2000) and mutuality of being (Sahlins 2013). This view of kinship resonates with the ways in which Nagovisi articulate the relational concept of *mono*, a concept that figures prominently in this chapter.

Where time is posited as an enduring and external frame in which agency is enacted, corresponding notions of crisis are provoked by a guarantee that time will continue nonetheless. Yet where temporality is made in people's actions, relations and movements, the question of continuity turns on the possibilities for enacting relations through the reciprocities and responsibilities of kinship and exchange. If all life comes through persons, and if relations provide vital supports for living, the curtailment or abandonment of relations removes the necessary bases for life to continue. This raises existential questions beyond ideas of crisis and time, for there are no such equivalent guarantees of continuing frames for life to rely upon: time for life must be made through movements and relations; cessation risks negating the possibility for life.

To external commentators, the 1990s Bougainville Crisis inevitably appeared as a time of crisis. Yet its effects on the ground entailed profound restrictions on movement, paralysed kinship and nullified the possibilities for projecting temporal momentum, for making time for life to follow. With spaces for relational flows extinguished, life's movement becomes impossible. A vernacular reading of Nagovisi ontology and kinship presented here (and see Kenema 2010) reveals how temporality is made in places and bodies that gather past and present constellations of relations and flows within and beyond the person. Nagovisi view land as endowed with a capacity for agency and relatedness, in that what is produced out of it, and the movements enacted upon it, are directly implicated in human interactions. With the Nagovisi, it is not uncommon to hear the claim that a certain parcel of land is related to such and such a person by virtue of a particular action. 'Spatio-temporality' appears inseparable from the enactment of kinship relations: moving in space is also moving in time, and implicates lives beyond a present moment. Neither time nor life appear guaranteed to continue.

The previous academic commentaries on the Crisis discussed below (beginning with Filer 1990), have tended to give little emphasis to the question of kinship and the relationship between land, kinship and vernacular conceptions of personhood, and the critical role each of these facets plays in the production of the islanders' social life. An ethnographic analysis exploring the conceptual life-world of the Nagovisi would have to deal with the centrality these categories, and their articulation in an inseparable amalgamation. This complex nexus of entanglements offers a novel understanding of the effects of the Crisis and why it should have drawn far removed and apparently unrelated people into a common cause (Kenema 2010, 2016).

The central question is how a localized set of grievances centred around the giant Panguna mine could have escalated into conditions of profound island-wide social and political upheaval. From an analytical and theoretical standpoint, my argument is motivated by a desire to transcend the descriptive paradigms of predominantly sociological explanations, such as that of Filer's (1990) 'social time-bomb' theory, or of ecological collapse (Lasslett 2014; Nash 1993; Ogan 1991) and state-centric notions of ethno-nationalism (Ghai and Regan 2000), all of which have the tendency to act as analytical vortices within which vernacular perceptions and understandings of the conflict become submerged.

While the origin of the Bougainville Crisis as a whole tends to be ascribed to landowner dissatisfaction over the distribution of economic benefits from the Panguna mine, how the conflict spread and how its effects registered in people's consciousness across the island in space and time warrants a nuanced understanding grounded in particular locations and experiences. This suggestion is based on the fact that, during the course of the war, many internal divisions arose among Bougainvilleans themselves, which in turn sparked multiple localized events, the two most prominent cases also being called 'crises', after the Bougainville Crisis. These were critical episodes of violence that arose from internal divisions that had little to do with the original concerns with the Panguna mine. These episodes can be thought of as products of competing temporal concerns: that is, of disagreements about whether the prevailing circumstances (which were questions of temporality) were appropriate for pursuing peaceful resolution to the conflict. Hence, a focus on how local people perceived time in the context of their daily struggles will allow us to understand the complex tapestry of motivations as to why particular actions were taken or not taken at different moments in the history of the conflict. It is true that the origin of 'the conflict' itself was spurred by a desire for a different kind of future, a different temporal horizon, where the economic inequalities (both imagined and real) engendered by the mine could be reset and rectified. Yet within this broader politics of violence, the way people related to the violence and its effects was shaped largely by forces that played out at the local level.

A brief overview of the Bougainville Crisis

Bougainville has had a long and tumultuous history in the general political landscape of the nation-state of Papua New Guinea (PNG). Figuring as a central dimension to this history is mineral exploration and development that predates PNG's political independence in 1975. When a large-scale copper mine was developed at Panguna in the mountainous interior of central Bougainville in the 1960s, many islanders had no prior experience of development on an industrial scale. From the early commencement of the giant Panguna copper mine, which was later to become the signature industrial behemoth on the island, the islanders' reactions to the project were mixed. For some, the mine ushered in a new era of economic opportunities whereby islanders could participate in the modern cash economy. While local communities in the vicinity of mine bemoaned the industrial-scale reconfiguration of their environment and landscape, others viewed the construction of the mine as a vehicle for attaining the novel social experiences that come with modernity, such as town life and wage labour. In 1989 historical grievances over the distribution of mining revenues exploded into a violent armed conflict, as dissatisfied landowners, with the help of other Bougainvilleans, took up arms and forced the premature closure of the mine. What initially began as a set of localized mine-lease area disputes among landowners, over the terms of benefit sharing, ultimately erupted into an island-wide secessionist conflict against the PNG state (Filer 1990; Regan 1998, 2019). In an effort to end the decade-long war, Bougainville was granted autonomous political status in 2005 under a series of amendments to the PNG constitution. These amendments paved the way for the implementation of the Bougainville Peace Agreement and the establishment of the Autonomous Bougainville Government. It also allowed for a political referendum to be conducted at a later date to determine whether Bougainville would remain part of PNG or become independent. The referendum was conducted in October 2019, when more than ninety per cent of the voters voted for independence.

The Bougainville Crisis, as it became known, had a considerable impact on people's practical uses and perceptions of time. One of the most significant shifts that occurred over the course of the Crisis was an observable alteration in the way people related to time and to each other. As freedom of movement became significantly curtailed, due to hostilities and intense fighting between the warring factions, the relationship between movement and time became a subject of bureaucratic management. People could no longer travel freely in and between places they had frequented without restriction before the conflict. During the war it became vital for people who lived in the PNG government-controlled areas to report their movements to the PNG security forces. As people's ability to move freely was constricted in response to heightened safety and security concerns, access to livelihood resources and strategies that would not have been problematic before the war proved increasingly challenging. Household activities that were once simple routines, such as families going to gardens to collect food, came under microscopic scrutiny from the security forces, who demanded a kind of temporal transparency regarding how and where people spent their time. Patterns of physical mobility at the care centres (refugee camps) came under close scrutiny. The PNG military monitored and surveilled every aspect of people's movements. All this was possible in an atmosphere that was shaped by fear, suspicion and a palpable inability to reconcile the divergent, heterogeneous and competing understandings of temporality and people's struggles to meet their daily livelihood demands. The Crisis considerably altered the times people moved in and between places, while it simultaneously redefined relations and the sense of mutual responsibility between close kin – particularly in cases where communities and families found themselves caught up in opposing factions.

The military landing at Nagovisi in 1993[2] introduced a significant shift in the dynamics of the Crisis, in several senses. For the first time the local Bougainville Revolutionary Army (BRA) splintered along two factional lines. Many members of the BRA who opted to remain in the care centre joined the local resistance force. The hardliners fled up into the mountain interior, from where they launched periodic attacks and ambushes, both against the security forces and the local population that had opted to move to the care centre under the care of the security forces and anti-BRA resistance fighters.

Before the arrival of PNG military personnel, the whole of Nagovisi was relatively calm and peaceful under the consolidated command of the

---

2   When the Bougainville Crisis erupted in 1989, Nagovisi was spared from much of the intense fighting that occurred in neighbouring Nasioi. There was no military base in Nagovisi. This changed in 1993, when the PNG army returned to Bougainville and established several military bases across Nagovisi.

BRA. Unlike the neighbouring Siwai to the south, who were beset by intense fighting as a result of earlier military occupation of the region, displacement and relocation were not in any significant sense defining characteristics of the Crisis for the local population. Most people lived in their villages simply going about their usual routines without the kinds of displacement-related struggles that came to preoccupy peoples' lives in care centres. The subsequent military occupation of Nagovisi was marked by rapid descent into violent conflict amongst the Nagovisi themselves, as people took sides between the PNG-defence-force backed anti-BRA militia (known as Resistance Fighters) and the BRA. It was a time marked by considerable confusion as communities, families and individuals were forced to make difficult decisions about which warring factions' control they wanted to live under. Yet, prior to the arrival of the troops, most Nagovisi did not anticipate that things would take a dramatic turn for the worse. People did not fully understand that the arrival and presence of the troops in Nagovisi would pave the way for community disintegration the likes of which they had never experienced before.

One development after the arrival of the security forces and the start of intense hostilities and fighting in Nagovisi was that, as the war intensified locally, the cycle of blame over who was responsible for the suffering became somewhat relocalized from the broader motivating factors understood to be the original cause of the Bougainville Crisis. The first few months after the army's arrival were extremely difficult. But what exactly was life like in the care centres? Many families had a rough time adapting to the new environment. It was impossible for people to return to their abandoned villages to collect food without fear of being attacked by the BRA or raising suspicion in the PNG military through their movement. Families struggled to gather basic necessities from the newly established centres to which several displaced villages had been relocated; for many people it was like starting all over again in life, having to build new houses and cultivate new gardens, sometimes amidst tensions with the landowners who owned land and other resources, such as coconuts, breadfruits and sago palms, within the vicinity of the centre. For families like my own that had close kin in a village that was transformed into a care centre (and to which my family was relocated), the difficulties were slightly cushioned by the support of other relatives who stepped in and made sure that there was shelter and food during the early transition period.

When the national army first came to Nagovisi, one immediate impact was the forced fragmentation of familial relations. The breakdown in family ties occurred as communities were forced to decide in a short period of time whether to flee into the mountains with local members of the BRA or relocate to the government-controlled care centres. This tumultuous time was accompanied by an omnipresent sense of siege, with people were unable to move about, whether to gardens or between different care centres to visit extended relatives and kin. This meant that normal familial and community routines were severely disrupted. The fulfilment of certain customary obligations, such as the hosting of mortuary feasts to signify the end of mourning for the dead, had to be suddenly abandoned. For some people the coming of the security forces felt like an end to an era, that of living under the control of Bougainville Revolutionary Army. While this may have felt liberating in one sense, to some Nagovisi, others remained silently suspicious of the presence of the government troops. To many people, the military surveillance and multiple layers of security check at each care centre felt humiliating .

Bougainville islanders and their Papua New Guinea compatriots unanimously agree that the event known widely as the 'Bougainville Crisis' is now etched forevermore into their political history. This chapter explores its interest for the concept of crisis via the notion of responsibility. I propose to re-orient the analysis of the armed conflict to local conceptualizations of the Crisis and to temporal concerns as to who ought to be responsible for the violent past and possible futures.

If we are to ask who is to be held responsible for the Bougainville Crisis, the answers and explanations may be as variegated as the diverse temporal unfoldings of the violent conflict itself. The question of responsibility in armed conflict and war is often complex, contradictory and polarized along factional lines. What is justifiable in the context of war may be subject to contrary views. Given this, a fixation on a singular origin or definition of the Crisis, or a singular attribution of responsibility for the effects of the conflict, as is largely present in the commentaries and analyses discussed above, has to be rethought and re-evaluated. At the local level in Nagovisi attribution of responsibility for the war and its consequences in the region was directed at multiple individuals, particularly the armed combatants who served on the front lines of the conflict. In other words, for the majority of egregious acts of violence that occurred on both sides of the conflict following the arrival of the army in Nagovisi, blame and responsibility tended to be broadly dispersed across several agents and actors. A key notion closely intertwined with the associational kinship idiom *mono* is the embeddedness of ideas of responsibility in the physical and relational bodies of persons. This concept of perceiving responsibility is much more complicated than orthodox understandings of the attribution of responsibility, which suggest that in order for an agent to be held responsible there ought to be demonstrable evidence of intention to act (Goodin 1987; Toumayan 2014). The former view is more attuned to a relational model of responsibility as espoused in the work of

Massey (2004:9), which posits responsibility as embodied, relational and dispersed (or extended).

War weariness, crisis and responsibility

One factor most commonly cited for the establishment of peace is 'war weariness'. This theory is most clearly advanced in Regan's (2019) analysis of the Crisis, which followed precedents found in Braithwaite *et al.* 2010; Jennings and Claxton 2013; May and Spriggs 1990. There is, however, little ethnographic evidence for it. These texts do not provide any concrete examples of what war weariness looks like, whether in temporal or subjective terms. Instead, we are asked to accept its theoretical basis without any guidance as to whether the category is an affective condition or a novel war-induced psycho-cognitive subjectivity. This chapter suggests an alternative reading of the motivations for ending the conflict and violence, one grounded in local ideas of kinship and the kinds of responsibilities demanded by these kinship ties.

There is another side to the story of war-weariness, and that is the view that kinship and concerns over kin relationships played a significant role in ending the violent conflict. Kinship aided people in their decision about which care centre to settle in. Kinship was central to their emotional support during the violent war. Fighters were forced by the sense of obligation they felt they had towards restoring these social relations. They felt deeply that if they failed to establish peace they would be seen as people without any moral concern over their obligations towards maintaining amicable kin relations and social relations of care. For the Nagovisi, kin relations are the bedrock of social life. People are known to be proper persons or beings by the names they are given at birth and via the kin relations within which their lives are enmeshed. Two ethnographic examples illuminate how responsibility is conceptualized as relational and necessarily embedded in the domain of kinship relations, particularly through the relational idiom of *mono* or *monompo* (hereafter *mono*).[3]

This essay thus attempts to open new horizons for understanding the armed conflict, without discrediting existing discursive constructions and explanatory models of the confrontations. Two ethnographic scenes demonstrate the complexities of what is entailed in local understandings of what it means to be responsible. I shall argue that responsibility for the Crisis among the Nagovisi is grounded on certain assumptions and ideas of kinship. I will demonstrate how the Nagovisi evaluate and view the notion of responsibility through the vernacular concept of *mono*, a relational kinship

---

3   A related term, *pioke,* denotes the umbilical cord in the Nagovisi language. It is
     also used to denote the genealogical descent of clan members.

terminology that invokes an image of the corporeal body as the site of multiple relations and responsibilities. The body is always entangled within prior social relations and social structures. The concept therefore implies that the socio-political conditions upon which responsibility is conceived for the Nagovisi is inherently intertwined with ideas of kin-making. It was on kin relations that the divisive force of violence placed enormous strain, subjecting existing social ties to the vicissitudes of a war where families, clans and villages were forced to splinter into opposing sides.

Scene 1: Wopele[4]

Following the initial withdrawal of the military across all of Bougainville in 1990, a personable villager named Wopele was summoned by the local branch of the BRA for coining a scintillating vernacular metaphor that placed the blame for the island's economic woes and lack of government services squarely at the feet of the BRA and its leadership. The sentiment was interpreted by the local branch of the BRA as a political statement intended to undermine the movement's leadership, criticizing its management of the economic chaos arising from the military blockade. The BRA leaders felt humiliated by this and summoned Wopele to their camp to explain what he meant, and why he said what he said in the manner that he did.

Wopele, a man in his mid-fifties, had savaged the BRA, metaphorically, for blocking the pathway or route for the timely and unimpeded flow of commercial goods with prickly bush cane, making it difficult to navigate, and impassable for the delivery of such basic items as batteries and vital services. The metaphor spoke to the frustrations people felt with the militarized economic blockade. The sentiments cast the responsibility for the blockade onto the BRA. Even though it was not overtly expressed in these precise terms, for Wopele the blockade was intimately connected to the economic and political collapse that followed soon after the withdrawal of the security forces. In this sense, the metaphor can be seen as a politically charged speech act intended to evoke the ensuing chaos and the failure by the BRA to meet peoples' basic needs. According to Wopele, the BRA was the source of the blockage of the flow of goods and services to the island. From the point of view of the BRA, Wopele's sentiments were interpreted as arising from an anti-BRA impulse. The BRA felt that they were unjustly accused of something they were not directly responsible for. Wopele's concerns were seen through as – following Walker's (2019:638) observation – an attempt to 'redefine the ways in which responsibility is allocated'. The sarcastic commentary was

---

4   The name is anonymized. At the time of my doctoral field research, Wopele had developed significant aural problems. He passed away not long after my fieldwork.

viewed as seeking to draw attention to the disruption of government services and to lay blame for the economic blockade squarely at the feet of the BRA. To speak this way was also taken by the BRA to entail the risk of galvanizing latent expectations among the civilian population and of mobilizing popular resistance against the revolution.

Many people would later describe the Wopele debacle as unnecessary, and as yet another demonstration by the BRA of their proclivity towards the arbitrary exercise of their new-found authority and power. The episode demonstrates the degree and scale of the limits to freedom of expression and speech that the BRA imposed, in order to stop people from openly expressing their dissatisfaction with their predicament. When the BRA later released Wopele without any penalties for his alleged provocative comments, he acknowledged that the decision to let him off freely was largely determined by the fact that he was connected to many of his interrogators through the associational idiom of *mono*. The local BRA was deterred from imposing harsh penalties because of a recognition of Wopele as a close relative; any effort to severely reprimand him could have had negative ripple effects on the kinship ties that entangle the BRA in the wider community. During my fieldwork in 2011, I asked Wopele, in a casual chat, how he diffused an otherwise confrontational and violent situation with the BRA, and he remarked that his comments were merely a personal musing and a reflection on the general sense of despair and deprivation resulting from the economic blockade. He responded by saying *tewo imaiko nekompo* ('they, my brother, are our relatives') in the local vernacular, which signifies a strong sense of encompassing affective ties between relatives.

This incident is typical of many, throughout the conflict, in which concerns over kin relations served to dampen hostilities between insurgents and those who lived in the so-called government-controlled areas. Faced with the real prospect of a retaliatory backlash galvanized through the idiom of *mono*, the BRA and the pro-government local militia were often careful in negotiating tense situations that might appear to offer one kind of solution, but which had the potential to set events in a completely different and unintended direction.

Scene 2: Fred and Frieda

A local school fete was the event that gave rise to a chain of actions resulting in a relational feud. It provides an ethnographic example of how *mono* acted as a conduit through which a simple boy-girl relationship flared into a conflict resulting in destruction and looting of property in the boy's village. The event involved two teenage students, Fred and Frieda, attending different secondary schools in Bougainville. Frieda went to a school in south Bougainville, while Fred, her boyfriend, went to one in Buka, the administrative capital in the north. According to informants, Fred and Frieda's relationship was largely a 'public secret'; many people (especially their young peers) knew about it, though Fred and Frieda's parents were initially unaware.

The chain of events began on the second day of a fete at Frieda's school. It involved two sporting events (football and volleyball) for both men and women, and the sale of assorted items and food. Participating teams were required to register by paying an admission fee that would go into raising funds for the school. Similarly, members of the community who opted to sell cooked food or loose grocery items in the school grounds also had to pay an admission fee. But the vast majority of those attending came as spectators and supporters of the competing teams from their local communities. Given the centrality of fundraising to the event, many of those present were also parents whose children attended the school.

Others came in order to socialize with relatives from adjacent villages, which gatherings such as school fetes enable by virtue of attracting a range of people to a particular location. The confrontation between Fred and Frieda's relatives unfolded after the 'disappearance' of Frieda at the end of the second day, when she failed to turn up at her village and parents' house. Frieda's parents did not initially take any notice of their daughter's absence, nor did any of her close family and relatives from the same village. Unbeknown to them, Frieda did not return to her village after the fete, having decided to go to a nocturnal rendezvous in the nearby bushes with her boyfriend, Fred. Her parents only became aware of her absence at 3 a.m., when her mother, Joan, realized that the door to Frieda and her younger siblings' room was ajar. She had woken at this time, as it is when her husband, Joe, usually gets up to prepare for his gruelling eight-hour return trip to Buka.[5]

At first Joan thought that the door was not properly shut, or that Frieda or one of her siblings had gone to the toilet. But as time wore on she realized that something was amiss. Initially, she was not overly concerned about her daughter's absence. She contemplated a number of places Frieda might have gone, including the homes of her maternal grandmother or her cousins. However, troubled by Frieda's ongoing absence, as the search continued, Joan decided to enquire at other houses where Frieda might have spent the night. She made her way in the darkness, guided by a torch, down towards the main cluster of dwellings. When these enquiries failed to yield her daughter's whereabouts, it became apparent that something quite serious might have happened to Frieda. Word spread rapidly within the village and a search was

---

5   This trip was a routine affair, as Frieda's family owns and operates a Public Motor Vehicle (PMV) business that frequently ferries passengers and cargo between Nagovisi and Buka.

immediately mounted. Soon the entire village was up searching for Frieda. Joe cancelled his trip to Buka.

As the search dragged on, Frieda's parents asked some of the young village girls if anyone could remember seeing her, or whom she might have been with at the school fete. There was an aura of optimism when someone remarked that Frieda was seen talking to Fred late in the afternoon. As the sequence of events and sightings began to fit together, like pieces of a jigsaw puzzle, from the recollections of individuals who had seen Frieda at some point during the day, it seemed more and more plausible that Frieda was somewhere with Fred. By now, Joe was fuming with absolute rage. He concluded that Fred had 'run away' with his daughter, and ordered the villagers to locate Frieda immediately and bring her back. He threatened to burn the family house with their belongings inside and return to his natal village if Frieda was not found and brought back.[6]

The search continued until dawn. The young couple parted just before dawn, once they realized that the entire village was looking for them. Frieda gave herself up to the search party. When she returned to the family house she was beaten by her parents, sustaining bruises on her body and a severe cut on one of her ears. According to informants, Frieda's grandmother came to her rescue.

The return of Frieda was not the end of the story, however, as a series of escalating events was about to be set in motion. Frieda's return had done nothing to appease her father's anger. Around midday, Joe mobilized his relatives and youths from his wife's village and they travelled in a two pick-up trucks to Fred's village. A group of around fifty to sixty assailants descended upon the village in a mighty display of public aggression, setting two houses alight. Several houses were looted of their contents. The assailants confiscated property and called for payment of K10,000 (c. £2,500) compensation before the loot would be returned.

Before anyone had the chance to imagine the possibility of an amicable resolution, the arson and looting of property by Frieda's relatives had set in motion a domino effect of retaliatory reaction from Fred's relatives. But Fred's relatives, those bounded by the relational concept of *mono*, were not

---

6   In Nagovisi, when a man marries he is expected to move and settle into his wife's village. Everything that derives from his productive labour after marriage is thought to be for the benefit for his children and wife. When an argument erupts between a married couple and the children, the father often returns back to his own village. This can be seen as a temporary withdrawal of support from his wife, children and affinal relatives. Joe's threat to burn the family house and return back to his village could be seen to have that implication.

living in the same village as Fred. Following the arson attack, relatives of Fred from Guava village, some thirty miles away from Fred's residential village, started constructing roadblocks at Panguna, along the primary vehicular road between Nagovisi and Buka. This was in retaliation for the destruction and looting of property. They warned that if either of the two vehicles used to transport the assailants to Fred's village passed through Panguna, they would be impounded. When Joe heard about the threat, he halted his PMV business for three weeks.

Mono: an ethnographic glimpse and analytical foray.

The two scenes recounted here are intended to serve as illustrations of the Nagovisi concept of *mono* as an organizing idiom of relatedness. Through them I show how *mono* implicates people in webs of responsibility. I shall highlight how this associational idiom of kinship is drawn upon to intervene in, or defuse, conflict or volatile situations, and the way it connects to local ideas of kinship and relationality. This brings to our attention the way in which kinship provides the grounding for eliciting and shaping particular actions in the context of conflict situations and other dimensions of social interaction. I take this analytical tack, partly, to unsettle and call into question prevailing assumptions about the role of state-centric approaches and institutions in restoring peace and normalcy on Bougainville; partly to recast a commonly held Nagovisi vernacular idiom (*mono*) through which people constitute and define their relations; and partly to appropriate it analytically as the social form through which particular actions, including notions about responsibility, are elicited. In order to make visible the constitutive elements that enable these relationships, I explore the nexus between Nagovisi ideas of personhood and the way relations are viewed through *mono* as an image of the body.

I now give a diagrammatic sketch of *mono*, to outline its relational contours; this exercise provides less an ontological representation than an amplification of its key feature as an encompassing relational trope. The semantic and symbolic meaning of *mono* in Nagovisi refers both to the corporeal human body and to the social form of the aggregate of relations encompassing persons, who are thereby relationally connected. The realization of *mono* is attained in part through a conceptual collapse of physical space, in a fashion similar to that of the northern Buka islanders, whose emphasis on this collapse of physical distance 'shows their thinking on one another because they are really one' (Schneider 2011:186). Similar to Wagner's (1991) image of the 'fractal person', *mono* personifies a scaled constitution of persons who embody a constant relational flux, much like a pendulum suspended in a sustained motion between opposite points of reference. The two scenes have revealed the ways in which *mono* is deployed to elicit both social and spatial

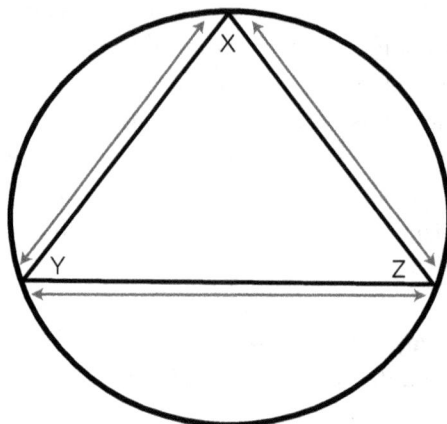

Figure 3.1 A schematic diagram of mono.

relations, thereby expanding the scope of responsibility between people who are encapsulated within its associational idiom. Figure 3.1 offers a simple analytical exposition of *mono* as it is conjured in Nagovisi kinship relations.

The sketch represents a hypothetical relation in which three notional persons, or *nado* (represented in the diagram with X, Y and Z) constitute and are encompassed in the *mono* relation. The imaginary persons, *nado*, viewed in their plural form, are represented here by the three points of linear convergence denoted by X, Y, Z. These symbolic variables are encompassed and encapsulated in an external circle, the analytic intention of which is to foreground *mono* as an aggregate relational form, as opposed to (say) providing a scaled model of relatedness in an enclosed domain of human interaction (Crook and Shaffner 2011:159). As the sketch illustrates, taken as singular individuals within an encompassing whole (as denoted here with the circle), X, Y and Z , being distinct and singular forms of the person (as *nam'me*), occupy different positions within what, in Dumontian terms (see Rio and Smedal 2009), might be described as a 'totalizing' image of relations. What needs to be stressed to reaffirm the emergence of the singular form of the person – even if the diagram presents a conceptually indivisible totality or encompassment – is that there is a clear ethnographic and conceptual re-appropriation of totality between the vernacular terms *nado* and *nam'me*. Basically, the two terms are conceptually bipolar (meaning they constitute two distinct aesthetic forms of persons), both in their mathematical nuance (*nado* denotes an aggregation of persons while *nam'me* denotes a single person) and in their vernacular usage as referent nouns for innumerable categories of people. For brevity's sake, our simple sketch also ignores the fact that in reality *mono* is difficult to model because of its ever-crystallizing qualities that implicate persons in interminable ways on the plane of social life.

Attentive readers might note my aversion to drawing an equivalence between *nam'me* and *mono*, although in a very limited ethnographic sense *mono* is substitutable for *nam'me*, such as when, for example, people refer to a dead person. For instance, where an argument or protest arises pertaining to disagreements over a burial site, the *mono* of the dead person (usually but not exclusively a married male) becomes the site of competing claims.

Having provided a description of a context in which *mono* attains the status of a near allegory of *nam'me*, I should however note that the refusal to conceptually conflate the two terms is deliberate, both to keep the vernacular distinction between them intact and to remain within the confines of the terms' deployment in everyday usage.

It is in explaining the emergence and the position of X, Y and Z in their discrete and singular form within the encompassing *mono* relation that our associational metaphor of *mono* becomes useful. If we imagine the connecting lines which form the shape of the triangle in the circle as the relation in which the oscillation or gravitation to a specific position, say X, Y or Z, is constant (the relational flux is denoted with the bi-directional arrows), it becomes easy to picture how the singular form of the person (*nam'me*) emerges from the multiplex field of human relations. It has to be noted, nonetheless, that the emergence of the singular form from the plural assemblage of persons (*nado*) and relations (*mono*) does not in any way form a mutually exclusive relation such that *nam'me* takes the form of a Western individual. It merely affirms *nam'me* as a relational singular person (Strathern and Stewart 2000:55) and not a 'self-defined monad of some kind' (Harrison 2006:7). Such a form is invested with agency and the human capacity for thoughtfulness, empathy, sorrow and a sense of personal responsibility for oneself and others. The idea of personal responsibility is often expressed in the vernacular idiom as *lakang kangkanelo*, meaning responsibility for one's own actions, especially where they are seen to be self-serving, and consequentially negative and disruptive to social relations. But of course, this does not mean that individual action is always assessed through the evaluative prism of whether one's action and its consequences are personal, as demonstrated by Fred and Frieda's story.

The notion of *mono* is also underpinned by a logic of binary juxtaposition: it hinges on the notion of the 'space outside' and 'space inside'. This dichotomization between exteriority (*ulono*) and interiority (*kuno*) is manifested through a metaphorical expression which deems that persons closely (the operative word here) related to one another ('inside') are *mono* to one another, while those deemed not closely related are 'outside' each other's *mono.*[7] *Mono* denotes physical and social proximity in another spatial sense, reflecting the 'density' of the relations concerned. This relational density is expressed and acted out through regular contact and close relations known as *malamala* (friendship) that entail a myriad of exchange relations. It is demonstrated through acts of kindness, empathy, solidarity and reciprocal support in material engagements. *Malamala* is the core social ingredient that imbues social relations with conviviality, for not all interactions are capable of fostering such friendship. For instance, close relatives with a history of intermittent social discord or disputes relating to land or other resources are said to lack *malamala* and its fusing qualities, which build and hold relationships together. *Mono* thus indicates physical proximity in distance in terms of the efficacy of exchanges between relatives.

Nagovisi indicate the importance of a set of individually and collectively recognizable social facts as essential for a person to be considered part of the *mono* relation. These social facts are marriage, birth, matrilineal kinship, friendship and the density and frequency of contact and exchange. Nagovisi thus create *malamala* partly through affective relations, partly through affinal and conjugal ties, clanship and various forms of reciprocal exchange relations. These exchange relations can be via any form of transaction, whether contributions to death and mortuary feasts, bride-wealth exchanges or, in the contemporary context, assistance with school fees. In other words, *mono* is the expression of relatedness made possible through birth, marriage, friendship and the density and frequency of exchange relations. It also expresses and denotes an aggregation of relations – at once plural and singular. To be related is to constitute and be part of the physical body of human persons to whom one is related. A similar linguistic term underlines the point: *nigompo* is derived from the root word *ni*, the equivalent in English being the 'self' or the 'ego' in relation to multiple 'others' (*mokopo*). The short word (*ni*) alters its meaning with a tonal inflection, through which the word expresses a collective 'us' or 'we'. Someone who is unrelated can also be referred to either as *mokamo* or *nam'me mokamo.*[8]

---

7   With respect to the attributes of the physical body, sexed bodily distinctions are made between female and male *mono*, expressed as *mono manikuma* and *mono nugang*. These basically refer to female and male bodies as distinctly sexed or gendered entities in a physical sense, although the context within which the phrases are commonly used can be one of vitriolic sarcasm.

8   The social process of fashioning relations on the basis of ideas about shared substance, the possession of relational bodies, along with the appropriation of similar totemic symbols is quite widespread across the entire island. In one of the more recent ethnographic studies in the northerly island of Pororan, Schneider (2012) notes similar ideas about tracing relations through the umbilicus, *ngorer,*

One way to better understand the power of *mono* as an encompassing and galvanizing relational metaphor is to consider how its logic works in instances where cultural notions of serious offence are at stake, as in the two scenes above. Scene two, in particular, described the ontological workings of the relational concept by demonstrating how a relatively localized family-level dispute resulting from the disapproval of a boy-girl relationship dilated outwards from its local node into an inter-village conflict. The mechanism by which the dispute was able to intensify and spread itself outwards between the entangled actors and parties owes its efficacy to the connections instantiated via the recognition of certain others as *mono*; that is, people who recognize themselves as ontologically constituted as persons sharing the same corporeal bodies. It is this very notion that also troubles simplistic ideas of ascribing and assigning responsibility. For in this model and view of the body, it is difficult to pin down a clear line of responsibility without upsetting the balance of relations between kin who view themselves as the extended skin, blood and bones of one another.

Conclusion: horizons of peace, kinship and bodily responsibility

The constitutive kinship idiom, *mono*, simultaneously denotative of the corporeal body and the network of kin relations, conjures an image of responsibility at its conceptual core. Responsibility is shared, as is evident in the trope's locus being distributed across multiple physical bodies, who are thereby regarded as connected via a powerful associational metaphor. This chapter has demonstrated as much through two ethnographic examples of how *mono* is central to constructions of responsibility as innately relational.

I have suggested that, at least in Nagovisi, contrary to widespread assumptions that the end to the Crisis on Bougainville was driven by sentiments for a 'political settlement', it was in actuality peoples' everyday concerns with the repercussions on their present and future kinship relations that moved them to search for an end to the divisive war. What the combatants were mainly concerned about, and acutely aware of, was the effect that prolonged warfare might have upon kin relations. As the conflict grew in intensity, and

---

and the adoption of the eagle as a totemic bird. I have heard people from distant localities, individuals as geographically distant as those from Tinputz, Buka and Siwai, using these ideas to claim that *mipela wanpela lain tasol* (Neo-Melanesian, 'we are all related') on the basis of these similarities. In Nagovisi and Siwai, moiety affiliation is thought to be the crucial organizing principle for exogamic marriage. More specifically, among the Nagovisi moiety affiliation is thought of as the axis or locus from which differential relations, especially those pertaining to marriage, are construed.

the loss of life of many young BRA and resistance fighters became all too common, people started looking for a pathway to combatant factions putting aside their differences and engaging in dialogue. This dialogue would largely come to be imagined, filtered and facilitated through the evocation of a model of kinship ties that, at its core, is understood to be relational and sedimented in peoples' physical bodies.

The impetus to end the conflict was thus a concern with kinship, and the risk of its potential loss or its reconfiguration beyond recognition by long-lasting hostilities. The implication is that as the war dragged on for years and decades, the kinship ties between combatants and families caught up in opposing sides would essentially lose their associational component. The extreme result of this, it was imagined, would be that members of future generations who were in the past *mono*, close kin, would turn into non-kin, and therefore into outsiders or strangers. If the temporal logic of war and its concomitant effects of separation held sway for a very long time, the Nagovisi feared that it would be near impossible for a mutually acceptable conclusion to the war.

It remains to offer a comment about the broader context of the academic production of knowledge in relation to the Bougainville Crisis. My research is the first Melanesian (and Bougainvillean) anthropologist's attempt to understand this infamous crisis by re-engaging with existing debates and commentaries through a focus on Nagovisi social life. Drawing on the combination of my lived experience, as a former combatant in the Crisis and later as an academic ethnographer, I have delved into the complexities of how the war has shaped people's ideas about the challenges and difficulties posed by armed conflict.

Insofar as the Nagovisi evaluate the notion of responsibility through the vernacular concept of *mono*, this being – as we have seen – a relational kinship that invokes an image of the corporeal body as the site of multiple relations and responsibilities, the body always carries entanglements with prior social relations. We have also seen that responsibility for the Nagovisi is inherently intertwined with ideas of kinship, and how the armed conflict was significantly unsettling to the practices of kin-making. As a war combatant, I was acutely aware of the receding horizon of relational ties with kin who were on the opposite side. The post-conflict reconciliations between kin and non-kin that followed soon after the end to active fighting, and which continue to take place between some communities, effects a reversal of the receding relational ties. The work of mending social relations via reconciliation is a way of reforming a new horizon of relational existence. For the Nagovisi, the contrasting or contradictory horizons brought about by war could also be a realm of multiple possibilities.

Just as people are moved through different relational positions by the movements of kinship exchanges, my own horizons – as a Nagovisi person, a war-combatant, an anthropologist – involve different positions in both time and analysis. Rather than being guaranteed by an external theoretical frame, my analysis here is made through Nagovisi conceptualizations and experiences. This creates a productive and illustrative analytical predicament – that is, my horizons are as if inside and outside a moment of time; inside and outside the Bougainville Crisis; inside and outside movements of kinship, and inside and outside different analytical horizons – and thus the possibilities by which arguments are enlivened and made possible.

Acknowledgements

A version of this chapter was presented at the 2021 ASA virtual conference hosted by the University of St Andrews. I am grateful to the conveners of the session on Attribution of Responsibility and Modes of Crisis Response, Dr Tony Crook and Professor Marilyn Strathern, for the opportunity to present a draft of the chapter and to test the ideas and arguments presented here. I also wish to acknowledge and thank my Nagovisi kinsfolk and extended relatives without whose generous support the ethnographic fieldwork this chapter is based on would have proven difficult to obtain.

References

Braithwaite, J., Charlesworth, H., Reddy, P. and Dunn, L. 2010. *Reconciliation and Architectures of Commitment: Sequencing Peace in Bougainville*. Canberra, ACT: ANU Press.

Carsten, J. 2000. *Cultures of Relatedness: New Approaches to the Study of Kinship*. Cambridge: Cambridge University Press.

Crook, T. and Shaffner, J. 2011. 'Preface: Roy Wagner's 'chess of kinship:' an opening gambit', *HAU: Journal of Ethnographic Theory* 1(1):159–64.

Filer, C; 1990. 'The Bougainville rebellion, the mining industry and the process of social disintegration in Papua New Guinea'. In J.R. May and M. Spriggs (eds), *The Bougainville Crisis*, pp. 73–127. Bathurst: Crawford House Press.

Ghai, Y. and Regan, A. 2000. 'Bougainville and the dialectics of ethnicity, autonomy and separation'. In Y. Ghai (ed.), *Autonomy and Ethnicity: Negotiating Competing Claims in Multi-Ethnic States*, pp. 242–65. Cambridge: Cambridge University Press.

Goodin, R.E. 1987. 'Apportioning responsibilities', *Law and Philosophy* 6(2):167–85.

Harrison, S. 2006. *Fracturing Resemblances: Identity and Mimetic Conflict in Melanesia and the West*. New York: Berghahn Books.

Jennings, P. and Claxton, K. 2013. *A Stitch in Time: Preserving Peace in Bougainville*. Canberra: Australian Strategic Policy Institute.

Kenema, S. 2010. 'An analysis of post-conflict explanations of indigenous dissent
relating to the Bougainville copper mining conflict, Papua New Guinea',
*Pacificurrents, eJournal of the Australian Association for the Advancement of
Pacific Studies*, 1.2 and 2.1 (April): intersections.anu.edu.au/pacificurrents/
kenema.htm (accessed 18 January 2024).

——— 2016. 'Experiences of gender-based violence from Nagovisi, Bougainville'.
In *Understanding Gender Inequality Actions in the Pacific: Ethnographic
Case-studies and Policy Options*. Luxembourg: Publications Office of the
European Union.

Lasslett, K. 2014. *State Crime on the Margins of Empire: Rio Tinto, the War on
Bougainville and Resistance to Mining*, London: Pluto Press.

Massey, D. 2004. 'Geographies of responsibility', *Geografiska Annaler* 86(B1):5–18.

May, R.J. and Spriggs, M. (eds) 1990. *The Bougainville Crisis*. Bathurst: Crawford
House Press.

Nash, J. 1993. 'Mining, ecocide, and rebellion: the Bougainville case'. Paper presented
to the Annual Meeting of the American Anthropological Association, DC.

Ogan, E. 1991. 'The cultural background to the Bougainville crisis', *Journal de la
Société des Océanistes* 92–3(1–2):61–7.

Regan, A.J. 1998. 'Causes and course of the Bougainville conflict', *Journal of Pacific
History* 33(2):269–85.

——— 2019. *The Bougainville Referendum: Law, Administration and Politics*.
Canberra, ACT: Department of Pacific Affairs. Australian National
University.

Rio, K. and Smedal, O.H. (eds) 2009. *Hierarchy: Persistence and Transformation in
Social Formations*. Oxford: Berghahn Books.

Sahlins, M. 2013. *What Kinship Is – And Is Not*. Chicago: University of Chicago Press.

Schneider, K. 2011. 'The one and the two: mainlanders and saltwater people in Buka,
Bougainville', *Oceania* 81:180–204.

——— 2012. *Saltwater Sociality: A Melanesian Island Ethnography*. Oxford:
Berghahn Books.

Strathern, A. and Stewart, P. 2000. *Arrow Talk: Transaction, Transition, and
Contradiction in New Guinea Highland History*. Kent, OH: Kent State
University Press.

Toumayan, A. 2014. 'The responsibility for the other and the responsibility to protect',
Philosophy and Social Criticism 40(3):269–88.

Wagner, R. 1991. 'The fractal person'. In M. Godelier and M. Strathern (eds), *Big
Men and Great Men: Personifications of Power in Melanesia*, pp. 159-173
Cambridge: Cambridge University Press.

Walker, H. 2019. 'Dislocating responsibility', *HAU: Journal of Ethnographic Theory*
9(3):638–41.

4

Investments without future, debts without past

Commodity horizons in Indigenous central Brazil

Bruno Nogueira Guimarães[1]

The Apanjekra clients of Brazilian patron-bosses, who manage government cash allowances on their behalf, seek to mould their relations in certain ways. In terms reminiscent of kinship, they want the bosses to keep 'thinking on' them, to perceive the needs to be satisfied and thus to show 'care', bosses being judged by their response to requests for help. The chapter forcefully elucidates just how this pressing claim to interpersonal responsibility creates a crisis for the bosses, a dilemma in terms of the (economic and other) choices they have to make concerning their own livelihood, while they in turn are seen by diverse commentators as harbingers of other crises. There is no shortage of critical accounts depicting the government-run system as enhancing rather than alleviating social vulnerability, with criticism coming from NGOs and anthropologists alike. These commentators nonetheless agree with government officials when it comes to the problematic existence of the bosses and the debt into which they put their clients. Unsurprisingly, the bosses and their Apanjekra counterparts entertain quite different apprehensions of what is at stake. The significant observation here is that clients do not seem to be in the cleft of the dilemmas – and their eruption into crises – that dog the patron-bosses.

1   This work, produced under the auspices of the Ethnographic Horizons project at the Centre for Pacific Studies, University of St Andrews, was supported by the International Balzan Foundation.

❀

It can be a commonplace to state that, over the past twenty years, the Bolsa Família Programme (PBF) became the most popular public policy in Brazil, assisting families facing hunger and alleviating the effects of poverty. Throughout those years, not only did PBF come to be the one of the largest Conditional Cash Transfer policies (CCTs) in the world, it was also deemed a very cost-efficient way to improve social-development indicators (Hall 2006; Martins *et al.* 2013; Reis 2010). Its results, in line with the efficacy of other CCTs worldwide (Gertler 2004; World Bank 2009), might be the reason why both left- and right-wing governments in the past two decades have maintained PBF functioning.[2] However, though CCTs went on to occupy the centre of debate on social programmes and economic inclusion due to their success, critics have pointed out how they are actually incapable of enacting structural change (Coraggio 2007). They attenuate the impact of neoliberal economic policies (such as the growth of social inequality or the precariousness of labour conditions), yet avoid targeting the source of the problem (Saad-Filho 2015).

CCTs deal with one crisis, extreme poverty, and prevent another, social upheaval. Not only that, they can be seen as an investment that countries make in their own economy:

> CCTs presumably alleviate poverty in the short and long run: while the transfers reduce destitution, the conditionalities strengthen the recipients' position in the labour market, eventually obviating the need for the programme.
>
> (Saad-Filho 2015:1231; see also World Bank 2009)

Setting out horizons

In recent years, anthropologists working in the South American lowlands have also joined the debate regarding the effects of cash-transfer programmes among

---

2   It is important to register that a lot of the criticism CCTs has received comes from academics, who consider the distribution of money to poor people as 'serving the cause of "commoditization", and thus capitalism', as Ferguson argues (2015:120). As Ferguson (2010) has also pointed out, many of these arguments are less structured around a constructive political agenda than they are organized against a particular system – that of capitalism or neoliberalism. As we will see, this is not completely the case with scholars discussing cash-transfer policies among Indigenous peoples in Brazil.

Indigenous peoples in Brazil.[3] Although some may concede the merits of PBF in addressing issues in urban centres and 'market economies', their assessment of the social-security system's application to Indigenous populations has been mostly critical (Bonilla and Capiberibe 2015; Borges, 2016; MDS 2015, 2016; Novo 2019; Pimentel, Bonilla and Guimarães 2017; Viveiros de Castro and Danowski in Brum 2014). Together with non-governmental organizations and media outlets that have historically supported Indigenous rights, they point out how PBF and similar programmes can actually enhance social vulnerability, lead to debt peonage and be regarded as part of a larger-picture development programme for the Amazon, one that draws on the outdated political projects for Indigenous peoples that marked most of the twentieth century.

Discussion regarding these programmes takes as a point of departure certain temporal assumptions. Analysts defending or criticizing these policies place them as part of an epoch that draws its features from the expansion of the neoliberal agenda after the end of the Cold War. Not only do they belong to a particular historical period, CCTs represent 'the emergence of new ways of thinking, new ways of reasoning about matters of poverty and distribution' (Ferguson 2015:10); in doing so, they encapsulate notions about the future they intend to build – and divergence regarding this future is where anthropologists' objections lie. But while scholars are at odds with what cash-transfer policies assume to be a step forward, they should also consider that the people on the receiving end of these programmes might not share their observers' temporal framework. To put in another way, it is possible that 'the best time to study (this or that) is not necessarily the time the researcher is in' (Strathern 2021:35). Indigenous peoples inhabiting the South America lowlands may not view themselves as living in a neoliberal era, and terms such as 'anthropocene' are unlikely to capture the defining features of their epoch.[4] Not only that, their temporal premises may derive from a set of ontological

---

3   I use the term 'Indigenous peoples', recognizing its potential issues (such as homogenization) and over other alternatives ('first nations'; 'first people'), because it is the vocabulary most employed by the Indigenous movement in Brazil and by the Apanjekra, the people with whom I conducted my fieldwork.

4   As Viveiros de Castro (1998) famously indicated, modern Western assumptions about the separation of 'natural' and 'cultural' domains of reality are not shared by the Indigenous peoples in South American lowlands, who suppose a multiplicity of 'natural worlds' determining the point of view of the agents in accordance with their body forms. Crook and Rudiak-Gould (2018:12–13) address this issue when dealing with climate change in the light of Pacific material, observing how the notion that human agency can affect the weather is not new for the Pacific Islanders, any more than the consequences are.

assumptions different from those that lead to the experience of cumulative or evolutionary time.

The way temporal perception is socially shaped is a long-lasting subject of anthropological investigation (see Munn 1992), which mostly addresses the question of how people deal with history (and concepts associated with 'the past'), construe memories or comprehend the succession of events in a logical sequence. Although these reflections influenced much of the academic production in South American ethnology, especially those of structuralist orientations regarding native perceptions of history, myth and time-making practices (cf. Carneiro da Cunha 2009; Carneiro da Cunha and Viveiros de Castro 1986; Fausto 2007; Gow 1991, 2001; C. Hugh Jones 1979; S. Hugh Jones 1979; Lévi-Strauss 1964; Matta 1970, amongst many others), the majority is more concerned with the cultural elaboration of what might have already happened than with the way people experience what is to come (Munn 1992; Robbins 2007). CCTs, however, evoke multiple concepts about 'the future'. For instance, policymakers and scholars debate whether they are good governmental investments or not, disputing whether one is to expect positive social-economic returns and when. The epoch to which they belong also draws attention to what might lie ahead: ecological catastrophe and the (im)possibility for us of avoiding it ('is it too late?'). 'Us': the pronoun gives away the ethnographer's own placement in a particular epoch and reveals their own temporal horizons and concerns about 'the future'.

The identification of certain features of cash-transfer policies depends on how distinct actors conceive them. First, I consider the view expressed by policymakers and their critics. Part of my data is bibliographical, as much has been published on governmental positions and the objections they have received; other parts are informed by my direct observations when dealing with government officials, scholars and activists.[5] A point of convergence for anthropologists and policymakers is the figure of the 'boss' (*patrão*), identified by both as an issue when it comes to Indigenous peoples' well-being. The

---

5   Since I started research among the Apanjekra in 2011, I have met with many people involved in development programmes and participated in a few of them, often as an observer. Between 2013 and 2014 I worked as a consultant for the Ministry of Social Development, responsible for programmes targeting extreme poverty in the first (and only) ethnographic study carried out by the Brazilian State on PBF among Indigenous Peoples (see MDS 2015, 2016). I also took part in the implementation of the Environmental and Territorial Management Plan (PGTA) at the Porquinhos Indigenous Land, and was an unofficial assistant in another PGTA in 2014, both collaborations with the Ministry of Environment and NGOs. My considerations on the views of policymakers come not only from documents, but also from these interactions and direct observations.

situation of the bosses, usually merchants or moneylenders who keep PBF beneficiaries' bank cards with them, is then analysed, looking at how they present a particular orientation towards labour, time and uncertainty. Then, I turn to Indigenous temporal registers and their relation to cash-transfer policies.

Between 2011 and 2019 I conducted fieldwork among the Apanjekra, an Indigenous people inhabiting the Porquinhos Indigenous Land on the transition between the Amazon rainforest and the Cerrado ('Brazilian savanna'), who seemed to experience drastic economic change after their enrolment in CCTs. During this period, nearly every family in the village was registered in CadÚnico (the governmental platform that gives access to PBF) and were making monthly trips to the largest city in the region, Barra do Corda, to withdraw their social allowances and buy food or commodities. But money from PBF hardly covered the costs of accessing it, so going to the cities and staying there for days posed challenges to travellers: entering into a client-boss relation was a way to manage the obstacles between CCTs beneficiaries and their allowances. These relations were marked by discussions on debt, credit and interest. However, as it will be clear, the debt the Apanjekra talked about was not the same as the one discussed by the bosses. Each contained different temporal assumptions. Local-government officials reasoned that the Apanjekra should save their money, buying later what they desired, instead of having it now and paying huge interest over time. It was hard to understand what seemed to be a lack of financial planning. Was the pressure to obtain a commodity in the present so intense that they could not do it in the future?

However, to talk about 'future' or 'past' may already suppose a particular set of ontological principles about time, one of which is that, as events happen, they have a cumulative effect in defining what will come. Besides that, modern Euro-American understandings about time presuppose its universality, non-reversibility and constant flow forward. One might wonder if it is possible to talk about the future without implying that it is the necessary result of (all) present-day actions – and what might happen if we do not share this supposition: 'Where the present is not tethered to an earlier epoch, then is there nothing ahead but a flat horizon of the ever-present?' (Strathern 2019:64). Although policies inscribed in a developmental framework are fundamentally based on an idea of the future, and both bosses and the Apanjekra make use of that word, employing this vocabulary to describe the temporal aspects of their experiences would lead to an 'uncontrolled equivocation' (Viveiros de Castro 2004). Instead, I draw on the image of the horizon, considering the possibilities of what is to come and what may already have happened from the actors' point of view. The concept evokes 'the interface between empirical perceptions and their orienting categories, values and epistemological ideas';

it is also defined by the fact that 'a basic property of horizon lies in fusing facts which are known with unknown objects, agents and forces. For this reason horizons are never just cognitive frameworks, but inherently symbolic in the sense of collapsing into each other different contexts of signification.' (Kaartinen and Sather 2008:9–10). Without committing to a particular temporal ontology or notions of future and past, 'horizon' allows us to discuss crisis, expectation and uncertainty.

What lies ahead may never come. Or, in trying to reach there, we may find ourselves returning to a place once considered behind us. It is in this dispute over the movements toward a horizon filled with the promise of progress that one finds the development advocates and critics.

Investments without future

'Brazil has an enormous past ahead of it'

(Fernandes 2002)

In order to access social programmes, their beneficiaries are required to fulfil a predetermined set of conditions. To be eligible to receive social allowances from PBF, a family (defined by the inhabitants of its household) must have a monthly income of less than 178 BRL,[6] secure attendance at school on the part of their children (up to sixteen years old) and have family members going through predetermined health consultations. These conditions are presented both as a counterpart contribution from the beneficiaries and as an investment in human capital (World Bank 2009). However, they are not the only requirements for accessing CCTs. To register for the programme, beneficiaries must hold ID documents for all family members; it is also important that they are close to a federal bank in order to make the monthly withdrawals, which additionally requires that beneficiaries know how to navigate the banking system. Both sets of conditions (be they explicit or implicit) are subjects of debate between government officials and scholars when assessing the effects of PBF among Indigenous peoples.

---

6   These numbers are from July 2020 and can be accessed at web.archive.org/ web/20201015173518/www.gov.br/cidadania/pt-br/acoes-e-programas/bolsa-familia/o-que-e/como-funciona (accessed 18 January 2024). In November 2021 the Brazilian government reformulated their social assistance programmes and created Auxílio Brasil ('Brazilian Aid'), in the place of PBF. After Lula became president for the third time, winning over Bolsonaro in October 2022, PBF was reinstituted in place of Auxílio Brasil. Novo (2019) explores in detail all the challenges posed by the PBF's conditions in Indigenous contexts.

Government officials in Brazil have traditionally stressed the role that cash-transfer policies play in stimulating sustainable development in poor and rural areas of the country. If once they were seen as a way to mitigate the effects of food insecurity, during the twenty-first century they have come to be regarded as a real driver of social mobility. Together with other social and economic policies, PBF was considered one of the reasons why social inequality actually diminished during President's Lula two terms (2003–10). Devised to deal with one aspect of the poverty crisis – hunger – PBF also managed to tackle another, helping to reduce social disparity. In doing so, it also led to the inclusion of millions of people in the banking system and allowed them to access commodities that were previously unavailable. In many places, the new influx of money was followed by infrastructure changes, with the Growth Acceleration Programme (PAC) taking electricity to rural areas and financing huge construction projects, from some of the world's largest river dams to the improvement of road networks and sanitation. Together with PBF, these development projects were presented by the government in the language of inclusion, a step towards a future in which none of the Brazilian population would be poor, as stressed by President Dilma's government's slogan: 'a rich country is a country without poverty'. They would bring Brazilian families to modernity.

In 2014 an engineer representing the Ministry of Mines and Energy visited Apanjekra village to start a report on development projects that had already been set up, tied to the Light for All Programme responsible for taking electricity to the Porquinhos Indigenous Land in previous years. The Apanjekra Association had submitted a project aimed at increasing the yield of rice crops for the whole village. Produce which exceeded community needs could then be sold and the surplus would generate a sustainable income. Some money would return to the business in order to pay for the maintenance of machinery, acquisition of new tools and other unforeseen costs. The fundamentals of the project lay in the idea that it was a social investment that would have a long-lasting economic impact. After two days of meetings with Apanjekra leaders, inspecting the buildings where the broken electric rice mills were located and failing to find the tractor or the computers that should have been bought with project resources, the engineer was disappointed. Crop production was the same as it was before the 'rice project' (as it was popularly known); there was no maintenance or repair as machinery suffered wear and tear; and pieces of a non-functioning mill and the small truck just lay on the floor, unused, as scraps from a plan that never came to fruition. Before the engineer left, he presented pictures of other projects that he had inspected, explaining how they were helping people to leave poverty behind and provide for themselves. He was moved by a women's association, which had started a sewing cooperative that had become a supplier to local markets: 'They were poor, but now they are not; they faced hunger, but now they eat.' People from the sewing cooperative no longer needed social assistance. In a private conversation with me when he was leaving Porquinhos, he remarked that the Apanjekra project failed due to a lack of leadership in the village: 'There needs to be a strong person capable of leading people to the future.'

The government representative anticipated a new epoch in which people would be able to provide for themselves. In the present, the state would play its part, acknowledging that so many people were marginalized and could not leave this position without assistance. However, true emancipation from poverty would only occur if people obtained a source of income that was not tied to public resources. In this sense, governmental aid was part of a transitional period: a bridge between a past of poverty and dependency and a future of development and self-reliance. Yet the engineer's horizon seemed to change as he delved into Indigenous life. His horizon, inscribed in so many political discourses and slogans, seemed antithetical to the way Apanjekra treated the 'rice project', in which the participants did not think ahead in an entrepreneurial manner at all. This project was not the only one that was considered a failure by external observers – other projects that should have had a lasting impact also failed to flourish in Porquinhos, as the one dedicated to the creation (and commercialization) of 'ema' (*Rhea americana*) exemplifies. The fifteen large birds given to the village by the National Indigenous Foundation (FUNAI) were eaten before they could reproduce, with Apanjekra arguing that they liked its meat better than the one they could have bought in city's market had they sold the animals. When questioned about why they did not try to breed the adults and sell the offspring, making a continuous profit and buying food out of it, Apanjekra responded that they were hungry at that particular moment – not in the future.[7]

There is no novelty in pointing out that development projects and cash-transfer policies do not generate the expected results among Indigenous peoples in Brazil. During the last decade anthropologists have openly criticized PBF, stating how the programme poses so many challenges to their participants that it can actually do more harm than good. Their remarks focus on diverse issues, such as the impact of cash and commodities on

---

7   Ironically, their answer was in line with a popular political motto in Brazil, from a campaign that inspired PBF: 'Those who are hungry are in a hurry.' This was the slogan for the Citizenship Action against Hunger, Misery and for Life, created in 1993 by the sociologist Herbert Souza. The motto was employed at the launching of the Zero Hunger Programme (2003) and in the creation of the Bolsa Família Programme by the Workers' Party.

local economies, the hardships many people face when travelling to urban centres, and the trouble beneficiaries go through when dealing with the intermediaries between themselves and the banking system (Athila 2017; Bonilla and Capiberibe 2015; Guimarães 2016; Novo 2019; Pimentel, Bonilla and Guimarães 2017). A detailed ethnographic study commissioned by the Ministry of Social Development described how common these issues were throughout the country (MDS 2015, 2016). This research is one of the very few collaborations in which social anthropologists worked with policymakers in order to diagnose the effects of PBF among Indigenous populations, and some of the concerns it voices are the result of the dialogue between state agents and scholars.

Although anthropologists and policymakers had different perspectives on some of the programme's demands and implications, there was one point about PBF that was apparently consensual – the problems posed by the existence of the 'bosses':

> In reports from all Indigenous Lands the 'boss' [*patrão*] figure was present
> as a key agent in the access to the financial resources given by PBF to the
> families enrolled in the programme. [...] Everywhere, bosses were local
> merchants who provided (paid) transportation and oriented beneficiaries
> to spend their money on their establishments. Control over the cards, kept
> by the bosses as collateral, is so overwhelming that people end up being
> alienated from the amount they should be receiving according to the rules of
> the Programme.
>
> (MDS 2015:7)

Government officials see bosses as obstacles to the functioning of PBF, inasmuch as they subvert the logic of the programme: they create a debt relation with beneficiaries and take part of their allowances, actually lowering the income of people who are possibly facing hunger. Not only does this make any social mobility for the poor much more difficult, bosses actually benefit by keeping their clients in a precarious situation, making sure that they continue to receive governmental money. These issues are of concern to anthropologists as well, who point out how food insecurity can emerge around the new social relations entailed by CCTs (Piperata, McSweeney and Murrieta 2016). Anthropologists, however, are less concerned with social mobility when it comes to PBF. Contemporary bosses evoke a kind of relation that has been present in Amazonia for centuries (Meira 2018), most notably during the economic booms of the rubber period (1870–1920): the *aviamento* economy. This had the figures of boss and client, with the latter working in the extractive economy to pay for the commodities they received from the former, in a classic debt-peonage model. Fundamental to this barter relation was a debt almost impossible to pay, forcing clients to engage continuously in a network of labour activities that not only had a lasting impact on the relational landscape of Indigenous peoples (Meira 2018), but which also shaped 'the economic basis of modern Amazonian peasantry' (Fraser *et al.* 2018:1388; see also Santos 1980; Weinstein 1983). Although nowadays certain fundamental features of the *aviamento* economy are no longer part of PBF client-boss relations (in a sense, government money is substituting Indigenous labour as payment for the bosses' commodities), other parallels remain, such as the insurmountable debt clients have and their lack of freedom to gain social benefits. In the end, bosses restrict market choices and can threaten the well-being of their clients. Even if there are some differences in the mechanisms, debt relations with bosses are seen as a throwback to outdated times by both government officials and social anthropologists.

However, for some scholars (Athila 2017; Bonilla & Capiberibe 2015; Guimarães 2017; Pimentel, Bonilla and Guimarães 2017), the boss figure is not the only matter of concern. In a capitalist context, CCTs mitigate hunger and extreme poverty, while failing to address the source of these issues; but what can be said of its palliative effects for Indigenous peoples, the ones who, in contrast with historical colonialists and present-day capitalists, are assumed to have an intrinsic relation with their land (Ingold 2000)?

Throughout the twentieth century official policies regarding the Indigenous population in Brazil aimed at their 'assimilation', becoming 'integrated to national society', as the law known as the 'Indian Statute' stipulated (Law 6.001, from 1973). Projects focusing on Indigenous communities' economic development were implemented in many regions, trying to bring these peoples into the market economy while also deploying them as cheap workforce. If they were considered assimilated, a community could lose their land rights, allowing the state to pass them on to private buyers. These policies, together with the violence of capitalistic expansion in most of the country and the constant register of decrease in the Indigenous population, informed the public perception (shared by many academics) that, in the future, if there were going to be Indigenous peoples in Brazil, they would not exist as culturally differentiated collectives. It was in the late 1970s that a major political movement with Indigenous activists, NGOs, scholars and scientific associations challenged this view and the government's position. Their lobby for change came to fruition under the form of the 1988 Federal Constitution, which recognized the right to cultural difference and rendered ineffective the previous assimilationist legislation. After the end of the military dictatorship and the start of the New Republic, a new set of health and education policies for Indigenous peoples tried to consider their local specificities. Deemed as advances for a pluralistic country, they attested the rupture with the assimilationist view that preceded the 1988 constitution.

Social anthropologists had been protagonists in the defence of Indigenous rights during the military period (Carneiro da Cunha 2018); as Peirano (1998:116) argued, a mainstay of Brazilian anthropology is 'a sense of social responsibility towards those observed'. Therefore, over the past two decades, anthropologists[8] have denounced in public forums the return of major construction projects from the dictatorship under the Workers' Party's (PT) presidential mandates (2003–16). River-dam projects once halted by the military were finally built (such as Belo Monte), even if at a cost to the Indigenous peoples who would have their lands and watercourses severely affected – not to mention the ecological damage caused by flooding in large regions of the rainforest.

PBF has been seen by some anthropologists (Athila 2017; Bonilla and Capiberibe 2015; Pimentel, Bonilla and Guimarães 2017) as an integral part of the present epoch of ecological degradation: concomitant with Indigenous territories being jeopardized by the advance of agribusiness, developmental projects and deforestation, cash-transfer policies offered an alternative to subsistence that does not require access to land. Inasmuch as in many regions of the country CCTs allowed for the acquisition of previously unavailable commodities and the local use of money in non-market economies, they could be considered partially successful in advancing the assimilationist programme, functioning as a gateway to market relations where Indigenous peoples would be classified as part of the 'poor segment' of the Brazilian population. Complementary to these issues, another point of criticism focused on PBF educational requirements that forced Indigenous children to attend regular schools, disregarding their own methods of knowledge production and transmission. By the same token, health requirements were also problematic.

Social anthropologists writing on cash-transfer policies often describe a horizon for Indigenous peoples filled with tropes from the past (Bonilla and Capiberibe 2015; Guimarães 2017; Meira 2018; Pimentel, Bonilla and Guimarães 2017): *aviamento* economy, assimilationist policies, environmental

---

8   These included the criticism from the Brazilian Anthropological Association on different occasions, from notes denouncing infrastructure projects in Indigenous Lands (the most recent being ABA 2023) to its dossier on the Belo Monte river dam (Pacheco de Oliveria and Cohn 2014), as well as academic symposiums on environment and Indigenous rights which criticized the Brazilian development policy (the most notable was the seminar, 'The thousand names of Gaia', organized by Viveiros de Castro and Danowski in Rio de Janeiro in 2015, with the presence of Bruno Latour, Isabelle Stengers and other international scholars).

catastrophes from major construction projects and public programmes that disregard cultural pluralism. If CCTs are, then, social investments, they are hardly investments in the future of the Indigenous population. The apparently similar criticism of the bosses, by government officials and scholars alike, is revealing of more fundamental divergences about their horizons. Whilst for the former the boss evokes a crisis for being regarded as an obstacle to progress, a figure from a different epoch breaching the road to progress; for academics criticizing CCTs the boss appears as a symptom of a distinctively other crisis – the advent of a colonialist epoch that has no place for Indigenous peoples.

Present work, future investment?

One night in 2014, right after I arrived in Barra do Corda to begin fieldwork, I ran into an old boss in a small restaurant. Octavio left his table and joined me, bringing me up to date on what had happened since my last visit to the region. When I first met him, three years before, he was a public servant working at the Apanjekra village, where he managed to amass over 10 PBF cards after he decided to 'help some families' with the acquisition of commodities and in dealing with bureaucracy. But now his career had changed and, with his new job requiring him to stay at the city during the weekdays, the number of clients he had was decreasing. Even though he told me he was considering quitting his activities as a boss, he still had four client families because, according to him, he liked them very much and they always treated him well in Porquinhos. Showing his appreciation, Octavio explained that one of the cards he held belonged to the woman who adopted him as her son in the village, making him his mother's boss. He listed the activities he did for his clients, taking them on his motorcycle to buy goods or to solve bureaucratic issues not limited to the scope of social allowances. When he worked at the village he would take various commodities with him, and for a short period he even had a small market in Porquinhos offering credit sales to his clients. When I asked if his family paid the same interest as other clients, he explained that it was only fair to charge them for his troubles, as he did not work less for them than for the others. Also, he was saving to buy a bigger house in the city: like many bosses, he had material goals to achieve through his activity. In 2015, Octavio was no longer a boss and lived in the same house as the year before.

Social-allowance bosses working with the Apanjekra are quite different from one another. During the last decade, small merchants, cattle-breeders, schoolteachers and other local public servants have all acted as bosses, with distinct trajectories leading to their activities as loan sharks and divergent outcomes afterwards. Observing the material conditions that made a boss succeed in Porquinhos, I wrote in a government report that what mattered most was their capacity to provide transportation between village and city (MDS 2016). Bosses who could not transport families in large vehicles faced a hard time in obtaining clients, and struggled to keep those they had for long, as the one talking to me at the restaurant exemplifies. This is why the clients of the store owners who were the first PBF bosses dropped out after a few years: the bosses could not arrange for people to go to the cities, leaving the clients waiting at the village for goods they had not chosen. Apanjekra complaints regarding these former bosses were mostly about the poor treatment they received from them, saying they only cared about selling things to their clients, rather than actually helping them satisfy their needs.

Bosses' activities can be broken down in two main aspects, which are enmeshed in everyday practice but appear as different features when they explain their relation with their clients: the work and the risk-taking. First, what they do is labour like any other. In driving PBF beneficiaries, mediating relations with other merchants and dealing with bureaucracy, they offer a service and should be paid for it. This is well attested by those who give up their current job to become a boss. They don't see themselves as quitting work; rather, they are opting for a different career that should be paid like any other regular work. Lucio worked for a company that had him travelling around rural areas close to Porquinhos, to where he had to go monthly. On his small truck, he took PBF beneficiaries with him to Barra do Corda as a favour. When explaining how he went on to leave his job and start driving Apanjekra passengers full time, he mentioned how much harder he had to work, as providing transportation was not enough for a boss to keep a client. Being an interpreter and helping people to manoeuvre the banking system was also time consuming, and he 'deserved' to be paid. The idea of justice present in many accounts of bosses' payments is of course rooted in a Euro-American notion of labour, in which the yield of a person's activities is potentially their property.[9] As Lucio was offering a service to his clients, it would be unfair if he did not receive anything in return – he would be alienated from the outcome of his labour. This sentiment is also strengthened by an opportunity-cost assessment, as being a boss is a demanding activity that makes it hard for someone to take on another job. But there is another central aspect of the boss-as-a-job rationale: the fact that the service happens in the present and should be paid accordingly. Before becoming a boss, Lucio began charging PBF

9　Strathern considers the personhood principles involved in this notion of labour, classically developed by John Locke. The idea that a person owns him- or herself and 'that rights can be obtained through purchase [...] opens the way for the capitalist premise that persons have a "right" to alienate their own labour for a wage' (1985:23).

beneficiaries a fare to drive them to the city – demand was too high for him to just let them hitch-hike. As most people could not pay immediately, Lucio registered in his notebook both who rode with him and the passenger's boss. He complained about the trouble he had to go through in order to receive what was due: not only could he spark conflict with his passengers' bosses, who tried to provide the same service; he would also wait for a long time to be paid. When Lucio explained his situation to me, he described feeling that he was 'working for free' when he was not paid immediately. This was a driving force for him to become a boss and keep his passengers' bank cards. Other bosses usually charged for the trip upfront, or deducted the fare from the monthly allowance. They seldom added it to their clients' long-term debts.

Complementary to the perception that bosses should be rewarded for their services is the idea that, in order to do so, they take risks. Besides having to secure their payment for transportation, the most obvious risk in their activity is the credit they offer to their clients, who can only pay them back through the social allowance. Debt relations are inscribed in the genesis of the boss-client relation, for usually one gives one's PBF card to a boss in exchange for goods in advance. If a family becomes enrolled in PBF and needs to go to the city, either to receive their bank card or to withdraw their cash for the first time, they are most likely to seek out a boss to help them with the trip and the bureaucratic procedures. Not only that, they will usually ask for a loan so that they can buy commodities. The boss will ask for card possession in order to secure payment. If the monthly allowance is not yet deposited in the beneficiary's account when they go to the city, the boss can pay for their expenses and save them from waiting.[10] On the bosses' horizon are the rewards of successful investments: they give up money in the present in order to receive more later. Investments such as the expense of vehicle upkeep and increases in the amount of credit they offer are ways to advance themselves towards their ideal future, allowing them to amass more clients, scaling up their gains and capacity to reinvest.

Although most of the time spent by bosses in their activity is considered 'work', most of the money they take from their clients is deemed 'interest' over the amount they offered as credit. All bosses and clients claimed that the agreed interest was twenty per cent on the loan value, but as many PBF beneficiaries do not know their allowances value, it is hard to verify how

---

10   PBF had a calendar that paid its beneficiaries on different days, according to the numbers on their bank cards. Therefore, a person could go to the city with their family before the payment date of all the family beneficiaries, with only a few being able to withdraw their cash. Bosses could advance the money, saving people from waiting to buy commodities and return to the village.

much the boss is actually taking, an amount that changes from month to month according to clients' demands. In any case, debt is never described in monetary terms: rather, when negotiating with a boss about how much they would have to pay for a particular good, Apanjekra discuss their debt by asking 'how long' the lender would keep their card. By the same token, when they are asked how much they owe, they always respond in terms of temporal length: 'For this refrigerator, my boss is keeping my card for eight months; to pay for the cloth and glass beads, he is charging me three months.' What is at stake is the duration of their relationship. Clients actually receive a very small part of their allowance in cash. Not only will bosses take a large piece of it as 'interest', they will also collect payment for the transport upfront and use another part of their clients' income to pay for commodities. The amount clients will receive (and what commodities they might obtain) is the source of everyday negotiation with those holding their cards. Apanjekra will try to show their bosses that they need a particular thing, like new cloth to dress up for a ritual, claiming that they will be extremely ashamed if the boss does not get it for them. Or they may ask for money while in the city, explaining that they have no food and are facing hunger. Bosses, however, often reply that there is little they can do, as they are limited by the budgetary restrictions of such small allowances.

By making their necessities visible, clients try to persuade bosses to assist them. When bosses give in, they usually claim that they 'are caring' for their clients, which is to say that they are going beyond what should be expected from them. The Apanjekra invariably feel abused by their bosses when they fail to meet their clients' 'fundamental needs'. Nevertheless, bosses may also complain that clients are trying to extract more from them than is fair. To bosses, the 'unpaid work' that is associated with the idea of 'care' encapsulates a particular notion of crisis. Their aspiration is to increase their net worth through their action, hence they invest in their business. Spending their time and resources helping people feels like a waste, as steps backwards away from their financial targets. As one boss put it for me, he would help the Apanjekra more if it did not mean that he would take a loss in doing so.

There is a grey area when it comes to differentiating work and care: bosses say that they are working when they are with their clients, but also that they are helping them. Part of this classificatory challenge comes from the fact that the only service the bosses can openly charge their clients for is transportation. They cannot price activities such as assisting people to enrol in social programmes or acting as an interpreter.[11] The justification for the fares

---

11   Although bosses do not speak the Timbira language spoken by the Apanjekra, they
       do mediate relations with state agencies and banks, putting in lay terms what their

is that the bosses pay for fuel and vehicle maintenance. After all, as Apanjekra know, non-Indigenous people only give you goods if they receive cash in return. But this argument cannot be used to justify clients paying for services that neither involve material things nor have a visible cost. If bosses do not provide the attention their clients need 'for free', then they will lose them. However, if they do not charge for their time, then they will waste hours that have financial value. The bosses' solution for this double-edged position seems to be to embed in the interest charges the costs that they consider themselves as having incurred when working/caring for the Apanjekra. Clients, however, might feel that they are receiving less than they need. Hence their daily negotiations start over again: clients asking for bosses to solve problems and bosses swaying from side to side in their course to accumulate wealth, a promised future fleeting in a distant horizon.

Debts without past

During the 1970s the Brazilian government initiated the process of recognizing the land inhabited by the Apanjekra (Maranhão state), naming it Porquinhos Indigenous Land. Its first limits were officially established in 1984 and since then have been disputed by the Apanjekra, social anthropologists and NGOs. In the 2000s government consultants identified the frauds that led to the reduction of Indigenous land and started administrative procedures to reclaim the area that was cut out from the previous demarcation. This process, which would have led to a massive increment in the Indigenous territory, was halted by the Supreme Court in 2014. It was during the late 2000s and the early 2010s that social allowances proliferated among the Apanjekra, coinciding with the most palpable moments in their struggle for their land. When conducting interviews on the land demarcation, my hosts in Porquinhos frequently asserted that establishing borders was important in trying to keep the *kupen* (non-indigenous peoples, the settler-colonialists)[12] out. From the advent of settler-colonialism onwards, new illnesses and accelerated ecological degradation had become an issue. Beyond the Apanjekra land that was left out of the 1984 demarcation, they have experienced losses in game and in fertile areas in their territory in recent years. Discussions on these issues

---

clients (who speak Portuguese as a second language) should do.

12   The term *kupen* was used by the Apanjekra and other Timbira peoples to describe people who are neither *mehin* ('same flesh', the term the Timbira people employ to describe themselves) nor a people they have already met. Therefore, it could be applied to other Indigenous collectives as well as settler colonialists, denoting an unclassified otherness. After two centuries of colonization, *kupen* has become used exclusively for settler-colonialists.

were frequent between 2011 and 2019, though they did not seem to carry any sense of novelty. Governmental documents on the land-recognition process show that these concerns were present among the Apanjekra decades ago (Guimarães 2012); lack of data makes it hard to know when they came about. From a historiographic perspective, it is reasonable to suppose that they are concomitant with the colonialists' advances on their territory, displacing people and turning their homes into pasture throughout the nineteenth century (Hemming 1978).

However, it is possible that concerns with the so-called 'environment' were ever present in a place where 'nature' does not constitute a domain without agency. Contrary to Euro-American assumptions, it is not human labour over inhuman matter that produces 'culture' – rather, the inhuman world is the source of it. The culinary fire that distinguishes humans from animals (who eat raw, see Lévi-Strauss 1964) was stolen from the jaguar; songs and rituals were taught to humans by the alligators; cultivated plants were obtained through the star-woman (who turned into a frog after she descended from the sky). Events that changed the Apanjekra relational landscape are described in mythical narratives, called by them 'stories from the ancient ones', which do not treat time as a cumulative chain of occurrences. Rather, these narratives speak of particular occurrences presented as ruptures in time, giving place to the present epoch and framing the way people signify their lived experience (Gow 2001). They come from a conception of an episodic time (Gellner 1964; see also Scaglion 1999; Strathern, 2019) that does not regard change as an ontological given, but as something that can only happen through a reality-warping event (such as those described in the 'history of the ancient ones'). Present-day events are inscribed in the horizons of these narratives, which contain the relational possibilities of the present epoch.

Apanjekra's 'history of the ancients' links the origin of commodities to settler-colonialist agency: after the young man Aukê is killed and burnt by people from his own village, becoming thereby the first *kupen*, he 'invents' all categories of industrialized food and goods. Thinking of his community, Aukê offers them his creations, letting them choose between their traditional bow or the gun he had made. Offended by their rejection of his inventions, Aukê gives them to the *kupen* – a people he is also creating – and makes a deluge to send people apart.

Different scholars have registered and analysed the Aukê myth over the decades (Carneiro da Cunha 2009; Crocker 1990; Matta 1970), often associating it with the emergence of a historical temporality among Indigenous narratives (Crocker and Crocker 1994; Matta 1970) or reading particular events through the lens of mythical propositions. One example comes from Carneiro da Cunha's structuralist analysis of a Canela[13] messianic movement in the light of the Aukê myth, showing how its prophet's actions are cosmologically grounded. In explaining how the prophet maintains her support even after her prophecies are unsuccessful, the author states that what was at stake was not the fulfilment of the expectations generated by her sayings, but whether 'the proposed action was cognitively satisfactory' or not (Carneiro da Cunha 2009:49). Carneiro da Cunha makes the case that the prevalence of movements, such as the Melanesian cargo-cult, over long periods of time are due to the fact that they 'satisfy intellectual demands', allowing people to 'understand' the reality they live in (ibid.). By the same token, one might ask if the persistence of the Aukê myth in its current form, with small variations in different places and from different speakers, is not the result of this long-standing horizon, in which the Apanjekra relation with the *kupen*, its 'orienting categories and values' (Kaartinen and Sather 2008:9), has remained the same from the Indigenous point of view. In this sense, what was new was the advent of *kupen* with commodities, as described in the 'stories of the ancients'; access to them through *kupen's* own terms (government money obtained in banks) is just a logical continuity of the very relational idiom that has been characteristic of ever-present interethnic contact experienced for more than a hundred years.

Fundamental to the Apanjekra conception of the *kupen* is their chronically ungenerous behaviour, something that was registered by Crocker (1990) with data from the 1950s and 1960s. A basic feature that distinguishes the Apanjekra from the *kupen* contributes to this lack of generosity. *Kupen* have a poor memory, which makes them frequently forget that they owe something to someone, or that they should behave in particular ways. *Kupen* writing is considered as a way in which to deal with this problem, and the fact that their knowledge transmission is done on paper seems to corroborate this. Hence going to school is less of a way to learn the content of *kupen* education than a means to master a technology to navigate through *kupen's* memory-less world of documents, contracts and projects (Guimarães 2018). When asking a *kupen* for a favour, many Apanjekra will politely ask for their request to be written down, so it is more likely to be remembered. Bosses' bookkeeping is actually encouraged, as is the ethnographer's registering of conversations or village activities. It is a commitment to not forgetting.

Bosses have a practical role in solving the issues the Apanjekra face when trying to obtain commodities – they facilitate transport between village and city, assist their clients in enrolling in social programmes and mediate their relations in the local market, often offering credit that allows for the purchase

---

13   There are two Timbira groups called Canela – the Apanjekra and the Ramkokamera.

of expensive goods. This dynamic leads to the debt relations that were characteristic of all Apanjekra families registered in PBF during the time of fieldwork (2011–19). To some anthropologists and policy-makers (MDS 2016), the prevalence of the client-boss duo was hard to explain, given the nefarious effects experienced when clients lose a huge part of their social allowance and potentially face food insecurity. For the Apanjekra, however, it does not seem that debts are just a result of their desire for commodities surpassing their purchasing possibilities, and causing subsequent negative impacts. As soon as one receives a social-allowance bank card, one looks for a boss and asks for goods with a higher monetary value than the immediate income – already negotiating away the payments in forthcoming months, when the boss will hold the client's cards and, eventually, other documents. There is intentionality in this process, which is executed by the vast majority of the village.

Debts are contracted not with reference to a prior event, but with a forthcoming relation in mind: from the Apanjekra point of view, the client-boss debt relation does not emerge from something bosses did previously, making them their creditors. A person becomes a client before they receive anything, be it a commodity or a favour; the client-boss duo is enacted when the client asks the boss to help them obtain certain things, offering in return participation in their social allowances. It is possible to be a client even when one does not yet have a PBF card, as the boss can assist the person in enrolling in a governmental programme, in order to receive future payment. What the Apanjekra are negotiating when contracting debt with bosses is an opening out of their relational horizons, both in the cities and in the village, for in the former bosses will help them navigate through a hostile environment and in the later commodities will circulate with an effect on personal capabilities and reputations.

To become indebted is a way to secure a *kupen* to work and care for them. Apanjekra expect bosses to keep their end of the deal. They understand their help as a service for which they are paying, with money from CCTs. However, there is another dimension to the client-boss relation. Apanjekra say that a person will act in favour of another, giving them gifts or aiding them to solve a problem, because they are thinking about that person. When one gives a present, it is customary to say something to the recipient such as, 'I have been missing you, I thought of you a lot, so I wove this basket for you.' Gift-giving is both a way to show affection for someone and a way to influence a person's actions by making them think about the giver. In this context, debt is the objectification of the giver's agency over the recipient's mind. When Apanjekra become clients, placing their bank cards in the hands of the *kupen*, they say that their bosses will think of them – not because they will remember their clients being nice (they are *kupen*, after all), but because they will have with them something they covet with their clients' names on it. By seeing their clients' agency over their money, they will be kind and care for the Apanjekra. Contrary to what may seem the case at first glance, it is the client who is taking the position of the gift-giver, taking on debt as a means to keep bosses thinking on them.

In this sense, debts in client-boss relations are never meant to be cleared (which some families could, but they only do so if they want to change bosses) and are not the result of a previous action from a boss in favour of a client; rather, they are used strategically to maintain a key relation operating. Equivocations between the Euro-American and the Apanjekra notion of debt can be exemplified by the way interest is conceived.

In 2019 I was asked to go to the school during the evenings to teach mathematics in the company of demographer Caio Bibiani. One night, we decided to teach compound interest, in an effort to render the content of our classes more useful. Most of our public (around twenty people of different ages and genders) did not have a hard time mastering the multiplying operations, but could not understand how that would happen in a non-theoretical relation. In our demonstration, a client took 100 BRL from a boss, paying the twenty-per-cent interest per month charged by most bosses. Although the students realized that after two months they would owe 144 BRL, and that after a year they would have to pay almost nine times the original value (891 BRL), it was difficult to make this seem plausible. Not only does this not happen in real life (the twenty-per-cent interest is not actually charged, let alone in a compound fashion), but it was counter to Apanjekra understandings. Their reasoning was that, if one receives an item, yet one's interactions with the giver becomes less frequent and even ceases, the parties could end up forgetting each other and the debts would fade. This had to be the case for debts that were never paid after a very long time. In these instances, previous transactions would disappear, the satisfaction from the giver and the recipient would be forgotten, giving place to new courses of action. In this opening of horizons, there is no past to tether the indebted.

Final remarks: development horizons

In 2018, Indigenous activist Marcos Terena gave an interview in which he spoke about the Indigenous struggle against development policies promoted by the dictatorship in the 1970s and 1980s.[14] The theme of Indigenous

---

14   The interview was given to Ricardo Ventura Santos, Bruno Nogueira Guimarães and Alessandra Traldi Simoni, under the scope of the 'Health of Indigenous Peoples in Brazil: Historical, Sociocultural and Political Perspectives' project, funded by the Wellcome Trust (203486/Z/16/Z).

existence in Brazil was central to the dispute between the government officials (who sought to eliminate the population as a culturally differentiated group, as a means of accelerating the country's progress) and anthropologists (who denounced policies that would make it impossible for them to exist in the future). But what to some was a period to come, for others had happened long ago. Reflecting on his own personal trajectory, Terena remarked that they 'were already the survivors' of late colonialism. Development policies were not ahead in time: Indigenous activists, Terena observed, had already experienced the deleterious effects of the 'interethnic friction' (Cardoso de Oliveira 1972) that was lurking on the horizon for many scholars. Another important Indigenous thinker restated Terena's observations when considering the election of President Bolsonaro: 'For 500 years we have resisted; my worries are if the non-Indigenous people will be able to resist,' said Ailton Krenak, after recalling all the attacks his people had suffered over the centuries, resulting in the near annihilation of the Krenak population.

Consideration of the underlying temporal dimensions of CCTs allows insight into the actions of people involved in them. Though many policymakers treat programmes such as PBF as social investments that will pay for themselves in the long run, improving the life condition of the general population and leading to better economic results, critics have pointed out that among Indigenous peoples they may constitute a movement backwards – not due to their inefficacy, but because they are particularly efficient in promoting a potentially harmful economic dynamic in an epoch marked by environmental challenges and disputes over Indigenous rights. As an integral part of this dynamic, bosses regard their own activities as both work and as an investment towards their personal future. In trying to convert their relations with the Apanjekra into interest rates they give their time and money in the present in order to receive more later, reproducing a market rationale with a crisis of their own: counterparts who do not operate by the same principles and who demanded bosses to 'care' for them, pressuring them to make the contrary movement of working for free or taking losses on their loans. There are some convergences in the temporal horizons of these three sets of actors: they all manifest a notion of a 'future' represented as a 'movement forward' in the direction of the improvement of life conditions, even though their concepts of a 'better life' differ. Social anthropologists and Indigenous-rights activists have measured progress in terms of multicultural policies and access to land, as established in the 1988 Federal Constitution. Economic growth is the token of advancement for government officials and bosses alike, be it on a regional scale or personal level. Each party sees the other as an obstacle to its own progress. To speak of horizons allows for the use of categories such as 'future', 'present' and 'past', not as ontological givens, but as native concepts through which some actors describe and experience their actions.

Apanjekra temporal horizons don't seem to consider notions of 'progress' or the idea of 'moving forward' in a cumulative timeline. The 'development epoch' was already there, long before the advent of distributive politics and development programmes. The relations that cash-transfer policies render possible are actually new, but they function within limits defined by the 'stories of the ancients': Apanjekra must bargain with *kupen* to acquire commodities, inventions they cannot access otherwise. If economic abundance is defined by a great capacity to obtain consumption goods, as one may formulate it in capitalistic terms, then that capacity has already been briefly experienced by the Apanjekra, right before they chose the bow over Aukê's gun. It does not belong to a teleological future; rather, it was losing the commodities they already had that gave rise to their lived world.

Acknowledgements

This chapter greatly benefited from dialogue with Marilyn Strathern and Tony Crook at the Centro Incontri Umani (Ascona, Switzerland); working with both of them has been a great privilege, as indeed was staying at the Centro. Fieldwork in 2019 was funded by the Wellcome Trust (grant 203486/Z/16/Z). Broader ideas on the Apanjekra material were also enriched through the comments of Priscila Santos, Simon Kenema and Virginia Amaral. The continuous interlocution on the relation between Indigenous peoples in Brazil and public policies with Aparecida Vilaça, Ricardo Ventura Santos, Carlos Coimbra Jr, James Welch, Maria Pederneiras and Hélio Sá made its way, into different forms, in some of my considerations. I thank them all.

References

ABA. 2023. 'Nota Técnica – Prosseguem as investidas contra direitos dos Povos Tradicionais em Belo Monte': portal.abant.org.br/nota-tecnica-prosseguem-as-investidas-contra-direitos-dos-povos-tradicionais-em-belo-monte (accessed 10 October 2023).

Athila, A. 2017. '"Gente que Anda" e os Percursos da "Cidadania" (Bolsa Família/Alto Rio Negro)'. In F. Ricardo and C.A. Ricardo (eds), *Povos Indígenas no Brasil 2011–2016*, pp. 236–9. São Paulo: Instituto Socioambiental.

Brum, E. 2014. 'Diálogos sobre o fim do mundo', *El País* (29 September): brasil.elpais.com/brasil/2014/09/29/opinion/1412000283_365191.html (accessed 15 December 2021).

Bonilla, O. and Capiberibe, A. 2015. 'Isolados ou cadastrados: os índios na era desenvolvimentista', *Revista DR* (12 November): revistadr.com.br/posts/isolados-ou-cadastrados-os-indios-na-era-desenvolvimentista (accessed 20 November 2021).

Borges, J.C. 2016. "'A sociedade brasileira nos fez pobres": assistência social e autonomia étnica dos povos indígenas: o caso de Dourados, Mato Grosso do Sul', *Horizontes Antropológicos* 22(46):303–28.

Cardoso de Oliveira, R. 1972. *A Sociologia do Brasil Indígena*. Rio de Janeiro: Tempo Brasileiro.

Carneiro da Cunha, M. 2009 [1973] 'Lógica do mito e da ação: o movimento messiânico canela de 1963'. In *Cultura com aspas e outros ensaios*. São Paulo: Cosac e Naify

——— 2018. 'Índios na constituição', *Novos Estudos Cebrap* 37(3):429–43.

Carneiro da Cunha, M. and Viveiros de Castro, E.B. 1986. 'Vingança e temporalidade: os Tupinambá', *Anuário Antropológico* 10(1):57–78.

Coraggio, J.L. 2007. 'Critica de la política social neoliberal: las nuevas tendencias'. Presented at the Congreso de Ciencias Sociales de América Latina y el Caribe: www.coraggioeconomia.org/jlc/archivos%20para%20descargar/ponencia%20FLACSO%202007.doc (accessed 10 December 2021).

Crocker, W. 1990. *The Canela: Eastern Timbira*. Washington: Smithsonian Institution Press.

Crocker, W. and Crocker, J. 1994. *The Canela: Bonding Through Kinship, Ritual and Sex*. San Diego: Harcourt Brace College Publishers

Crook, T. and Rudiak-Gould, P. (eds.). 2018. *Pacific Climate Cultures: living Climate Change in Oceania*. Warsaw/Berlin: De Gruyter.

Fausto, C. 2007. 'If God were a jaguar: cannibalism and Christianity among the Guarani (16th–20th Century)'. In C. Fausto and M. Heckenberger (eds), *Time and Memory in Indigenous Amazonia: Anthropological Perspectives*, pp. 74–105. Gainesville: University Press of Florida.

Ferguson, J. 2010. 'The uses of neoliberalism', *Antipode* 41(SI):166–84.

——— 2015. *Give a Man A Fish: Reflections on the New Politics of Distribution*. Durham: Duke University Press.

Fernandes, M. 2002. *Definitivo: Uma Antologia de A Bíblia do Caos*. Porto Alegre: L&PM.

Fraser, J., Cardoso, T., Steward, A. and Parry, L. 2018. 'Amazonian peasant livelihood differentiation as mutuality-market dialectics', *The Journal of Peasant Studies* 45(7):1382–409.

Gertler, P. 2004. 'Do conditional cash transfers improve child health? Evidence from PROGRESA's control randomized experiment', *The American Economic Review* 94(2):336–41.

Gellner, E. 1964. *Thought and Change*. London: Weidenfeld and Nicholson.

Gow, P. 1991. *Of Mixed Blood: Kinship and History in Peruvian Amazonia*. Oxford: Clarendon Press.

——— 2001. *An Amazonian Myth and its History.* Oxford: Oxford University Press.

Guimarães, B. 2012. Os Caminhos da Terra Indígena Canela: História e Transformações. Masters thesis in Social Anthropology. Rio de Janeiro: UFRJ.

——— 2017. O Outro Lado da Moeda: Dos Benefícios Sociais dos Brancos ao Parentesco dos Apanjekra. Ph.D. dissertation in Social Anthropology. Rio de Janeiro: UFRJ.

——— 2018. 'Projetando a Humanidade: observações sobre a educação apanjekra', *Revista Pós-Ciências Sociais* 15:181–94.

Hall, A. 2006. 'From Fome Zero to Bolsa Família: social policies and poverty alleviation under Lula', *Journal of Latin American Studies* 38:689–709.

Hemming, J. 1978. *Red Gold: The Conquest of the Brazilian Indians*. Cambridge, Mass: Harvard University Press.

Hugh Jones, C. 1979. *From the Milk River: Spatial and Temporal Processes in Northwest Amazonia.* Cambridge: Cambridge University Press.

Hugh Jones, S. 1979. *The Palm and the Pleiades: Initiation and Cosmology in Northwest Amazonia.* Cambridge: Cambridge University Press.

Ingold, T. 2000. *The Perception of the Environment: Essays on Livelihood, Dwelling and Skill.* London: Routledge.

Kaartinen, T. and Sather, C. (eds) 2008. *Beyond the Horizon: Essays on Myth, History, Travel and Society* (Studia Fennica 2). Helsinki: Finnish Literature Society.

Lévi-Strauss, C. 1964. *Mythologiques: Le Cru et le Cuit.* Paris: Plon.

Martins, A.P., Canella, D., Baraldi, L. and Monteiro, C. 2013. 'Cash transfers in Brazil and nutritional outcomes: a systematic review', *Revista de Saúde Pública* 47:1–12.

Matta, R.D. 1970. *Mito e Linguagem Social: Ensaios de Antropologia Social.* Rio de Janeiro: Tempo Brasileiro.

MDS (Ministério de Desenvolvimento Social) 2015. *Estudos Etnográficos sobre o Programa Bolsa Família entre Povos Indígenas – Sumário Executivo.* Brasília: MDS.

——— 2016. *Estudos Etnográficos sobre o Programa Bolsa Família entre Povos Indígenas – Relatório Final.* Brasília: MDS.

Meira, M. 2018. *A Persistência do Aviamento: Colonialismo e História Indígena no Noroeste Amazônico.* São Carlos: EdUFSCar.

Munn, N. 1992. 'The cultural anthropology of time: a critical essay', *Annual Review of Anthropology* 21:93–123.

Novo, M. 2019. 'As políticas de transferência de renda e o desenvolvimento: o caso Kalapalo do Alto Xingú', *Maloca Revista de Estudos Indígenas* 1(1):78–97.

Peirano, M. 1998. 'When anthropology is at home: the different contexts of a single discipline', *Annual Review of Anthropology* 27:105–28.

Pimentel, S., Bonilla, O. and Guimarães, B. 2017. 'A diferença e o benefício'. In: F. Ricardo and C.A. Ricardo (eds), *Povos Indígenas no Brasil (2011–2015)*, pp. 107–10. São Paulo: Instituto Socioambiental.

Pacheco de Oliveira, J. and Cohn, C. (eds) 2014. *Belo Monte e a Questão Indígena.* Brasília: ABA.

Piperata, B., McSweeney, K. and Murrieta, S. 2016. 'Conditional cash transfers, food security, and health: bicultural insights for poverty-alleviation policy from the Brazilian Amazon', *Current Anthropology* 57(6):806–26.

Reis, M. 2010. 'Cash transfer programs and child health in Brazil', *Economic Letters* 108:22–5.

Robbins, J. 2007. 'Continuity thinking and the problem of Christian culture: belief, time, and the anthropology of Christianity', *Current Anthropology* 48(1):5–38.

Saad-Filho, A. 2015. 'Social policy for neoliberalism: the Bolsa Família programme in Brazil', *Development and Change* 46(6):1227–52.

Santos, R. 1980. *História Econômica da Amazônia: 1800–1920.* São Paulo: T.A. Queiroz.

Scaglion, R. 1999. 'Yam cycles and "timeless time" in Melanesia', *Ethnology* 38(3):211–25.

Strathern, M. 1985. 'John Locke's servant and the hausboi from Hagen: thoughts on domestic labour', *Critical Philosophy* 2:21–48.

——— 2019. 'A clash of ontologies? Time, law, and science in Papua New Guinea', *Hau: Journal of Ethnographic Theory* 9(1):58–74.

——— 2021. 'New and old worlds: a perspective from social anthropology', *European Review* 29(1):34–44.

Viveiros de Castro, E.B. 1998. 'Cosmological deixis and Amerindian perspectivism', *Journal of the Royal Anthropological Institute* (NS) 4(3):469–88.

——— 2004. 'Perspectival anthropology and the method of controlled equivocation', *Tipití* 2(1):3–22.

Weinstein, B. 1983. *The Amazon Rubber Boom.* Stanford: Stanford University Press.

World Bank 2009. *Conditional Cash Transfers: Reducing Present and Future Poverty.* Washington, DC: The World Bank.

5

'Papua New Guinea was the last, but now is our time'

Priscila Santos da Costa[1]

A particular kind of time and a counter view from another vantage point are exemplified in the intertwining of two kinds of repetition in the thinking of a Papua New Guinean reformist movement. The Unity Team within the national parliament battled against the ungodliness of the institution and thus its dire condition. But their narrative took two different courses. The identification of a crisis, or rather of repeated crises, was made in terms of an account that historicized successive rises and falls of national virtue. Linear history was here understood in terms of certain key replications of moments of power. Yet crisis and linearity were also, in another sense, off stage. Rather than only emphasizing a future trajectory towards end times, the Unity Team also understood themselves as already living in an expansive present. What was immanent in their present condition was made evident on the occasion of a Bible presentation that appeared as a defining moment. That event propelled the nation into a particular epoch, its horizon established by a new generation of believers; Parliament must be made to recognize the situation ('accept' the Bible). Rather than a crisis about the future, what figured in this part of the Unity Team's narrative were re-enacted characters from a biblical past.

1   This work, produced under the auspices of the Ethnographic Horizons project at the Centre for Pacific Studies, University of St Andrews, was supported by the International Balzan Foundation.

❋

My fieldwork in 2015 coincided with the arrival of an antique King James Version (KJV) Bible in Papua New Guinea (PNG).[2] The Bible was donated by the Reverend Gene Hood – an American missionary pastor of the Independent Nazarene Church and owner of multiple radio stations across the developing world – who often travelled to PNG. In 2014, during a trip as a PNG Bible Church guest, Hood heard about the 'Restoration, Reformation and Modernization Programme' (RRMP) spearheaded by the speaker of the ninth Parliament (2012–16), Theodor Zurenuoc, and supported by an entourage of bureaucrats, liberal professionals and pastors (henceforth Unity Team). The programme aimed at reforming the Parliament and the nation according to Christian values and was deeply influenced by Pentecostal and charismatic Christianity. The RRMP envisaged the bureaucratic reform of a Parliament often accused of corruption and nepotism (Walton 2018:31), and its most famous and controversial measures against the present state were grounded in Pentecostal ideas, such as spiritual warfare (Rio, MacCarthy and Blanes 2017:3). For Pentecostal Christians, morally reproachable practices, especially corruption, are traced back to the intervention of bad or satanic spiritual forces in the material realm, and actions against it must, accordingly, be dealt with both materially and spiritually (Marshall 2009:204; Meyer 2010).

In 2013 the Unity Team removed a lintel carving that decorated Parliament's façade and partially dismantled the assemblage of carved wooden poles entitled *Bung Wantaim* ('coming together') from the grand entrance hall. Their reasoning was that those objects represented non-Christian worshipping practices and therefore exerted an ungodly influence on Parliament and, by extension, Papua New Guinea as a whole (Eves *et al.* 2014; Rio, MacCarthy and Blanes 2017:2). The Unity Team's plan was to substitute the assembled wooden poles with a 'Unity Pillar'. Both objects (Figure 5.1) were intended to represent national unity. The poles were designed and carved in the wake of PNG's independence by Papua New Guinean artists, and represented PNG's different traditions on a single object (Rosi 1991:302). The Unity Pillar was designed by the Unity Team to represent PNG's diversity by engraving the word 'unity' translated into all the languages spoken in PNG. However, their main goal was to point to the moral force they thought linked the diverse groups, namely, the 'Word of God' (Zurenuoc 2015). A stone representing the Word of God was to

---

2   I conducted most of my fieldwork in the National Parliament of Papua New Guinea between 2013 and 2015 (Santos da Costa 2018 and 2021; Pickles and Santos da Costa 2021).

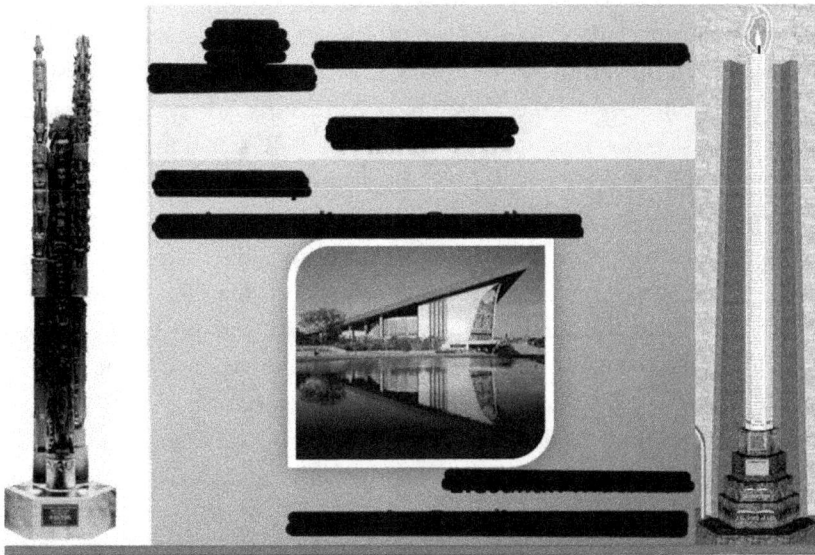

Figure 5.1 A PowerPoint slide used by officials shows the carved pole on the left and an image of what the Unity Pillar would look like on the right. The slide was provided by a member of the Unity Team in 2015.

support one representing the constitution, which in turn supported the pillar with the translations of 'unity'.

In 2014 Hood visited Parliament and met members of the Unity Team. During that visit, he also saw the dismantled carved poles at the Parliament's grand entrance hall. By its side, he saw a poster maintaining that the pole represented idolatry, with a picture of what the new pillar would look like and the symbolism behind it. A member of the Unity Team explained to him the changes that the Speaker of Parliament, Theodor Zurenuoc, wanted to make to Parliament and to the country, and how they wanted God and Christian values to be officially recognized as the foundation of the nation. My interlocutors, members of the Unity Team, agree that it was during this visit that Hood, a Bible collector, decided that he had a 'gift' for PNG – a 1611 KJV Bible – a suitable donation for a programme that would like to have the Word of God as the foundation of the nation. What happened subsequently placed Zurenuoc and the Unity Team back in the public spotlight.

In April 2015 a delegation of around fifty people, including five Members of Parliament, two parliamentary officers, various clergy and members of the interdenominational Christian network, the PNG Bible Church and Body of Christ, left PNG to receive Hood's donated Bible in the United States. The trip, funded by the PNG government, was criticized by some as a use of public funding for private religious purposes (Kamu 2015; Ove Jr 2015). In contrast, as was to be expected, those supporting Zurenuoc's Christian-led initiatives told me that the government had finally spent money on a 'noble cause'. The delegation returned with the Bible on 27 April 2015, when it was solemnly received at Jacksons International Airport in PNG's national capital, Port Moresby. A red carpet was laid from the airplane and on it walked the MPs followed by four pastors carrying the donated Bible. A crowd, estimated at 20,000 by the media (Cochrane 2015), watched the Bible's arrival, praying and praising. A stage was set out near the airport. There, the then Prime Minister O'Neill, the opposition leader, the Governor General and other MPs gathered, delivering speeches about the importance of Christianity and the Word of God to Papua New Guinea and Papua New Guineans.

In this chapter I analyse the discourse surrounding the Unity Team's acceptance and treatment of the KJV Bible in order to understand the notions of crisis and time underlying their Pentecostal political ideology. The first part focuses on what I call the journey of the Bible. For the Unity Team, the Word of God, which is revealed in the KJV Bible, is a powerful force that brings about riches and opulence; but its absence also produces decay and crisis. This oscillation is predicated on the way in which the Bible and its principles were embraced or denied by nations around the world and through history. The Unity Team understands world history as linking Israel, England, the United States and, finally, Papua New Guinea in a sequence of rises to prominence that follow the movement of the Bible from one country to the other. Hence, time appears as linearly propelled forward by the force of the Word of God. But time only takes this linear form against the background of recurrent and congruent crises, which allows temporal difference to be perceived. The Unity Team did not put full eschatological emphasis onto any of the crises. Rather, they were seen as endings to someone somewhere, and evidence that God is powerful and will continue to influence the world of men. Their focus was solely on the present, pushing the notion of 'end times' into an almost invisible future. As a matter of fact, as I will argue, a lack of concern with the eschaton made political action desirable and necessary.

The second part of the chapter explores how the Unity Team saw their own place in the present. It considers the dynamic between repetition and linearity in the way that my interlocutors understood the history of Papua New Guinea's national politics. The Unity Team uses the Bible as a scripture to map out PNG's history by equating prophets that appear in the Old Testament to PNG's past and present leaders. The effects of leaders in the formation of Israel, for instance, becomes a framework for understanding the effects that politicians have had in Papua New Guinea (Haynes 2020; see also Halvorson and Hovland 2021:513). As Haynes observed (2020:71), this type of scriptural reading collapses the biblical past into the believer's present, and is therefore more than an exercise in finding potential likelihoods: 'through these narrative practices, Pentecostals are inserting themselves into the text, and in so doing bringing the biblical past into an expansive present where the stories of the Bible are lived over and over again' (ibid.:59). This typological reading applied to PNG's political history brings up a temporal model in which there is a visible repetition of movements of approximation and distancing from God and of types of people and their fates. But it is also these recurrences that make each epoch and moment appear different from the one that came before. More importantly, it is the recognition of yet one more crisis and break from the past that enables further broadening of the horizons in which new presents are made possible.

The journey of the KJV Bible

The arrival of the donated Bible in Port Moresby prompted public and private discussions about its value and meaning. Many, both in news outlets and personally (to the ethnographer), questioned the importance the Unity Team attributed to it. There were two main critiques. The first was directed at Zurenuoc's use of public funds to fly a group of pastors and politicians to the United States to receive the Bible. The second focused on accusations of 'cargo cultism' and 'idolatry',[3] as Zurenuoc was seen to be proposing that the simple presence of an object would bring prosperity to Papua New Guinea.

Members of the Unity Team were eager to deny these accusations. My presence in Parliament at the time, I have no doubt, served as an outlet for them to explain the significance of the Bible's arrival; but, as I circulated among different groups supporting the Unity Team's initiative, it became clear that publicizing their rationale for the acceptance of the donated Bible was important for other reasons too. As one member of the Unity Team, Carl[4], told me in a conversation in Parliament in 2015, people criticize Zurenuoc because they do not 'understand the value ... the meaning of the KJV Bible'. He noted that the comprehension of the value of the donated Bible is impossible if 'you do not understand the events that brought it here [to PNG]'. This interpretative work ('understanding') was not only aimed at external validation; it was also part of my informants' practice of evaluating events among their Christian peers. One event that Carl highlighted, for example, was the encounter between missionary Hood and the Team that eventually brought the KJV Bible to PNG. The Unity Team's reception of the donated Bible was evidence

---

3   See nancysullivan.typepad.com/my_weblog/2015/05/the-emperor-wears-no-clothes-.html (accessed 23 January 2024).

4   Whenever possible, pseudonyms are used.

of God's approval of their programme to reform Parliament and the nation, as well as evidence of the Team's efficacy, as it was their actions that 'prompted' Hood to make the gift (Pickles and Santos da Costa 2021:361).

I focus now on another series of events that solidified the Bible's importance for the Unity Team and many of its supporters, particularly regarding the significance of the KJV Bible in framing Papua New Guinea's place as a Christian nation in the international landscape. The Unity Team inferred this 'significance' from personal and generalized testimonies about the KJV Bible and its past that circulated among various groups of the Christians who supported the Team. A version of the general testimony of the importance of the arrival of the KJV Bible for Papua New Guinea was stated by a Unity Team member, Phil, while we talked in his parliamentary office:

> The historical value of the Bible is that it is a first edition, and one of the five existent in the world. Its importance lies in the fact that it was the first bible to be translated from Latin and Hebrew to English, under the supervision of King James.

But historically, I told him, there were inaccuracies in his account. For example, there are not just five first-edition KJV Bibles, rather several hundred, and the Bible had already been translated into English before the KJV translation of 1604. Phil dismissed my comments, 'Indeed, but that was the culmination of all other translations that were already there.' As I came to understand, for my informants, what they called the Bible´s historical importance could only be understood in the context of its spiritual importance: as the translation with the most 'integrity' it yielded powerful effects. Possibly repeating what they had heard during services, I was repeatedly told that the KJV recognized God and Christ as equals (Philippians 2:6), whereas other versions allegedly undermined that identity or perverted the Word of God. I suspect that claims about the integrity and superiority of the King James Version were influenced by reading websites such 'Dial-the-Truth Ministries', containing texts by Terry Watkins,[5] an American Baptist and member of the King James Only Movement, a conservative Christian movement that believes the KJV Bible to be the most perfect translation of the Bible in English.

My interlocutors believe that the KJV is the most faithful reproduction of the Word of God and that the translation was inspired and guided by God himself. Hence, as Bielo (2008:9) observes in relation to the North American

---

5   See, for example, 'Bible version comparison', www.av1611.org/biblecom.html (accessed 7 December 2021) and 'Counterfeit', www.av1611.org/nkjv.html (accessed 7 December 2021).

Lutherans he studies, the Bible is 'the absolutely authoritative "Word of God"'. However, unlike his informants' approach to the various translation of the Bible as equally valid, some of the people that I met were inclined to give prominence to the KJ Version. This belief enabled them to ground and unpack the spiritual impact that the KJV Bible had in the world, and its relevance for their and Papua New Guinea's present. This spiritual value was predicated on the KJV's past. As Phil proceeded to tell me in one of his conversations in his office in Parliament in 2015:

> Regarding its spiritual importance, this Bible was kept in King James' Palace and it actually contains the principles and strategies that inform the organization of the Constitutional monarchic system. This Bible was called The Glory of England, and while it was there, England was a superpower and colonized all other countries.

To reiterate, the spiritual importance of the KJV Bible was that it correctly translated and registered the Word of God, according to Phil, and consequently offered guidance to the monarch and allowed England to be successful. This power manifested itself repeatedly, leading him to consider it evidence of the efficacy of Word of God. It was believed that the integrity of the translation was substantiation for the claim that the KJV had a particular power in comparison to any other Bible, and that the effects of the arrival and the acceptance of the Bible, and thereby the Word of God, were demonstrated throughout history.

One way of explaining the power of God in a national context was to map the journey of the Word of God and its effects as it changed places and ownership:

> The Word of God was captured from Israel and transferred to England, and when it was there, they compiled it into this book here, the KJV Bible, that is the Glory, somebody said, that is the Glory of England, and that is because God was transferred from Israel to England, and that is why they became a superpower and when people started to move to America, they decided to take the Bible over there and that is why America became a superpower.
> (Pastor Michael's sermon, meeting of the Christian Parliamentary Fellowship, PNG Parliament, 2015)

Demonstrating the importance of the KJV Bible's arrival to PNG was an exercise in laying out the power of God's Word through time and showing its effects on the material world. As the pastor continued to say in the same meeting, 'the movement of power is equal to the movement of the Bible'. The

Word of God was defined as politically productive, its effects ranging from efficient government organization to power over other nations to colonial liberation (Marshall 2009; see also Santos da Costa 2021). Importantly, believers recognized these powers as being replicable in different places and, in this ethnographic case, as forming a linear history through its replicability.

Conversations with interlocutors and attendance at meetings indicate that the succession of events are as follows: from the Israelites, the Word of God was 'transferred' to England, where it was translated from the Greek, Latin and Hebrew to become the seventeenth-century KJV Bible, serving as the foundation for the British government and constitution. It then travelled with the Puritans to the New World, where it became, yet again, the base upon which another 'superpower' (as my interlocutors labelled the United States of America) was built.

Discourses about the 'transfer of powers' and the Bible as grounding the nation and offering principles of governmental organization echo those of two American Christian movements, the New Apostolic Reformation (NAR) and Christian Reconstructionism. Despite their theoretical differences (Haynes 2021:223) both movements focus on processes of social transformation that radiate outwards from individuals to society. They can loosely be described as propounding 'dominionism' (McVicar 2013),[6] a belief that God made Earth for men to have dominance over, and that therefore Christians should assert dominion over different spheres of society and rebuild according to God's Word.

The Unity Team's view of their programme as a plan to redesign the nation according to Christian principles shares more than passing similarities with 'dominionistic' ideals. The view that Christians should influence the seven 'mountains of culture' (business, art and entertainment, government, media, religion, education and family), which is used by NAR (Haynes 2021:222), is also in a manifesto written by the Unity Team:

> We have seven distinct systems in which our people are trapped, which we must take complete control [of]. These systems are (1) the political system, (2) the economic system, (3) the education system, (4) the social systems, (5) the media, (6) the entertainment world, and (7) the religious systems. Our crossing over must be to take over these systems. As we begin the

---

6   Inspired by the passage in Genesis 1:26 (King James Version) which says, 'And God said, Let us make man in our image, after our likeness: and let them have dominion over the fish of the sea, and over the fowl of the air, and over the cattle, and over all the Earth, and over every creeping thing that creepeth upon the Earth.'

new era, these systems must be radically reformed to reflect our belief and convictions – to be in charge of these systems for our full benefit.

(Zurenuoc 2015:1)

Citizens who supported the Unity Team and who went weekly to Parliament to pray for the institution, for Zurenuoc and for the nation were also influenced by this ideology. The idea of the seven mountains of influence originated in the 1970s with two American self-described apostles (Cunningham 1988:134). In addition to separating and defining spheres in which believers can act upon in the world, the seven-mountain prophecy also describes social intervention as mandated by God, indicating the templates and directions for it in the Bible. During my fieldwork a document inspired by the seven-mountains-mandate ideology, called 'Template for kingdom establishment',[7] circulated among Unity Team supporters. The document says the Bible contains 'strategies and a blueprint' to 'capture domains', such as the nation, and to transform them. Although interlocutors who self-identified as being part of the Unity Team have never mentioned this document, they did refer to the Bible as a 'blueprint', a moral guide for both the individual and for Parliament, which would ultimately guide the 're-designing' of the nation (Santos da Costa 2018).

One striking idea from the 'template' is that by receiving and following God's blueprint, PNG will fulfil its mandate of being a 'role-model nation', as other nations were before. The notion that there is a mandate to be fulfilled by Papua New Guinea shows how both past and future are brought to work in the present. This process is called 'replication' in the 'template' itself: PNG is not only replicating choices (and its effects) from previous times, but by becoming this role model – as the Kingdom of God on Earth – it will prompt other nations to copy it for the prosperity brought by following God's plans. This replication of effects resulting from openly accepting the Word of God was clear in the Unity Team's narrative of the way different countries have risen to power through history. From Israel to the United Kingdom and

---

7   The document has around twenty pages and seems to have been written by more than one person. Although authorship is not clear, the writers are associated with the PNG Rhema Bible Training College, a ministry-training programme founded in in the 1970s by the North American pastor, Hagin. He is known for his work in strengthening a global network called Faith Movement, which puts great emphasis on ideas of prosperity (Coleman 2006:164). Hagin (1993) has written about the individual's authority (understood as mandated power bestowed by God) or dominion over himself against evil. His focus, however, was more on the individual level, whereas the seven-mountains-of-influence ideology developed the idea of dominion outwards to society and the nation.

then the United States, the Word of God arrived to offer guidance for the creation of a nation's 'superpower', shifting and shaping the balance of power on the international landscape as it travelled. Carl, the public servant who contextualized the relevance of the KJV Bible's arrival to PNG, noted the importance of understanding what had brought it there in the first place. His explanation identified a crisis:

> ... you look at the relationship between moral ethics and the rise and fall of
> civilizations and countries. The rise, the upholding of moral ethics ensures
> the continuity, sustenance and rise of civilizations. If there is a decay in
> moral ethics, eventually there will be a decline in society, imbalance.
>
> (fieldwork notes, July 2015)

When moral standards fail to be upheld, there is a crisis of morality; this is the moment when the Bible and the power of the Word is 'transferred' to another location. My interlocutors had descriptions for what caused the transfer of the Bible for each place it moved from. The Bible's departure from Israel, according to Phil, was due to 'the people's denial of Christ as God's son ... [for] they thought that he was another prophet, not his son. They did not receive him.' This referred to the difference in canonical scriptures used in Judaism and Christianity. England, on the other hand, had accepted the New Testament and Christ's equality to God. However, King James, who was responsible for commissioning the KJV translation, then became greedy and 'wanted to be more powerful than God ... and did not allow for freedom of faith.' Here, Phil is referring to the fact that King James I persecuted Puritans, who for this reason fled to North America, 'carrying the Bible with them.'

According to the narrative, the Bible did not stop in the USA, and members of the Unity Team had no difficulties finding evidence of a North American moral crisis that prompted its departure. For example, my interlocutors highlighted the nine African Americans who were killed in a Charleston church shooting that same month.[8] Even before this, they claimed they saw 'signs' of crisis. Examples included other instances of gun violence, increased numbers of drug addicts and Obama's alleged distancing from Israel and his support for Arabic countries. As a side effect of not following the Word of God, it was no surprise to the Unity Team that the Bible had left the USA for the benefit of another chosen people. The future, as the Unity Team understood it then, remained to be made as the KJV Bible landed in Papua New Guinea. As one member of the Team told me in an interview in 2015:

---

8   See www.cbsnews.com/pictures/charleston-south-carolina-church-shooting
     (accessed 22 January 2024).

I had not thought about it before, but since the Bible arrived, I started thinking about what it means when people say that Papua New Guinea is a Third World country. People usually think that it is because we are underdeveloped, while Western countries are not. But this is not what it means. Maybe it is about the order that each people received the Word of God. I think [the fact] that we were considered as being a Third World country was not about being inferior, but the meaning was the order in which the Word of God would arrive here. First Europe, second United States and, third, PNG. Papua New Guinea was the last, but now it is our time.

The crisis here is a moral one, connected to the commitment to God. The various crises that the Unity Team identified throughout history are seen as indexes of a poor relationship with God that repel blessings and direct them elsewhere. The biblical story of Israel, the Promised Land, as an outcome of God's blessing irrupts into world history through the Unity Team's accounts, and it is repeated in their recounting of the past until it encompasses Papua New Guinea's present. Believing that nations can 'rise and fall' according to their commitment to God's Word, the Unity Team acted accordingly when the KJV Bible was donated to PNG: they had to make sure that their commitment was acknowledged and visible to God, to other nations and to Papua New Guineans. Hence, in the months after the Bible's arrival, the Unity Team prepared what they saw as evidence of Papua New Guinea's commitment. In July 2015 a motion was passed in Parliament, after MP Powi read a statement on the floor on behalf of the Speaker and the House Committee. It stated that Parliament accepted the donated KJV Bible 'as a national treasure and the property of the people and the government of Papua New Guinea and [it should] be placed in the chamber of the national parliament on the clerk's table' (fieldwork notes, July 2015). The Unity Team and its network of supporters organized a big event for the 16 September 2015 (Independence Day), leading to the placement of the Bible in the chamber of the parliament. After the routine celebrations, the donated Bible toured around Port Moresby and it solemnly entered the parliament building in a chest, similar to the Ark of Covenant built to carry the Ten Commandments.

The Unity Team drew a parallel between the ability to receive God and the ability to receive the KJV Bible, which is modelled on the Unity Team's belief that a moral commitment to God has consequences. The impact of the type of commitment is only knowable as one looks to the past and to the past's future. Their perception and analysis of a US crisis that precipitated the departure of the Bible during the Obama administration show how the Unity Team's narratives interweave a very immediate past with a very distant biblical one, that of the Promised Land. Regardless of how distant these pasts are, each has another crisis on the horizon, and another place the blessings and growth are destined to move to. Considering this, and believing appropriate actions would deliver positive outcomes, the Unity Team organized the present in order to precipitate a desired future.

A genealogy for Papua New Guinean politics

> It is not as much about the historical past of this Bible but more so it is our joint action in receiving it, which makes this occasion and its challenges worthy, Prime-Minister. Our action today, Prime Minister, Ministers of State, and people of God, ladies and gentlemen, is a symbol of respect and honour to the Word of God. We have taken a major action in faith and that is the most significant thing that matters to God and an honourable act in the eyes of God. We as leaders are now making a statement that we are recommitting this nation and its people to God and to the values and to the principles of the Christian faith.
>
> (Zurenuoc, April 2015, Port Moresby)

This is an extract from the speech given by then Speaker of Parliament at the airport during the arrival of the KJV Bible. The Unity Team and their supporters organized the event, ensuring that MPs from Government and Opposition parties would be present to show that 'being Christian' and committing to God brought people together and bridged differences. This was the ideological premise of their programme. But another bridging was also being enacted in that speech: as Zurenuoc stated, the action of receiving the donated Bible was one of 'recommitting' to God, of re-establishing a link that had been lost.

The Speaker was alluding to, and claiming continuity with, a commitment to God once made by another politician, Sir Michael Somare. Previously, in May 2014, he had released an advertorial recognizing Sir Michael Somare and Sir Julius Chan, among others, as central to the process of PNG gaining independence:

> Since Parliament stands as a symbol of national unity, an emblem of collective wisdom and the pinnacle of political decision-making in which noble dreams of great men and women have been and will continue to be, translated into reality through legislation that will transcend to the Executive, Judiciary and the rest of the society, it needed the reformation, restoration and modernization to be undertaken. The idea of National Unity

was taken from the courageous actions of our Founding Fathers who united our very difficult and fragmented tribes of a thousand languages to give us Independence. Inspiration was also drawn from the spirit of unity still alive and active in two of our remaining Founding Fathers, Rt. Hon. Grand Chief Sir Michael Somare and Rt. Hon. Sir Julius Chan.

(Zurenuoc 2014:35)

One can see how the RRMP's goals of bringing the nation together are presented as echoing those of long-standing politicians.[9] The continuity with Somare's legacy and commitment to Christianity is explicit:

Our Grand Chief Sir Michael Somare not only delivered us Independence, but also made two decisions of far-reaching ramifications that cements the unity of this country. ... The second was his dedication of PNG and [its] covenant with the God of the Holy Bible in 2007. ... This second action was in my view the most important of all the actions he had taken since the founding of this nation.

(Zurenuoc 2014:37)

But the claim of continuity might appear at odds with what was happening at the time. In 2013 Somare and the Director of the National Museum were in a legal battle with Zurenuoc.[10] They alleged that the Speaker's order to

---

9   The piece was written after the dismantling of the carvings that decorated Parliament. As such, it also addressed the widespread criticism that the Speaker and the RRMP actions were based on the irrational or senseless assumption that the carvings were endowed with traditional spirits. It used the work of curator and anthropologist Barry Craig as evidence (Zurenuoc 2014:36) for their presence. Craig (2010:4) quotes Somare as saying, in the context of art repatriation, 'I would ask you all to cooperate with us in returning our ancestral spirits and souls to their homes in Papua New Guinea. We view our masks and our art as living spirits with fixed abodes.' Craig (2010:3) sees irony in the fact that evangelicals who want to destroy 'traditional cults ... and objects associated with them' end up giving evidence of the power of the objects destroyed. There is, however, little irony to be found; evangelical iconoclasm indeed assumes that spiritual forces are embodied in objects. To the Unity Team, that passage gives evidence that it is known and recognized that these forces exist, including by Somare, as highlighted in the 'Tribute' (Zurenuoc 2014:36).

10 After the partial removal and destruction of the carved lintels and pole in 2013, the Director of the National Museum of Papua New Guinea and the then Prime Minister, took legal action against Zurenuoc. They claimed that Zurenuoc's actions infringed Section 45 of the National Constitution, which guarantees freedom of religion, and Section 9 of the National Cultural Property (Preservation) Act which

dismantle the totem pole and the carvings that decorated the façade of the Parliament was illegal, as these were cultural artefacts protected by law. In addition, the Speaker's Pentecostal claims that the carvings represented evil traditional spirits and therefore should be removed is something that Somare disagreed with. In fact the architecture of Parliament takes inspiration from traditional Sepik motifs, Somare's home region (Briggs 1989; Rossi 1991).

Both the Unity Team's iconoclasm and litigation with opposing figures appeared to be (Pickles and Santos da Costa 2021:359) enacting a 'ritual of rupture' (Robbins 2003:224) and a 'breaking with the past' in the realm of politics (Schram 2014). This type of Christian politics points to a model of temporality defined by ruptures (Eves *et al.* 2014; Rio, MacCarthy and Blanes 2017; Santos da Costa 2018) and, as Haynes points out (2021:57), rupture has been the focus of anthropology concerned with evangelical Christianity (Bialecki, Haynes and Robbins 2008:1144). This interest stems mostly from evangelicals' concern with 'breaking with the past' and becoming 'born again' (Meyer 1998), whether at an individual or collective level. But Zurenuoc and the Unity Team did not only display a political theology concerned with temporal rupture, as in Zurenuoc's speech of 2015. Nor was PNG's political past and its protagonists made to appear in the present solely as spectres of an ungodly past that needed to be expunged (Marshall 2009:88).

The 'Tribute' delineated how the Unity Team performed what Engelke (2011:179, see also Meyer 1998:318) called 'realignments of rupture', an operation of re-inscribing themselves into a Christian past through practices of rupture. The 'Tribute' refers to the 'New Covenant', a document crafted on the occasion of an All Peoples Prayer Assembly (APPA)[11] meeting in Port Moresby and signed by Somare in August 2007 (Patrick 2015). This document is connected to the creation of 'Covenant Day' in PNG, which in 2011 would become the 'National Repentance Day', a day for prayers established by Somare. Somare signed the New Covenant document and created the Repentance Day in response to the request of Christian churches and in recognition that PNG is a country with a Christian majority,[12] but the Unity Team both understood this event differently and incorporated it into their 'ongoing social production of

---

protects objects of cultural importance. Zurenuoc's actions were deemed unlawful (see the court decision: Somare v Zurenuoc [2016] PGNC 124; N56308 on vlex. com/vid/sir-michael-somare-v-922773445).

11   The APPA was initially a prayer movement created by Maeliau (Bond and Timmer 2017:137; Timmer 2015:17), a prophet from North Malaita, in the Solomon Islands, which became a global movement. The document Somare signed reflects the APPA's beliefs in evangelical ideas of establishing covenants with God and sustaining them through prayer (Haynes 2015; Timmer 2015:18).

12   www.youtube.com/watch?v=DkoRMllERdo (accessed 21 December 2021).

accounts of' (Hirsch and Stewart 2005:262) PNG's political past and therefore of its present.

In the Bible God initiates various covenants, so that one can speak of an Adamic, a Noahic and an Abrahamic Covenant, for example. Covenants[13] are a form of relationship. They are an exchange between God and humans in which the former expects loyalty and the latter receives blessings. Throughout the biblical narrative, humans are repeatedly depicted as straying from the covenant, worshipping other gods and then being reminded of their commitment (see, for instance, Jeremiah 22:9). For Pentecostals covenants with God can be made by individuals and by nations (Coleman 2004:421–2; Haynes 2015:18) as a way of compelling God to act on their behalf and to bring prosperity to themselves or the nation. The 'New Covenant' indeed has the vocabulary of a contract:

> I, Michael Somare, Prime Minister, hereby concur with the Terms and Conditions of this Covenant and do entreat the Lord on Behalf of the people of Papua New Guinea, that God would fulfil the stated intent of this Covenant.
>
> (Patrick 2015)

According to Zurenuoc (2014:37, 2015), after signing this document on 5 September, Somare makes a prayer in which he declares he will renounce all gods and idols – and therefore past covenants – and commit himself in the following words:

> on behalf of the people and the nation of Papua New Guinea, I make this New Covenant with you and Almighty God, we acknowledge you as One and the ONLY God, we acknowledge you as the holy God in whom Papua New Guinea stands.
>
> (Zurenuoc 2015:2)

As mentioned, Somare's reasons for signing the 'New Covenant' were different from those presented by the Unity Team. From the Unity Team's point of view, Somare's attempts to commit with God were similar to the commitments made by different biblical leaders, and the extent to which he succeeded or failed was like a repetition of distant biblical times in PNG's present.

---

13 I focus here on the covenant between men and God, but the form can also be extended to other partnerships such as marriages and communities (see Handman 2014:S207–11).

This was made clear to me when I commented to a member of the Unity Team, Dan Costa, that I found the message that they were sending in the 'Tribute' incoherent in relation to the RRMP. If Somare had committed PNG to God, then why was there any need for the RRMP, and why had the donated Bible been accepted in Parliament as a national treasure in order to affirm PNG as Christian nation? Dan's answer was that Moses had freed Israel from an authoritarian rule and led them through the wilderness, unifying them under God's law, 'but,' he continued, 'the Israelites were Gentiles and had not accepted God fully, they had their own cultural beliefs ... This is the relevance of the Moses generation.'

Dan makes sense out of Papua New Guinean politics, past and present, through a typological reading of the Bible (Harding 2000; Tomlinson 2010:754;). Exodus (3:8) narrates the story of Moses and his leadership, about how he freed the different tribes of Israelites from slavery, led them through decades in the desert and ultimately gave God's ten commandments to them. The parallel between the Exodus narrative and the history of PNG's independence are perhaps obvious and so is the analogy between Moses and Somare. Somare, as Moses, is seen as a leader in the struggle for liberation and as a lawgiver (Zurenuoc 2014:36).

The reference to the 'Moses generation', however, was not only about applying typology to leadership (Murphy 2011). The Unity Team also used it to characterize an epoch and therefore everyone living it. Importantly, as Dan highlighted, the 'Moses generation' shares similar constraints as those at the time of the biblical Moses (and perhaps, according to the Bible, ones that humankind of any epoch shares), in particular in their tendency to relapse into 'past' or 'traditional' worship and ways of life, thus straying away from God (Exodus 32:4). Dan was indicating that ritually accepting the donated Bible, as they did in September 2015 after Somare's New Covenant, was a recommitment to God.

Indeed, when asked the same thing, another member of the Unity Team answered that Somare's New Covenant was more like 'courting' with God instead of what the Unity Team was proposing with the declaration of the Bible as a national treasure, namely, a 'formalized marriage'. While Somare, Papua New Guinea and Papua New Guineans belonging to the 'Moses generation' had a commitment to God, the Unity Team believed it was not as wholesome as it could be. To supersede the previous generation and, therefore, continue its work, a new generation was necessary:

> The year marks the end of a forty years journey since PNG attained
> independence from Australian rule in September 1975. Generationally, a
> 40-year period speaks of the END of one generation and the BEGINNING

of a new one. It denotes passing on of leadership baton by the older generation to the new.

(Zurenuoc 2015)

This 'new' generation is the 'Joshua generation'. According to the scriptures, Moses had led the Israelites for forty years in the desert towards the Promised Land, never achieving it. Joshua, Moses' successor, is the prophet that led the crossing over the River Jordan to the Promised Land. If then, the Moses generation had led Papua New Guineans from slavery to freedom (independence), putting in motion a nation-making process, the Unity Team saw themselves and their supporters, the 'Joshua generation', as having the task of completing it.

The association between Joshua's story and that of Zurenuoc and the Unity Team was widespread. For instance, during a meeting of the Parliamentary Christian Fellowship taking place in Parliament in 2015, a pastor explained:

> The call of God is upon this nation.... He waited for the time, this time, and it is now, the time when we cross over.... God said to Joshua, Joshua was the man at that time with a mandate by God to cross over, and He told him, I am going to take you to new places you have never been. Now, when you are in new places you need someone more experienced than you to take you.... When the Bible came in, it was God speaking.... He [the Speaker], they never told him that the Bible was very significant, 400 years, he did not know this family [Dr Hood's family], but it was God. When he [Speaker], was doing the Totem [dismantling it], God brought this man [Gene Hood] and he brought the Bible. So, when we are moving to a new area, and you are in the new land, you need the guide of a very experienced person. That is why Joshua says: meditate on the Word of God, day and night.

The pastor's speech blends Joshua's story with that of Zurenuoc, and that of the Israelites with that of Papua New Guineans. In doing so, pasts and futures coalesce to supply an understanding of the present. The pastor understood, through the Bible, that the Word of God guided Joshua as he went to 'new places', and guided him successfully. If this was so, then it could do the same for Zurenuoc. The scripture of the Bible was used both as a moral guide and as a framework for interpreting contemporary events in PNG. The event of God communicating with Joshua and supporting him as a leader re-emerges in the event of the arrival of the KJV Bible. It is the same story and the same characters, but in different times and with different players.

As Munn remarks, 'people operate in a present that is always infused, and which they are further infusing, with pasts and futures' (1992:115). In the case of the Unity Team, bringing Joshua to the present means both articulating and connecting themselves to the past, the 'Moses generation' epoch, and pre-empting the future of Zurenuoc and Papua New Guineans. During Repentance Day in August 2015, one of the church representatives making a public speech in the Parliament brought up Joshua once more:

> An important principle was when Joshua was leading the nation of Israel to conquer. And the first city they faced was Jericho.... It was a fortified city, with mighty men, military power, knowledge, capacity, weaponry to fight the nation of Israel. When a key man dies halfway into achieving a dream, it is the worst nightmare for the next men coming up.... Joshua [encountered] this kind of situation. All these people with Joshua, they had no training, no schooling, no work ethics, don't know how to fight, how to do anything. These were children born in the wilderness.... Follow cloud and fire, it was all they knew. Moses is gone, now there is Joshua, so there is also criticism. But God encouraged Joshua and said: Joshua, Moses is dead. If you were Joshua, you would ask: how? I don't have capacity, the think tanks, the military power, that kind of people around me.... PNG! What is totally impossible is possible with God.... People tell us that we cannot grow rice. They [Australians] told us. And they continue to tell us that you are not good at this, not good at that... You all have degrees here. Is your degree yellow and theirs blue? It is the same kind of degree, the same knowledge, we got to believe in ourselves!

Joshua won the battle of Jericho against all odds. The parallels being drawn with Zurenuoc, the Unity Team and Papua New Guinea are clear. The message is that PNG is a poor country, perhaps unprepared to oppose more powerful developed countries, but God is on their side, and those who follow the divine word should persist despite difficulties and, above all, despite criticism. This sermon echoes the Unity Team's discourse of 'taking back PNG' by taking over the seven mountains of influence, through God, and by the pastor's comparison of Zurenuoc to Joshua, who has the task of going to places – or of taking a people to places – that seemed impossible to reach. As was the case with Joshua and Moses, God had given the tool, the 'blueprint', to achieve what seemed impossible: his Word.

That the effects and power of God's word can only be known through biblical stories, which are precisely about God's interventions, strengthens the argument that the Unity Team experiences God's presence through models provided by the Bible. Living biblical stories 'over and over' (Haynes 2020:60), however, does not mean pure repetition. These biblical stories are themselves about transformation: the passage of one generation to the other, the gradual accomplishment of God's promises, or a 'sacred history [that] unfolds in a series of stages or dispensations, each with its own (increasingly greater) degree of revelation' (Bercovitch 2012:13). Hence, the irruption and enaction of these stories, characters and types change because the context of their application changes, as does the results of the actions modelled upon them (Tomlinson 2018).

The horizon of the present

Temporality holds a special place in discussions about Pentecostal Christianity. The Pentecostal stress on conversion and practices of 'making a complete break with the past' raises interesting questions about continuity, ruptures and the way Pentecostal Christians experience them (Bialecki, Haynes and Robbins 2008; Robbins 2007). The trope of rupture points to a radical discontinuity. It can be enacted in relation to a traditional, non-Christian past or be expected to happen in the future, for instance, in the apocalyptic expectation of the second coming of Christ.

Haynes (2020) offers a detailed account of the ways in which anthropologists talk about Pentecostal temporality and suggests a model that she called the 'expansive present'. Noticing how her interlocutors in Zambia were profoundly interested in acting in the present and how their reading of the Bible framed this interest, she described how the biblical past is constantly brought to the present in a 'shared timespace' (2020:60–1). This was achieved through a typological, but non-fundamentalist and non-dispensionalist reading of the Bible. The Zambian Pentecostals with whom Haynes worked would bring stories and characters of the Bible into their lives, identify with them and acting in ways influenced by them. In this sense, the biblical narrative could happen repeatedly and in many different contexts with no linearity.

Haynes' model of the expansive present has deeply inspired the way I interpret notions of temporality underlying the Unity Team's narratives of the arrival of the KJV Bible in PNG, and their assessment of where they stand in Papua New Guinean politics. The first part of this chapter described how the Unity Team understood the arrival of the donated Bible to PNG as part of a broader journey that the Word of God has made in time. The biblical story that is repeated in this case is the story of an effect: that God gives the Israelites land and enables them to be a prosperous nation provided they remain committed to him. In the Unity Team's narratives, this nation-making effect leaps out of the biblical narrative and shapes their understanding of world history: that this same effect has been repeated in the ascensions of England and the Unites States of America. As the Bible often describes, God's favour is denied for lack of loyalty, commitment and trust. These crises of faith are moral, as are the crises and decay that the Unity Team see as the reasons for the Word of God leaving Israel, England and then the United States. The Unity Team's use of the biblical story does create a linear world history but, as Gell (1992:35) argues, recurrent events 'assume a linear time-axis, because it is only with respect to such a linear time-axis that any event could ever be said to have "repeated" itself'. The linearity of the Unity Team's story is fabricated as the background for their attention to the recurrence of God's manifestation in the history of the 'rise and fall' of nations, including the recurrence of crises pointing to the disappearance of his favours. These recurrences, however, also pull the past into the present leavening the 'now' with meaning and inevitably reorganizing what came before. This is clear from the insight of a Unity Team´s member that the 'third' in 'third world' perhaps means not a stagnant position down the ladder of development, but an apex only to be achieved after other pieces have been laid. The analogies are spatial, and are only made possible by a change to the meaning of a temporal sequence. Here, messianic time reinterprets linear time and what was supposed to be the 'third' – or the last – becomes the first, looking towards the future.

The second part of the chapter moves the scale down from that of world history to focus on the dynamics of repetition of linear sequences as expressed in the Unity Team's framing of national politics. The Unity Team's iconoclasm in 2013 and confrontation with PNG's cultural traditions can indeed be understood as a break with the past. Their goal of solving the government's moral crisis is confronted by Somare, who is from the Sepik region and who was directly involved with the design of the Parliament. Somare, in turn, joined with the National Museum, an institution that protects and conserves culture. From a Pentecostal point of view, the spiritual battle against the forces of traditional culture could not be more palpable. What I have shown, however, is that the rupture and discontinuity look different once the Unity Team infuses PNG's political history and present with the biblical past. Their texts link prominent leaders described in the Old Testament to PNG's leaders. Seeing Papua New Guinean characters as biblical characters is based on a paradigmatic (Valeri 2014) reading of the Bible. The effects of biblical leaders in the formation of Israel, for example, are used as a framework to understand the effects that politicians have had and continue to have in Papua New Guinea as a nation. Again, as was the case in the first part of the chapter, there is a repetition of effects.

In some ways, the linear succession of leadership from the 'Moses generation' to the 'Joshua generation' entails a qualitative change that is absent from the discourses about the journey of the KJV Bible. This is how the Unity Team established continuity against the foregrounded rupture involved in their iconoclasm. Somare, as the 'Moses generation', becomes a past promise of total commitment to God that only encounters its fulfilment in the 'Joshua generation', of which the Unity Team is a part. But it is important to notice that the two qualitative progressions of epochs (Moses – Joshua = Somare – Zurenuoc) can only be framed as equating to each other if the linear development from the biblical past is fused together with the historical horizons of the Unity Team. This enables the Unity Team to compare their history to what happened in the past while differentiating it from what they encounter in the present.

Finally, this organization of time into generations or epochs, in which God is present each time in different ways, is typical of dispensionalist or fundamentalist Christian readings of the Bible (Bialecki 2017:50; Harding 2000). However, Haynes (2020:59–61) observes that while a fundamentalist reading of the Bible may be typological, it differs from the one she describes in Zambia. A fundamentalist reading looks at the Bible as a story that happens in a linear form, tending towards the end of times. Fundamentalists interpret reality as a search for signs that this end is near. Despite the linearity and the 'punctuation' (Guyer 2007), the members of the Unity Team I met were not interested in the end of times. Some of them, when pressed, commented that they did not know when Jesus would come back and that they were acting with the present in mind. As a matter of fact, the overall feeling I sensed in 2015 among the Pentecostal Christians was of seizing the moment, appropriately encapsulated in one of the Unity Team's theories that PNG's 'time is now' (see also Coleman 2011:443). In this sense, the Unity Team is closer to the model of an expansive present that 'foreshorten[s] the horizon of Christian expectation considerably, focusing the possibility of divine intervention on the here and now rather than the end of time' (Haynes 2020:62). This seizing of the moment and desire to claim what is one's own also transpires in the Unity Team's (and their supporters') self-identification with the Joshua generation. I transcribed in the second part of this chapter a sermon given by a pastor during Repentance Day in August 2015; here is another quotation from it that reiterates this idea:

> Jericho was the gateway to the land of Canaan, and it was extremely secured. But what God says? The Lord tells Joshua: 'See. The first principle is of seeing, having a vision and focus. What are we seeing here? See, I have given Jericho into your hands, something impossible, something beyond thinking, something outside our capacity, that you are not prepared for.... Something that the children of Israel are not educated enough to do, their military means cannot measure up. These people [in Jericho] are advanced in thinking and technology. I am giving Jericho into your hands.' I believe this is what God is saying to PNG. I am giving back your inheritance back

into your hands! Your people, back into your hands! Your industries, back into your hands! Your forestry, back into your hands! Your mining industry, back into your hands! Your agriculture, back into your hands!

Theodor Zurenuoc left Parliament in 2016 and was not re-elected. The Unity Team did not see a unity pillar replace the totem pole, and many of my interlocutors are no longer working in Parliament. They did tell me, however, that their goals and visions preceded them and would succeed them. Interestingly, when Prime Minister Marape started his mandate in 2019, he pledged to make PNG 'the richest Christian black nation' and incorporated the motto 'take back PNG' as his goal, as a means for social reform (Bal Kama, 8 August 2019).[14]

In 2021, Marape launched a constitutional inquiry on whether to declare Papua New Guinea a Christian Nation, explaining that Christianity is what binds a country of a thousand tribes as a nation.[15] Finally, during the Repentance Day of 2021, the Prime Minister reaffirmed his commitment with the Christian community to place a 200-metre tall unity pillar facing Parliament 'under a Christian Banner of "One People, One Nation, One Country".[16]

Acknowledgements

Santos da Costa's contribution has benefited from discussions with Molly Rosenbaum, Steffen Dalsgaard and the editors of this volume. Thanks also to L.L. for the careful reading and insights.

References

Bercovitch, S. 2012 [1978]. *The American Jeremiad*. Wisconsin: University of Wisconsin Press.

Bialecki, J. 2017. 'Eschatology, ethics, and ēthnos: ressentiment and Christian nationalism in the anthropology of Christianity', *Religion and Society* 8(1):42–61.

---

14 "'Take Back PNG": Prime Minister Marape and his audacious vision for PNG', DevpolicyBlog: devpolicy.org/take-back-png-prime-minister-marape-and-his-audacious-vision-for-png-20190808 (accessed 7 November 2021).

15 www.pmnec.gov.pg/index.php/secretariats/pm-media-statements/283-prime-minister-marape-launches-inquiry-on-declaration-of-png-as-a-christian-country (accessed 30 August 2021).

16 www.looppng.com/png-news/k5mil-national-unity-pillar-103811 (accessed 30 August 2021).

Bialecki, J., Haynes, N. and Robbins, J. 2008. 'The anthropology of Christianity', *Religion Compass* 2(6):1139–58.

Bielo, J.S. 2008. 'On the failure of "meaning": Bible reading in the anthropology of Christianity', *Culture and Religion* 9(1):1–21.

Bond, N. and Timmer, J. 2017. 'Wondrous geographies and historicity for state-building on Malaita, Solomon Islands', *Journal of Religious and Political Practice* 3(3):136–51.

Briggs, M. 1989. *Parliament House Papua New Guinea*. Port Moresby: Independent Books.

Cochrane, L. 2015 'Thousands welcome arrival of 400-year-old King James Bible in Papua New Guinea', *ABC News* (28 April): www.abc.net.au/news/2015-04-28/thousands-greet-bibles-arrival-in-papua-new-guinea/6428856 (Accessed May 15 2021).

Coleman, S. 2004. 'The charismatic gift', *Journal of the Royal Anthropological Institute* 10(2):421–42.

——— 2006. 'Materializing the self: words and gifts in the construction of charismatic Protestant identity'. In F. Cannell (ed.), *The Anthropology of Christianity*, pp.163–84. Durham: Duke University Press.

——— 2011. '"Right now!": historiopraxy and the embodiment of charismatic temporalities', *Ethnos* 76(4):426–47.

Craig, B. 2010 (ed.) 'Introduction'. In B. Craig (ed.), *Living Spirits with Fixed Abodes*, pp.1–4. Honolulu: University of Hawai'i Press.

Cunningham, L.1988. *Making Jesus Lord: The Dynamic Power of Laying Down Your Rights*. Seattle: YWAM Publishing.

Engelke, M. 2011. 'Past Pentecostalism: notes on rupture, realignment, and everyday life in Pentecostal and African independent Churches', *Africa* 80(2):177–99.

Eves, R., Nicole, H., May, R.J., Cox, J., Gibbs. P., Merlan, F. and Rumsay, A. 2014. 'Purging parliament: a new Christian politics in Papua New Guinea?', *State, Society and Governance in Melanesia Discussion Paper* 1. Canberra: The Australian National University.

Gell, A. 1992. *The Anthropology of Time: Cultural Constructions of Temporal Maps and Images*. Oxford: Oxford University Press.

Guyer, J.I. 2007. 'Prophecy and the near future: thoughts on macroeconomic, evangelical, and punctuated time', *American Ethnologist* 34(3):409–21.

Hagin, K.E. 1993. *The Triumphant Church: Dominion Over All the Powers of Darkness*. Tulsa: Faith Library Publications.

Halvorson, B. and Hovland, I. 2021. 'Reconnecting language and materiality in christian reading: a comparative analysis of two groups of Protestant women', *Comparative Studies in Society and History* 63(2):499–529.

Handman, C. 2014. 'Becoming the body of Christ: sacrificing the speaking subject in the making of the colonial Lutheran church in New Guinea', *Current Anthropology* 55(S10):S205–15.

Harding, S.F. 2000. *The Book of Jerry Falwell: Fundamentalist Language and Politics.* Princeton, NJ: Princeton University Press.

Haynes, N. 2015. '"Zambia shall be saved!": prosperity gospel politics in a self-proclaimed Christian nation', *Nova Religio: The Journal of Alternative and Emergent Religions* 19(1):5–24.

——— 2020. 'The expansive present: a new model of Christian time', *Current Anthropology* 61(1):57–76.

——— 2021. 'Taking dominion in a Christian nation: North American political theology in an African context'. *Pneuma* 43(2):214–32.

Hirsch, E., and Stewart, C. 2005. 'Introduction: ethnographies of historicity', *History and Anthropology* 16(3):261–74.

Kamu, M. 2015. 'The strange and mysterious case of the donated King James I Bible to Papua New Guinea', *PNG Blogs*: www.pngblogs.com/2015/04/the-strange-and-mysterious-case-of.html (accessed 25 October 2021).

Marshall, R. 2009. *Political Spiritualities: The Pentecostal Revolution in Nigeria.* Chicago: University of Chicago Press.

McVicar, M. 2013. 'Let them have dominion: dominion theology and the construction of religious extremism in the US media', *The Journal of Religion and Popular Culture* 25:120–45.

Mead, S.M. (ed.) 1979. *Exploring the Visual Art of Oceania.* Honolulu: University Press of Hawai'i.

Meyer, B. 1998. '"Make a complete break with the past": memory and post-colonial modernity in Ghanaian Pentecostalist discourse', *Journal of Religion in Africa* 28(3):316.

——— 2010. 'Pentecostalism and globalization'. In A. Anderson, M. Bergunder, A. Droogers and C. van der Laan (eds), *Studying Global Pentecostalism: Theories and Methods*, pp. 113–30. Berkeley: University of California Press.

Munn, N. 1992. 'The cultural anthropology of time: a critical essay', *Annual Review of Anthropology* 21:93–123.

Murphy, J.M. 2011. 'Barack Obama, the Exodus tradition, and the Joshua generation', *Quarterly Journal of Speech* 97(4):387–410.

Ove Jr, S. 'Speaker referred to ombudsman', *EMTV Online*: emtv.com.pg/speaker-referred-to-ombudsman (accessed 14 September 2021).

Patrick, J. 2015. 'Tear down the idols', *James Patrick's Blog*: alabastertheology.files. wordpress.com/2015/09/somare-covenant-for-png-26-aug-2007.jpg (accessed 21 December 2021).

Pickles, A.J. and Santos da Costa, P. 2021. 'It is Christ or corruption in Papua New Guinea: bring in the witness!', *Oceania* 91(3):349–66.

Rio, K., MacCarthy, M. and Blanes, R. 2017. 'Introduction to Pentecostal witchcraft and spiritual politics in Africa and Melanesia'. In K. Rio, M. MacCarthy and R. Blanes (eds), *Pentecostalism and Witchcraft*, pp. 1–36. London: Palgrave Macmillan.

Robbins, J. 2003. 'On the paradoxes of global pentecostalism and the perils of continuity thinking', *Religion* 33(3):221–31.

——— 2007. 'Continuity thinking and the problem of Christian culture: belief, time, and the anthropology of Christianity', *Current Anthropology* 48(1):5–38.

Rosi, P.C. 1991. 'Papua New Guinea's new parliament house: a contested national symbol', *The Contemporary Pacific* 3(2):289–323.

Santos Da Costa, P. 2018. 'Re-Designing the Nation': Politics and Christianity in Papua New Guinea's National Parliament. Ph.D. thesis, University of St. Andrews, Scotland.

——— 2021. 'Postcolonial nationalism and neo-Pentecostalism: a case from Papua New Guinea', *Nations and Nationalism* 27(3):895–909.

Schram, R. 2014. 'A new government breaks with the past in the Papua New Guinea Parliament's "haus tambaran"', *Material World: A Global Hub for Thinking About Things*: www.materialworldblog.com/2014/02/a-new-government-breaks-with-the-past-in-the-papua-new-guinea-parliaments-haus-tambaran (accessed 10 November 2021).

Timmer, J. 2015. 'Heirs to biblical prophecy: the all peoples prayer assembly in Solomon Islands', *Nova Religio: The Journal of Alternative and Emergent Religions* 18(4):16–34.

Tomlinson, M. 2010. 'Compelling replication: Genesis 1:26, John 3:16, and biblical politics in Fiji', *Journal of the Royal Anthropological Institute* (NS) 16(4):743–60.

——— 2018. 'Repetition in the work of a Samoan Christian theologian: or, what does it mean to speak of the perfect pig of God?', *History and Anthropology* 30(2):149–169.

Valeri, V. 2014. *Rituals and Annals: Between Anthropology and History*. Manchester: HAU Society for Ethnographic Theory.

Walton, G. 2018. *Anti-corruption and its Discontents: Local, National and International Perspectives on Corruption in Papua New Guinea*. New York: Routledge.

Zurenuoc, T. 2014. 'A Tribute to the founding fathers Sir Michael Somare and Sir Julius Chan', *Business Melanesia*: www.parliament.gov.pg/images/misc/May-2014-Speaker-Section-compressed.pdf (accessed 12 December 2021).

——— 2015. '2015 – the year of crossing over to the other side', *National Parliament of Papua New Guinea*: www.parliament.gov.pg/index.php/news/view/2015-the-year-of-crossing-over-to-the-other-side (accessed 20 November 2021).

6

Al Gore's horizons, hockey sticks, holograms and hope

Plotting nature and time in a crisis

TONY CROOK[1]

✳

That time and crisis implicate each other, this volume's starting point, reflects their relation in a naturalist cosmology and corresponding experiences of processual time. Here it is given ethnographic weight. Much of the subtlety and imagination with which the US thinker-politician, Al Gore, approaches the crisis in 'nature' entailed twinning it with a crisis in 'time': the world is running out of both. These endings are all too imminent. Gore figures temporal horizons as too short for long-term future planning, too short-sighted to grasp historical legacies, but offering salvational hope of freedom from crisis itself. Together with figurations of nature and time through images of hockey sticks and holograms, the exposition here serves as reminder of taken-for-granted assumptions, and the risk of projecting or transposing these to Amazonian and Melanesian examples. When read in light of the preceding four chapters, it provides a counterpoint exemplification of orthodox past and future speculations – and a depiction of the limiting horizon of epistemic connections that have produced the climate crisis and equally failed to produce solutions.

1 This work, produced under the auspices of the Ethnographic Horizons project at the Centre for Pacific Studies, University of St Andrews, was supported by the International Balzan Foundation.

❀

One way of defining the climate crisis is the tragedy of the horizon.

(Al Gore 2015)

Despite appearances, ideas – including those of time and crisis – never travel alone: causes, consequences and connections become partially disguised. An exposition of the forms of time produced by ideas of nature – the motivating implications in shaping meaning and action – will provide a counterpoint to the volume's contributions from Amazonia and Melanesia. It is also a decolonizing mirror to such taken-for-granted Euro-American assumptions about conceptualizations of time and nature, and a reminder of the risks of transposing these when reading Melanesian and Amazonian accounts. Taken alone, this chapter is an ethnographic exposition of the cultural thinking that assumes that ecological and climate crises have, inevitably, pitted assumptions about nature and time against each other. This 'inescapability' has real-life consequences for how causes and consequences are perceived, and how solutions are formulated in response. Rather than singling out an example for critique, Al Gore's analytical synthesis and advocacy is taken here as articulating and exemplifying widely held cultural ideas and responses. Euro-American notions of time and nature and crisis endorse a normative configuration that guides responses to climate crises, and articulates distinct limits to such thinking and to the motivation of actions. Any critique goes beyond Gore himself.

Within this mainstreamed narrative of epistemic causalities and connections, nature's diminishment has disrupted and enhanced the importance of time – both literally and figuratively. In this lived and conceptual collapse, the present lives in the future's shadow, as if all time were converging in the present, creating heightened perceptions of crisis. Nature and time provide the coordinates for this epoch of urgency: when plotted against each other, the shape of modernity's conflictual relation to the earth emerges. What has happened to nature can be seen vividly when plotted against time: nature no longer appears in balance, time no longer appears linear. Now, as if in retrospect, we can begin to see how each interlinked concept operated through a particular linear and irreversible directionality; how each participated in ideas of genealogical flow and relational sequencing; and how each provided a grounding context and limiting horizon for social action. For those raising and responding to the alarm, there is both less time and less nature, and an increasing sense that each is fast running out. As a consequence, what remains of time and what we have left of nature is all the more vital. The rates of change have altered: accelerating habitat degradation, species extinction and biodiversity losses elicit demands for immediate rather than cautionary responses; and the seemingly exponential rise in atmospheric carbon dioxide levels outruns the pace of political progress. For participants in these ideas, the taken-for-granted forms of time produced by ideas of nature likely appear all too familiar, and this should serve as a cultural and analytical reminder that ethnographic writing entails 'staying with the expositional trouble' (Strathern 2020:173).

Al Gore

In an age of climate urgency, Gore has come to be known as 'the popular prophet of global warming'[2] and continues to play a major role in successfully raising the profile of the climate crisis – and how we think and respond to it – in popular imagination and in international agendas. Of course, as a former US Vice-President and continuing prominent public figure, Gore's Euro-American epistemology has a distinctive and vibrant United States cast. For example, and to place and introduce how 'horizon' figures in the scheme, *Earth in the Balance: Ecology and the Human Spirit* (Gore 1992), penned and published ahead of the 1992 US election that took President Clinton and Vice-President Gore into office, makes a series of characteristic analogic linkages. For example, Gore recalls Vaclav Havel's 1990 address to Congress, writing that 'we in the United States have not yet reached our goal and still travel toward "the eternally receding horizon of freedom"' (1992:172); and elsewhere bemoans an 'unwillingness to make decisions with an eye to their long-term effects, coupled with our insistence on basing strategy on short-term time horizons' (ibid.:351). In Gore's holistic analysis striving, destiny and freedom characterize the place of horizon in space and in time, and configure motivations, movements and meanings.

Gore's subsequent depiction of the climate crisis as a 'tragedy of the horizon' in 2015 followed and referenced a speech entitled 'Breaking the tragedy of the horizon – climate change and financial stability' given the previous month by Mark Carney, then Governor of the Bank of England:

> We don't need an army of actuaries to tell us that the catastrophic impacts of climate change will be felt beyond the traditional horizons of most actors – imposing a cost on future generations that the current generation has no direct incentive to fix.
>
> (Carney 2015)

---

2   'Al Gore's new campaign', 60 Minutes (27 March 2008): www.cbsnews.com/news/al-gores-new-campaign (accessed 23 January 2024).

Here, Carney pointed to the consequences of monetary policy operating on horizons of two to three years, perhaps a decade at most, and thus externalizing costs and consequences, so to speak, onto future generations. Gore, having previously written about how 'the future whispers while the present shouts' (1992:170), and repeatedly about the limitations of short-duration political cycles and short-sighted business cycles in *The Future* (2013:xxviii, xxix), again segued to spatial horizons:

> One way of defining the climate crisis is the tragedy of the horizon. Meaning that we all share the atmosphere, but we also all see the horizon as a distant place, perhaps far enough away that we need not engage our attention with it directly and immediately. But the horizon is not that far away and the sky above us is not as vast as it seems – it's a thin shell surrounding the planet. We need to pay attention to protecting it and, in the process, protecting the future of human kind.
>
> (Gore 2015)

Characteristically, Gore renders Carney's temporal horizons through vivid imagery: humankind's interdependent relations through a shared atmosphere that appears as a thin shell when viewed from space – 'rising above the moon's horizon' (1992:205). Horizons become a problem of seeing and the revelation of unacknowledged intimacies, proximities, relations and responsibilities – and become a problem of inertia, abeyance and inaction in movements toward the rewards of freedom from crisis.

Any ethnographic engagement should take conceptual work and cultural theorizing seriously: in this instance, former US Vice-President Gore's writings, documentary and wider climate advocacy provide a productive vantage point and reveal an innovative synthesis of ecology, theology and politics. Here, in particular, my analytical ethnography focuses on *Earth in the Balance: Ecology and the Human Spirit* (1992, hereafter *EB*); *An Inconvenient Truth: The Planetary Emergency of Global Warming and What We Can Do About It* (2006); and *The Future: Six Drivers of Global Change* (2013). Gore depicts multiple crises as overlapping – their causes and consequences necessarily interlinked – and uses a part-whole metaphor of 'holography' to portray both ecological interdependence and theological indwelling (*EB*:11, 265). I take the corpus of Gore's public-oriented productions, books, documentary film and global concerts as an exposition that vividly explicates and exemplifies certain themes in contemporary responses to the crisis of anthropogenic climate change (Crook 2018). The work of establishing Gore's credentials as a cultural theorist of 'climate cultures' (Hulme 2017) involves the exploration of a distinctive climate ontology, in Schnegg's terms 'the nature of what exists' (2021:261). Gore's work offers an intriguing glimpse of 'native cultural structures of the long term', as Sahlins (1996:395) puts it.

Whilst attending a natural sciences class by Roger Revelle at Harvard University in 1968, Gore was discomforted by the climatologist 'drawing on the blackboard a dramatic upward shift of carbon dioxide' (Gore 2006:40; Kennedy White and Duram 2012:485) – an early depiction of research underpinning the 'Keeling curve' (Wilson and Matthews 1971:234). Gore co-organized early congressional hearings on global warming in 1981 and 1982 (Weart 2008, 2022). He served as Vice-President throughout the Clinton administration, from 1993–2001, and stood unsuccessfully in the 2000 presidential election. Gore's slide show on the climate crisis provided the basis for the Academy Award winning documentary *An Inconvenient Truth: A Global Warning* (Guggenheim 2006), which was highly influential in raising international public awareness about global warming, and highlighted Gore's long-standing environmental advocacy, for which he jointly won the Nobel Peace Prize in 2007. Gore founded the Alliance for Climate Protection in 2006, and co-organized Live Earth 2007: 'the biggest global media event of all time – and by far the largest climate awareness event in history' (Heffernan 2007). Any figure capable of simultaneously connecting with more than two billion people – transcending languages, dissolving cultural divisions and generating a tangible feeling of oneness – is obviously a figure that anthropology needs to take seriously.

Although one was first published in 1992, and the other first screened in 2006, Gore's book *Earth in the Balance* and film *An Inconvenient Truth* emerged from the same thoughtful, wide-ranging and evolving body of work: 'While writing this book, I started giving the slide show that would later become the basis for the documentary movie.' (2007:ix). *Earth in the Balance* has since been reprinted and updated (in 2000 and 2007), the slide show continuously developed and the charismatic film presents the culmination of Gore's 'focus on the mission of solving the climate crisis' (2007:x). As his biographer puts it:

> *Earth in the Balance* is the essential Gore: thoughtful, earnest, ambitious, crammed with facts, moralizing, hyperbolic, and breathtakingly grandiose. The pages are charged with the evangelistic fervour of a man who believes he can save the world.
>
> (Turque 2000:230)

Whilst constantly refreshed through scientific updates and presentational changes, this body of work builds upon the philosophical foundations and synthesis of its initial creation. Even the form and substance of Gore's hopeful message, as manifested in Live Earth 2007, which drew a world-wide audience of more than two billion people, is anticipated in his earlier work. As the books and movie attest, the specific origins in 1989 are crucial to Gore's story: the writing of *Earth in the Balance* was begun in a hospital, while caring for his son in the weeks following a serious accident (*EB*:371). *Earth in the Balance* provides the background, the mission's intellectual and ontological groundings. Gore's synthesis of politics, ecology and theology can best be read in the original – and what extraordinary, strangely important and oddly neglected words they are.[3]

Gore's conceptual synthesis and personal beliefs illustrate how 'the cosmological, religious, political, economic dimensions cannot be disaggregated' (Tambiah 2013[1973]:508). Rather than taking analytical issue with the way a world has set itself up, attention is drawn here to the problem of acknowledging the disguised effects of specific cultural origins. That nature and creation are inseparable in Gore's thinking only serves to emphasize and illustrate the fundamental importance of time and the character of crises, and how – as if inescapably – they never travel alone in this mode of thought. Gore's imagistic syntheses depicting ecological, theological, political and climate crises also provide vantage points on theorizations of time emerging from a contemporaneous ethnographic horizon. Gore's depictions and scholarly conceptualizations (in the epoch of Gell 1992 and Munn 1992) demonstrate how, in this thinking, time operates as a dimension of nature: whether as externalized context or as internalized immanence Alongside Latour's *We Have Never Been Modern* (1993), and Strathern's *After Nature* (1992), which both analyse then contemporary changes in the concept of nature, Gore's demonstrations are also instructive. Certainly, the (un)hinging of time and nature is a premise in his work. The analysis of Gore's own multidimensional ethnographic horizons provides vignettes of time served in four ways: the proximity of indwelling horizons; in the shape of a hockey stick; in the form of a hologram; and in the character of hope. Each of these illustrate how forms of time are internalized in forms of social action, each providing mutual motivation and empowered by moving from without to within. The examples provide a vantage point on Gore's own temporal framework, which characterizes and exemplifies particular figurations of crises.

---

3   As one of the few anthropologists to have written on Gore, Harding places Gore's documentary film *An Inconvenient Truth* (2006) in the genre of an 'American jeremiad', which 'works as an alternative precisely because of its aggressively religious and specifically Christian Protestant undertows' (2007:132).

The times they are a-changin'

> Nature, we believe, takes for ever. [But] our reassuring sense of a timeless
> future, which is drawn from that apparently bottomless well of the past,
> is a delusion. In much the same comforting way that we think of time as
> imponderably long, we consider the earth to be inconceivably large. Our
> comforting sense, then, of the permanence of our natural world, and our
> confidence that it will change gradually and imperceptibly, if at all, is the
> result of a subtly warped perspective.
>
> (McKibben 1990:3, 4, 5, 7)

At the time of McKibben's and Gore's earlier writings, climate debates
still turned on whether or not past records, present measurements and future
predictions provided scientifically dependable evidence of natural variability
or of unnatural anthropogenic carbon emissions. In a state of balance, the
plotted line either side of any given point would be linear – discounting
seasonal, cyclical and periodic variability – and things would be as they ever
were. It is this extended pre-industrial period of time that resembles the shaft
of a 'hockey stick' (Gore 2006:65). But in this epoch of crisis, any balanced
equilibrium is replaced and betrayed by a line that is no longer equalized
along its length. The timeline from nine-hundred years in the past to the
recent present is linear, but the timeline since and into the near future shows
a dramatic non-linear upswing. It is this period of time that resembles the
club-face or blade of a hockey stick. The future now rises out of balance with
the past and the present. Rather than lying on, below or beyond the horizon
– the future now rises above it, impinging upon the present, seemingly move
visible than ever before. What has happened to nature can be seen vividly
when plotted against time: nature no longer appears in balance, time no longer
appears linear in quite the same way. Nature and time now share the same fate.

Time appears to have lost its direction and lost its footing: what once
afforded a reassuring guide to how things unfold in sequence, seems to have
folded back upon itself and revealed uncertainty and instability in its place.
If modernity ever perceived time to occupy a separate domain, dependably
set apart from and comfortably beyond the meddling reach of social life,
then that is clearly no longer the case in depictions of time as immanent. As
Munn described in 1992, 'the topic of time frequently fragments into all the
other dimensions and topics anthropologists deal with in the social world'
(1992:93). This shift is crucial, for rather than forming a staged backdrop
to social performances, Munn views time as no longer external, but rather
as a 'symbolic process continually being produced in everyday practices'
(ibid.:116). Social and temporal practices have been re-apprehended as

mutually constitutive and reciprocal. Time is brought into, and produced by, the social moment; in Munn's view, time has moved from without to within.

Of his time of writing, McKibben acknowledged that 'we live too close to the year 2000', which had long 'become a symbol of a bright and distant future' (1990:6). This was a particular and a curious moment from which to be apprehending time: 'We live in the shadow of a number, and this makes it hard for us to see the future.' (ibid.:7) . That a renewed anthropological interest in time (e.g. Gell 1992; Munn 1992) and a new anthropological interest in comparative Christianity and theology (Cannell 2006; Robbins 2006) became prominent before and after this temporal shadow is instructive. Writing even closer to the number, Stewart and Harding suggested that:

> Apocalypticism and millennialism are the dark and light sides of a historical
> sensibility transfixed by the possibility of imminent catastrophe, cosmic
> redemption, spiritual transformation, and a new world order.
>
> (1999:286)

As we shall see, Gore's *Earth in the Balance* (1992) gives us all of this, and more. But although it appeared in this same epoch, alongside Latour's (1993) and Strathern's (1992) writings on the changing place of nature, as we might expect they each account for change in these times in quite different terms.

Latour's account registers the consequences of a transformation of nature and time as follows: 'The asymmetry between nature and culture then becomes an asymmetry between past and future.' (1993:71, emphasis removed). The old order plays against the new here, for an incomprehension amongst the moderns of new kinds of actors connected in unfamiliar ways is more than matched by their ability, nonetheless, to impose familiar order:

> The notion of an irreversible arrow – progress or decadence – stems from
> an ordering of quasi-objects, whose proliferation the moderns cannot
> explain. [...] This beautiful order is disturbed once the quasi-objects are
> seen as mixing up different periods, ontologies and genres.
>
> (1993:73)

Time as the context for modern ordering might continue, but it does so alongside new actors who appear to carry their own temporal context within them, in defiance of any imposed external order. This takes the reciprocity between social and temporal forms one step further. When Latour spells out the implications, it is as though it is now in the nature of things for quasi-objects to be their own time: 'Time is always folded. So the idea of any synchronic interaction where all the ingredients will have the same age and

the same pace is meaningless.' (2005:201). Perhaps with the collapse of nature
and time as ordering contexts, both become lodged within the proliferating
new actors? With every quasi-object – a teacher's desk, dress and thoughts
(2005:200) – being of a differing age, interactions are constituted by different
times congregating on the present. Here it is as if a temporal context had
collapsed into itself, such that there is no longer anything outside of time, for
time is newly indwelling and located inside everything.

Strathern's account is rooted in unfolding changes in English folk models
of kinship, in which they have made explicit previously taken-for-granted
assumptions.

> It is not that the English cannot imagine time going back on itself – but that
> they cannot imagine relationships going back on themselves. For them the
> temporal sequencing of generations is irreversible. Indeed, the English are
> able to point to the 'biological' experiencing of temporality as vindicating a
> linear interpretation of it.
>
> (1992:62)

The linearity appearance of time derives from a particular kind of linearity
in relations conceived by virtue of the biological character of nature. Things
might well unfold in multiple directions, but persons unfold in a singular
sequence. We might, with Bamford and Leach (2009:19), who ask why the
genealogical method 'now appears as a "natural" way of interpreting the
world', ask the further question of why the direction and irreversibility of time
once appeared natural in a way that it no longer does? Genealogy, in these
models, appears natural because of an inseparable connection to biological
reproduction: 'A life has a demonstrable beginning and an end in this view,
and biological time is irrefutable evidence of linearity.' (Strathern 1992:62).
Questions of nature and questions of time are bound up with each other here.
As Cassidy puts it (2009:24), 'The genealogical model is a theory of attribution.
It fixes the direction of time by granting special status to temporal anteriority.'
Kinship and anthropological reckoning through models of 'natural' genealogy
have lost their motive force, because nature is no longer set apart and can
therefore no longer provide a model for relational reckoning – it too has moved
from without to within. As such, these moves involve shared consequences for
nature and time. In conclusion, Strathern suggested (1992:194) that nature had
'constituted both the given facts of the world and the world as the context for
facts'. In that, it was 'a prior fact, a condition for existence. Nature was thus
a condition for knowledge.' (ibid.). Time is connected to nature in a further
dimension, as having similarly lost its grounding function, just as '[Nature]
no longer provides a model or analogy for the very idea of context.' (ibid.:195).

Time no longer merely provides a context for social action, but has become a process and an object of social action itself – such that, in this thinking, forms of social action reveal the shape of time.

Hockey-stick time

For Gore, the planetary emergency of global warming, and what we can do about it, has a definite shape: a grid-like non-linear timeline curve culminating with an exponential uplift. The shape is unified as an 'overall pattern of worldwide environmental degradation' (*EB*:44), and will be familiar to readers of Gore's books and viewers of his documentary film:

> When one considers the relationship of the human species to the earth, not much change is visible in a single year in a single nation. Yet if one looks at the entire pattern of that relationship, from the emergence of our species until the present, a sharp and distinctive contrast beginning in the very recent past clearly signals the dramatic change to which we must now respond.
>
> (*EB*:43)

For Gore, the pattern is both everywhere and ubiquitous, rather than restricted to levels of atmospheric carbon dioxide: for example, in the 2007 edition of *Earth in the Balance*, graphs of this shape depict CO_2 (*EB*:xv, 5), species extinction (24), human population (32–3) and changes in atmospheric temperature (94, 95). As much as the rising levels, it is the rates and dynamics of change that concern Gore: because 'nature exhibits a recurring pattern of interdependency among the parts' (*EB*: 50), upsetting the balance causes runaway consequences:

> The phenomenon of interdependency is probably best illustrated by what scientists call positive feedback loops, which magnify the force with which change occurs. In fact, almost everywhere you look throughout the ecological system, natural mechanisms tend to accelerate the pace of change once it is set in motion.
>
> (*EB*:50)

Change is not just change, for it changes the very nature of change itself: timelines and nature's balance no longer unfold in a predictable linear manner. Timelines in these hockey-stick shaped graphs show Gore the 'entire pattern' of the relationship of the human species to earth, and give urgency to his quest to save us before 'our momentum carries us past the point beyond which an ecological collapse is inevitable' (*EB*:50).

But this hockey-stick shape of the ecological and climate crisis also operates in a second way in Gore's thinking: as the entire pattern of politics – the shape of the political process, awareness, will, change and action. For example, in 'The shadow our future throws' (*EB*, chapter 2:36–55), Gore uses two models from science (chaos theory and relativity) and one from music (*EB*:47–8), to give operational shape to this conception of political dynamics. As he puts it, 'time is relative in politics as it is in physics' (*EB*:47). Gore presents these scientific and musical models as part of his search for a new language to speak about the shadow our future throws, and takes a leaf from the way 'Newtonian physics led to a revolution in our understanding of cause and effect' that 'was lifted wholesale into politics, economics and society at large' (*EB*:47). Clearly, Gore's vision of science is political: science determines, predicts and provides a template for the reality and the relativity of societal relations, and he is trying to forecast the future shape of political economy through these models. Here too, science provides the imagistic shape of the hockey stick:

> Chaos Theory describes how many natural systems show significant changes in the way they operate even as they remain within the same overall pattern ('dynamic equilibrium'). According to this theory, certain critical boundaries define that overall pattern and cannot be exceeded without threatening the loss of its equilibrium.
>
> (*EB*:47)

As with Newtonian cause and effect, and relativity theory, there is a social and political counterpart, described here in terms of a rate of change in the emergence of ecological thinking:

> This change in thinking will also follow the pattern described in Chaos Theory, with little change evident until a threshold is passed, and then, as key assumptions are modified, a flood of dramatic changes will occur all at once.
>
> (*EB*:48)

When Gore moves onto Einstein, he knows that his readers will find themselves on rocky ground:

> Einstein's Relativity Theory. Bear with me: although complicated, Relativity Theory can easily be explained with the help of a picture showing how time and space are shaped by mass. An especially dense mass like a 'black hole' is

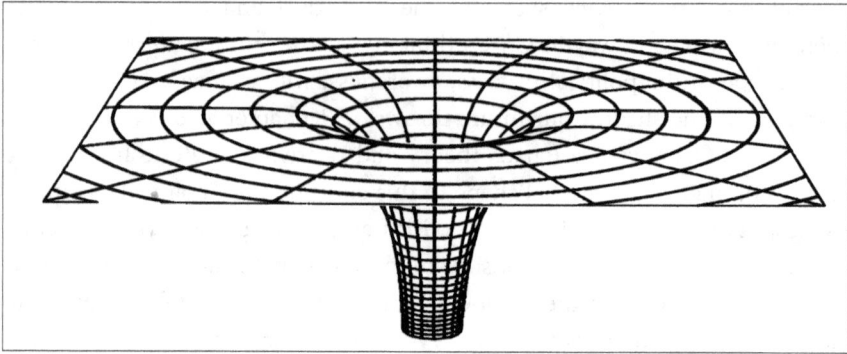

Figure 6.1 Black hole shape.

shown as a deep well, with space and time arrayed around it like a grid that
slopes down to the center.

(*EB*:48)

Gore provides and describes such a picture (*EB*:48, similar to Figure 6.1):

A black hole as portrayed by physicists, who explain that the continuum of
space and time represented by the flat grid is bent by the dense mass of the
black hole that pulls the grid down into a deep well of space and time. Large
historical events shape political consciousness in much the same way.

Singular examples of just such a large historical event that 'exerts a
powerful gravitational influence on every idea and other event close to it
in time and space' are the Second World War, the Holocaust, the fall of
Communism in 1989, the prevention of nuclear holocaust and, of course, the
global environmental crisis (*EB*:49). In spelling out his black-hole analogy,
Gore describes the dynamics of time in the future:

The potential for true catastrophe lies in the future, but the downslope that
pulls us toward it is becoming recognizably steeper with each passing year.
What lies ahead is a race against time. Sooner or later the steepness of the
slope and our momentum down its curve will take us beyond a point of no
return. But as the curve becomes steeper and catastrophe's pull becomes
stronger, our ability to recognize the pattern of its pull is greatly enhanced.

(*EB*:49)

There is, then, both danger and virtue in the steepness of the shape of
time here. Gore sees the very steepness of the hockey-stick-shaped curve
as enhancing our ability to recognize the pattern, just as it also precipitates

action. He is obviously displaying agility with the imagery here: a black hole in cross section, a musical crescendo before the harmony, and a downslope with a point of no return, all creatively stand as analogues of the shape of a hockey stick, which in other guises registers the timeline of increasing rates of concentration, population and extinction.

The political nature of Gore's vision of science has a further dimension: it as if a change in political consciousness will reveal the true significance of the shape of the science. Like his attempted epistemological reconciliation of so many other dualisms, science and politics are simply the same thing in this sense: Gore's scientific graphs measure and depict a political process, as if they were a polling result of a likely outcome, and a prediction of tipping points and thresholds indicating a change of intention. The non-linear shape of time here tracks the intra-planetary conflicts that have caused the ecological and climate crisis and brought us 'closer to the edge of history' (*EB*:50). The urgency of the curve suggests that a tipping point is close – and that the response is similarly reaching a threshold of consciousness and a critical mass of awareness and action. Seen in terms of chaos theory, Gore has figured out how the hockey-stick shape and dynamics of the response can be a match or solution to the shape of the problem. The nature of time here is relational and derives from the shape that politics and science borrow from each other, and that consequently now provide the shape of time for each other. Conceptually, their separation has been collapsed. Time provides the basis of Gore's reconciliation: this gives rise to his real question of whether a terrestrial reconciliation can be made quickly enough.

Hologram time

Earth in the Balance presents the deliberate and progressive revelation of a vision, through a powerful perceptual device that organizes words and images into something more than the sum of the parts:

> I am reminded of a new form of holistic photography that captures three-dimensional images of people and objects called holograms. One of the curiosities of this new science that makes it useful as a metaphor is that every small portion of the photographic plate contains all the visual information necessary to recreate a tiny, faint representation of the entire three-dimensional image. The image becomes full and vivid only when that portion is combined with the rest of the plate.
>
> (*EB*:11)

Earth in the Balance is organized into three parts, and begins from the premise that we do not properly see the damage caused in front of our very

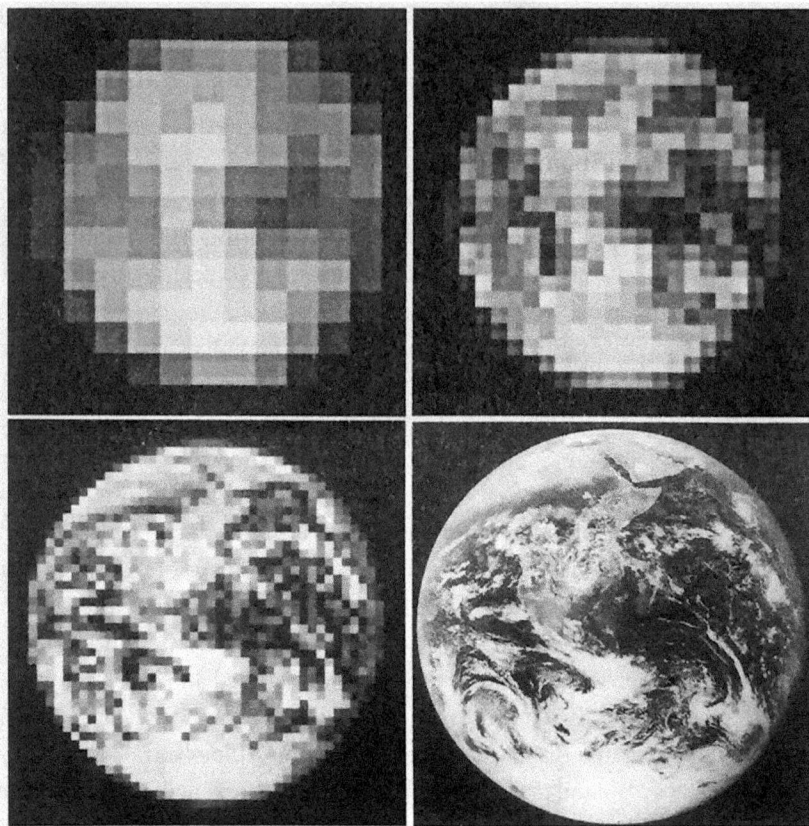

Figure 6.2 © Todd Gipstein, reproduced with permission.

eyes (as Gore puts it, 'a journey in search of a true understanding of the global ecological crisis and how it can be resolved' – *EB*:1). Part I 'Balance at risk' could be characterized as looking to the past; part II 'The search for balance' as looking to the present, and part III 'Striking the balance' as looking to the future. The frontispiece to each of the three parts carries an image of planet Earth set against a black background, with each having progressively more component parts carrying greater information about the bigger picture. Clearly, the intended effect is to mimic the realization of the vision: the image for part I is very blurry (*EB*:17), that for part II less so (*EB*:165); though it is still blurry when compared to the resolution achieved by the start of part III (*EB*:267). These three frontispiece images are reproduced again immediately following the conclusion (*EB*:367), and set alongside a fourth and finally sharp image of the Earth. The combined quadrant of images recapitulates the journey from tiny and faint portions to full and vivid image.

Gore's particular design for holographic part-whole relations receives its first description early in *Earth in the Balance*: 'The ecological perspective begins with a view of the whole, an understanding of how the various parts of nature interact in patterns that tend toward balance and persist over time.' (*EB*:2). Having spelled out this core organizing principle in words here, it is also resolved in images – the intended effect of the book's unfolding revelation is that the Earth itself comes sharply into new focus in the moment that Gore's vision is realized.

These Apollo moon mission images 'of the earth floating in the blackness of space were so deeply moving because they enabled us to see our planet from a new perspective – a perspective from which the preciousness and fragile beauty of the earth was suddenly clear' (*EB*:44). The conclusion to *Earth in the Balance* begins with the words 'Life is always motion and change.' (*EB*:361), and on the final page Gore hints of 'a deeply personal interpretation of and relationship with Christ':

> my own faith is rooted in the unshakeable belief in God as creator and
> sustainer, a deeply personal interpretation of and relationship with Christ,
> and an awareness of a constant and holy spiritual presence in all people, in
> all life, and all things.
>
> (*EB*:368)

Appropriately, the page facing this final composition carries words that bring us as close as possible to Gore's three-dimensional vision. Here, Gore makes a marriage of ecology and theology, and spells out how we might conceive that 'we are part of the whole too' (*EB*:2).

Gore deploys a sophisticated and enduring interest in holography as a visualizing technique for revealing relations between parts and whole, and for revealing creation by giving us more than just a glimpse of a Creator. This is more than wordplay: *Earth in the Balance* is a systematically theological text, radically so, because of Gore's unorthodox location of God inside Man (*EB*:264), his commitment to both a type of creationism (*EB*:254) and a form of process theology (e.g. Cobb 1965; Woodward 2000; Whitehead 1926) in which every human and non-human interaction is creation in the making. Cobb's outline of process theology illustrates the resonances here through Whitehead's view that 'God is in all creatures, although only very fragmentarily so.' (Cobb n.d.). Many commentators have noted infusions between ecology and theology (e.g. Ross 1991; Spretnak 1986; White 1967), but in Gore's holography, the union is achieved by parts that carry a faint image of the whole:

> It is my own belief that the image of God can be seen in every corner of
> creation, but only faintly. By gathering in the mind's eye all of creation, one

can perceive the image of the Creator vividly. Indeed, my understanding
of how God is manifest in the world can be best conveyed through the
metaphor of the hologram [...] Each tiny portion of the hologram contains
a tiny representation of the entire three-dimensional image, but only
faintly. However, due to the novel and unusual optical principles on which
holography is based, when one looks not at a small portion but at the entire
hologram, these thousands of tiny, faint images come together in the eye of
the beholder as a single large, vivid image.

(*EB*:265)

Gore imitates this holographic effect in the form and the substance of *Earth
in the Balance*, deploying it figuratively to reveal his vision of how his Creator
is manifest in the world, and literally in the series of pixelated digital images
of earth. The resolving-image-of-earth device progressively emerges from the
discussion in which a powerful new perception of nature is revealed, and which
also progressively reveals a vision of God. The book aims to bring us into a
position where we can as if see Creation from the perspective of a Creator –
and in doing so we see that one is a manifestation of the other. This reciprocal
double vision of seeing both at the same time is because, for Gore, they are
one and the same thing. In this view, it is necessarily impossible to separate
out considerations of the natural world from considerations of the Creator. In
Gore's 'environmentalism of the spirit' (*EB*: chapter 13, 238–65), especially, it is
as if he intends to restore a faint image to a state of renewed vividness.

In Gore's view, holographic imaging is merely one of a number of devices
supporting his efforts to help other people visualize the ecological crisis for
themselves. Gore is thinking of nature in a particular way here: at a meta,
ecological or theological level that 'tends towards balance', as if adhering to
some greater plan, rather than the arbitrary messiness of lived nature. Gore
wishes he could bring the two into proper alignment, again. Time serves as the
enabler here, restoring the alignment of the act and process of creation, and
extending it from an origin point into a constantly unfolding present. Equally,
drawing all time and all nature into the present moment affords proximity
to God in the very moment of Creation. Gore ultimately relies upon a hope
that this realization alone will re-instantiate the critical relationship between
humanity and the earth: 'We are, in effect, bulldozing the Gardens of Eden'
(*EB*:144). Gore uses the metaphor of holography to exploit its facility to expose
what might otherwise remain illusive: Creation is in crisis. The critical distance
required to visualize the ecological crisis and to bring the solutions into focus is
enabled by holographic imagery and an eco-theological synthesis affording the
co-inherence of creator and creation in all people, life, things and time.

Hope time

Gore's enduring fascination, and figurative relationship, with the metaphor of holography was vividly literalized at Live Earth 2007, the biggest global-media event and largest climate-awareness event in history, as Heffernan put it (2007). A hopeful moment for those involved, the Live Earth 2007 concerts were held on 07.07.07, connected events from seven continents, and were geared to a seven-point commitment to action that included a seven-point petition-pledge. The different sevens each manifested a part with which to make the whole more vivid, carrying and reconstituting the form of the original design:

> 'The general theory behind Live Earth is we need to get this information about the crisis and solutions to it to every person on the planet, as many of them as we can reach', said Gore. 'And then they will, armed with knowledge, put pressure on all political leaders.'[4]

Live Earth 2007 was 'part of a campaign, Save Our Selves – the campaign for a climate in crisis',[5] and a 24-hour event broadcast live from seven continents. In addition to over one hundred artists, there were appearances by 'celebrities and thought leaders', and the whole event was watched by more than one million audience members and more than two billion viewers.[6] Live Earth's ten concerts represented and substantiated connection on a global scale: the live flow of digital signals, and of relations, were intended to generate a new phase of life for audience members and for planet earth. The technological connection of music events on all seven continents[7] was intended to produce, and make manifest, an ecstatic personal feeling of

---

4   'Gore urges "7 Point Pledge" ahead of Live Earth': www.nbcnews.com/id/wbna19502465 (accessed 18 October 2023).

5   'The campaign's identity is based on SOS, the international Morse code distress signal: three dots, followed by three dashes, followed by three dots. SOS is the most urgent, universal message we have, and SOS will use that signal as a continuous distress call to prompt individuals, corporations and governments around the world to respond to our climate crisis with action.': web.archive.org/web/20081202092528/http://liveearth.org/2007/02/3rd-news-post-test (accessed 28 November 2023).

6   Celebrities and thought leaders were defined as: 'Entertainers, athletes, scientists, government leaders and CEOs helping engage their constituencies with SOS.':web.archive.org/web/20081202092528/http://liveearth.org/2007/02/3rd-news-post-test (accessed 28 November 2023).

7   'Nunatak', a group of researchers, performed from the British Antarctic Survey's Rothera Research Station: web.archive.org/web/20070712100650/http://www.antarctica.ac.uk/indepth/nunatak/index.php (accessed 28 November 2023).

connection for its participants: both within oneself, amongst the billions and with all life on earth. Live shows across the globe came into focus at different times, as if receiving and passing on a baton in relay, and kept pace such that it was always – holographically speaking – the same Live Earth time and space. By these means, Live Earth brought its intentions and ambitions into being: they created 'One World'. With this, a relational form emerged and materialized through which to deliver the message about 'one climate', and to ask those who experienced and felt the connection to 'Answer the Call, and Be the Change'.

> 'We hope the energy created by Live Earth will jump start a massive public education effort', Live Earth Co-Chair Vice President Al Gore said. 'Live Earth will help us reach a tipping point that's needed to move corporations and governments to take decisive action to solve the climate crisis'.[8]

Politicians or televangelists could only dream of connection on such a scale. If Live Earth could deliver or administer inspiration through this relational form, then there would be no knowing the power of the spirit it had summoned.

The progressive revelation of the importance of holographic thinking in Gore's engagement in the world was most vividly literalized during the Live Earth concert held in Tokyo, where he made a personal appearance in the form of a hologram.[9] Gore's rather unworldly apparition was achieved by the use of Musion® Eyeliner™ Holographic Projection to create a virtual hologram.[10] When Gore made his appearance, it was as if he had travelled through time, though the effect was to powerfully ground a vision in the immediate present. As Kevin Wall, co-founder of Live Earth, put it: 'Global warming is the greatest environmental challenge facing humanity – not in the future and not somewhere else, but right here, right now'. (de Rothschild 2007:154). As Gore's sparkling parts resolved into a vision of a transported whole – a virtual hologram of the man also in America – the resemblance

---

8   web.archive.org/web/20100621034753/http://liveearth.org/en/press/pressrelease/
     usa-live-earth-revealed (accessed 28 November 2023).

9   See web.archive.org/web/20080907143438/http://musion.co.uk/Al_Gore_Live_
     Earth_Tokyo.html (accessed 28 November 2023).

10   Musion Eyeliner uses a specially developed foil that reflects images from high
     definition video projectors, making it possible to produce virtual holographic
     images of variable sizes and incredible clarity, using industry standard software.
     Infinitely configurable, the virtual hologram appears within a stage set: web.
     archive.org/web/20080912010440/http://www.musion.co.uk (accessed 28
     November 2023).

was striking: the holographic effect looked and sounded uncannily like Gore. His three-dimensions had been recomposed and brought together. This materialization was apparently really him, but only faintly, at least at first:

> Thank you. Hello... I'm Al Gore. What an amazing world we live in – I love it that I can stand here on this stage in Tokyo and speak to you in holographic form. It is astounding that in just these recent few decades we have seen the invention of technologies that enable us to connect and instantly communicate our ideas and intentions and feelings with people on the other side of the globe. [...]
>
> The human race is also connected by the climate crisis. It is a global problem that transcends boundaries, languages and culture. The climate crisis has an impact on everyone, everywhere on earth. [...]
>
> With Live Earth we hope to connect people through the power of music, and engage them with a simple, universal message: SOS – Answer the Call. The Live Earth concerts are intended to inspire you and a mass audience all over the world to take immediate action and build a global movement for change. You can launch this movement today, by pledging to take meaningful and lasting action to make changes in your life.
>
> (Al Gore, Live Earth 2007, Tokyo Concert)[11]

Live Earth 2007's seven-point pledge took two seven-point forms: one focused on people taking personal action to reduce CO2, spreading the word and adding their name to the 'Live Earth 7 Point Pledge',[12] which in turn constituted a petition urging governments into action.[13]

But it was not immediately apparent to which governments, and by what means, the pledge would be sent. Yet this was hardly the point: rather, as much

---

11   web.archive.org/web/20080907143438/http://musion.co.uk/Al_Gore_Live_ Earth_Tokyo.html (accessed 28 November 2008).

  12   I will change four light bulbs to CFLs at my home.

     I will ride public transit or carpool one or more times per week.

     I will shop for the most energy efficient electronics and appliances.

     I will forward a Live Earth email message to 5 friends.

     I will shut off my equipment and lights whenever I'm not using them.

     Add my name to the Live Earth pledge.

               www.liveearthpledge.org (accessed 18 October 2023)

  13   I PLEDGE:

     1.   To demand that my country join an international treaty within the next 2 years that cuts global warming pollution by 90% in developed countries and by more than half worldwide in time for the next generation to inherit a healthy earth;

as it demanded action of would-be recipient governments, it also directed this SOS to those very people who were in a position to do something about it, those people ready and able to 'answer the call' – who signed up by entering their personal details and then pressing the red button marked 'I commit to make this change'. As much as the seven-point pledge looked as though it were addressed to a collective of separate entities, following the form of traditional adversarial protest, it actually amounted to a demand upon oneself for action – 'to be the change'. Self-activation shifted the agency from without to within.

Live Earth reworked the SOS international distress call for immediate assistance, by challenging the intended recipients to 'answer the call'. Rather than a call to 'save our souls', aimed at someone else who might be in a position to assist precisely because they were external, beyond or outside the emergency and not directly involved in it themselves, Live Earth's rewording to 'save our selves' was a call for self-help directed at the collective billions, and directed individually: in Gore's words, 'The Live Earth concerts are intended to inspire you and a mass audience all over the world to take immediate action and build a global movement for change'. This mass of people may have been attending in person or watching from a distance as part of the global audience, but this was no guarantee that they were yet inside, yet inspired by or yet committed to the Live Earth campaign message: 'One world. One climate. Be the change'.

Live Earth's SOS distress call was not aimed at other people. It was as if any and all external agencies were no longer in a position from which to help,

---

2. To take personal action to help solve the climate crisis by reducing my own CO_2 pollution as much as I can and offsetting the rest to become "carbon neutral;"

3. To fight for a moratorium on the construction of any new generating facility that burns coal without the capacity to safely trap and store the CO_2;

4. To work for a dramatic increase in the energy efficiency of my home, workplace, school, place of worship, and means of transportation;

5. To fight for laws and policies that expand the use of renewable energy sources and reduce dependence on oil and coal;

6. To plant new trees and to join with others in preserving and protecting forests; and,

7. To buy from businesses and support leaders who share my commitment to solving the climate crisis and building a sustainable, just, and prosperous world for the 21st century.

web.archive.org/web/20070711210631/http://www.liveearth.org/thank_you_pop.
htm (accessed 28 November 2023

and the only effective agents for change were 'within' – and this was a test of whether the required response could be actualized.

> Our climate crisis affects everyone, everywhere, and that's who SOS is
> aimed at. Only a global response can conquer our climate crisis. SOS asks
> all people to Save Our Selves because only we can.[14]

Pressing the red button would make the commitment, one inspired by and arising from the inside, and registered inside the Live Earth website, which acted as the recipient agency, witnessing the act. This commitment, made for the 'whole world', was made in front of the 'whole world'. Once made, the committer's name joins the scroll of other newcomers, now on the inside, who had felt 'the call inside' and who had 'answered from within', and whose names and actions ran across at the bottom of the pledge screen.

Clearly, Live Earth 2007 was a hopeful moment and shared a genealogy with Barack Obama's 2008 'campaign of hope' for the US presidency. In suggesting that 'the general appeal of hope seems to reside in its embrace of the radical uncertainty and indeterminacy of the present moment', Miyazaki traces Obama's outline of a theory of hope to the keynote speech delivered from the national stage of the 2004 Democratic National Convention: 'God's greatest gift to us, the bedrock of this nation; the belief in things unseen; the belief that there are better days ahead.' (2008:5). Live Earth 2007 could join Miyazaki's other examples of how 'hope has emerged as a way to redefine the ethical contours of the social and the relational', not least by aligning a 'call for change as a call for personal change' (ibid.). This was Obama's appeal in his 2008 Super Tuesday speech: 'Change will not come if we wait for some other person or some other time. We are the ones we've been waiting for. We are the change that we seek.' (cited in Miyazaki 2008:5). Bringing the future into the present enables societal change to be brought in as if stemming from the personal. In Gore's reckoning, perhaps the event also exemplifies Miyazaki's earlier insight that 'it is not God that is the source of hope but hope is the source of God' (2004:18). Alongside the predictions and testaments to climate crisis, Live Earth 2007 also sought to draw the future into the present through the mimesis of making terrestrial time and the time for change into a singularity. Again, Gore seeks to solve multiple, interconnected crises by giving time new shapes.

---

14 web.archive.org/web/20081202092528/http://liveearth.org/2007/02/3rd-news-
post-test (accessed 28 November 2023).

Conclusion: Gore-dian knots

Time has been central to Gore's depictions of holographically interconnected crises. That kinds of time are co-produced by ideas of nature may be too obvious for words. Not only do they equate to nature in terms of how much of each is left, time also measures out a field for action, giving shape to urgency and providing a form for hope. Gore's depiction of the temporal thresholds for negative feedback loops amongst the molecules, and positive feedback loops amongst the masses, gives the ecological and climate crises a particular shape, and consequently gives particular characteristics to the motivation and momentum seemingly required from humanity to deal with it. In this way, even faint changes in the parts might produce vivid effects in the whole. The personal character given to the steps required and parts played suggests that humanity's relationship to creation, and to a creator, is a matter of personal commitment. For Gore, this appears to be natural to Protestant faith and action. Gore finds a match for the global pattern of destruction in a global pattern of creation. The problems of the future rise out of line and out of balance, and these are addressed by imagining the present political context as in the alternate forms of tipping points, thresholds and feedback loops. By bringing together a host of concerts and happenings in a singular event, one that makes a singularity of time and a congregation of personal commitment, Gore is also able to relocate change, making it and those who answer the call a personal exercise in collective hope.

This chapter has been concerned with ethnographically analysing Gore's logic, and has stayed with the expositional trouble by tracing cultural interconnections perhaps taken for granted by convention. The ethnography explored our examples of Gore's shaping of time: the proximity of indwelling horizons, the shape of a hockey stick, the appearance of a hologram and the character of hope. Each of these illustrate how forms of time are made manifest as immanent motivations for social action. Gore's eco-theological synthesis provided a pivot to the exposition plotting the crises of nature and time, by drawing attention to partially disguised causes, consequences and connections, and by showing how crises are interconnected in holographic and theological forms. As such, the exposition provides a counterpoint to the volume's contributions from Amazonia and Melanesia whose own holographic equivalences, conceptual figurations and lived co-inherences are just as distinctive and vibrant.

Acknowledgments

Research presentations on these materials have been given in St Andrews, Cambridge, Durham, Ljubljana, Aberdeen, LSE, Ascona and the Open University. I am grateful to the organizers and participants for the many interesting and challenging insights and fruitful exchanges, including those involved in the International Balzan Foundation funded Ethnographic Horizons project.

References

Bamford, S. and Leach, J. 2009. 'Introduction: pedigrees of knowledge, anthropology and the genealogical method'. In S. Bamford and J. Leach, (eds), *Kinship and Beyond: The Genealogical Model Reconsidered*, pp. 1–23. Oxford: Berghahn Books.

Cannell, F. 2006. 'The anthropology of Christianity'. In F. Cannell (ed.), *The Anthropology of Christianity*, pp. 1–50. Durham: Duke University Press.

Carney, M. 2015. 'Breaking the tragedy of the horizon – climate change and financial stability'. Speech by Mark Carney, Governor of the Bank of England, Chairman of the Financial Stability Board, Lloyd's of London, 29 September 2015: www.bankofengland.co.uk/-/media/boe/files/speech/2015/breaking-the-tragedy-of-the-horizon-climate-change-and-financial-stability.pdf (accessed 23 January 2024).

Cassidy, R. 2009. 'Arborescent culture: writing and not writing racehorse pedigrees'. In S. Bamford and J. Leach (eds), 2009. *Kinship and Beyond: The Genealogical Model Reconsidered*, pp. 24–49. Oxford: Berghahn Books.

Cobb, J. 1965. *A Christian Natural Theology Based on the Thought of Alfred North Whitehead*. Philadelphia: Westminster Press.

——— n.d. 'Process theology': www.religion-online.org/article/process-theology (accessed 18 October 2023).

Crook, T. 2018. 'Earthrise +50: Apollo 8, Mead, Gore and Gaia', *Anthropology Today* 34(6):7–10.

de Rothschild, D. 2007. *The Live Earth Global Warming Survival Handbook*. Emmaus: Rodale Books.

Franklin, S. 2013. 'From blood to genes?: rethinking cosanguinity in the context of geneticization'. In C. Johnson, B. Jussen, D. Warren and S. Teuscher (eds), *Blood and Kinship: Matter for Metaphor from Ancient Rome to the Present*, pp. 285–320. New York: Berghahn Books.

Gell, A. 1992. *The Anthropology of Time: Cultural Constructions of Temporal Maps and Images*. Oxford: Berg.

Gore, A. 1992 [2000, 2007]. *Earth in the Balance: Ecology and the Human Spirit*. Boston: Houghton Mifflin Company [rev. edn. 2007. *Earth in the Balance: Forging a New Common Purpose*. London: Earthscan].

——— 2006. *An Inconvenient Truth: The Planetary Emergency of Global Warming and What We Can Do About It*. London: Bloomsbury.

——— 2013. *The Future: Six Drivers of Global Change*. New York: Random House.

——— 2015. *Beyond the Horizon*. TV series with J. Leto. Episode 3 (October).

Guggenheim, D. 2006. *An Inconvenient Truth: A Global Warning.* Paramount
    Pictures.

Harding, S. 2007. 'After the Falwellians'. In A. Szántó (ed.), *What Orwell Didn't Know:*
    Propaganda and the New Face of American Politics, pp. 122–34. New York:
    PublicAffairs.

Heffernan, O. 2007. 'Creating a c-change?', *Nature Reports Climate Change* 3:1.

Hulme, M. 2017. *Weathered: Cultures of Climate.* London: SAGE Publications.

Kennedy White, K. and Duram, L. (eds) 2012. *America Goes Green: An Encyclopedia*
    of Eco-Friendly Culture in the United States. Santa Barbara: ABC-CLIO.

Latour, B. 1993. *We Have Never Been Modern.* Cambridge: Harvard University Press.

——— 2005. *Reassembling the Social: An Introduction to Actor-Network-Theory.*
    Oxford: Oxford University Press.

McKibben, B. 1990. *The End of Nature.* New York: Viking.

Miyazaki, H. 2004. *The Method of Hope: Anthropology, Philosophy, and Fijian*
    Knowledge. Stanford: Stanford University Press.

——— 2008. 'Barack Obama's campaign of hope: unifying the general and the
    personal', *Anthropology News* (November):5, 8.

Munn, N. 1992. 'The cultural anthropology of time: a critical essay', *Annual Review of*
    Anthropology 21:93–123.

Robbins, J. 2006. 'Anthropology and theology: An awkward relationship?',
    Anthropological Quarterly, 79(2):285–94.

Ross, A. 1991. *Strange Weather: Culture, Science and Technology in the Age of Limits.*
    London: Verso Books.

Sahlins, M. 1996. 'The sadness of sweetness: the native anthropology of western
    cosmology', *Current Anthropology* 37(3):395–428.

Schnegg, M. 2021. Ontologies of climate change: reconciling indigenous and
    scientific explanations for the lack of rain in Namibia', *American Ethnologist*
    48(3):260–73.

Spretnak, C. 1986. *The Spiritual Dimension of Green Politics.* Santa Fe: Bear &
    Company.

Strathern, M. 1992. *After Nature: English Kinship in the Late Twentieth Century.*
    Cambridge: Cambridge University Press.

Strathern, M. 2020. *Relations: An Anthropological Account.* Durham: Duke University
    Press.

Stewart, K., and Harding, S. 1999. 'Bad endings: American apocalypses', *Annual*
    Review of Anthropology 28:285–310.

Tambiah, S. 2013 [1973]. 'The galactic polity in Southeast Asia', *HAU: Journal of*
    Ethnographic Theory 3(3):503–34.

Turque, B. 2000. *Inventing Al Gore.* Boston: Houghton Mifflin Company.

Weart, S. 2008. *The Discovery of Global Warming.* Cambridge, MA: Harvard
    University Press.

——— 2022. 'Money for Keeling: monitoring CO2 levels': history.aip.org/climate/
    Kfunds.htm (accessed 19 October 2023).
White, L. 1967. 'The historical roots of our ecologic crisis', *Science* 155(3767):1203–7.
Whitehead, A. 1926. *Religion in the Making.* Cambridge: Cambridge University Press.
Wilson, C. and Matthews, W. (eds) 1971. *Inadvertent Climate Modification. Report
    of Conference, Study of Man's Impact on Climate (SMIC), Stockholm.*
    Cambridge, MA: MIT Press.
Woodward, K. 2000. 'Finding God', *Newsweek Magazine* (6 February): www.
    newsweek.com/finding-god-162445 (accessed 19 October 2023).

Afterword

'Crises in time' from the perspective of an Amazonianist's ethnographic horizon

APARECIDA VILAÇA[1]

✺

What do different Indigenous peoples of Amazonia and Papua New Guinea have to say about the notion of crisis? How do they relate these events or states to specific temporalities? How do these societies perpetuate themselves as such in the face of various historical events that imply ruptures (such as deaths, wars, revolts, invasions by whites)? How do anthropologists incorporate these specific conceptions of memory and temporality into their ethnographic horizons? These are some of the questions posed by the authors who compose this collection.

The universe studied is quite diverse, not only with regard to the ethnographic areas themselves, but also with regard to the different peoples within them. Amazonia and Melanesia have only in the last few decades become the object of systematic comparisons, especially after the collection on the question of gender organized by Gregor and Tuzin (2001). This correlation is not exactly due to the discovery of common cultural practices, as the differences between the two regions are substantial, but mainly due to a convergence in the concepts used for the analysis of the ethnographic data, a consequence of an intense dialogue between specialists of the two areas, especially through the works of Roy Wagner, Marilyn Strathern and Eduardo Viveiros de Castro. Thus, for example, the concept of the dual person explored by Strathern (1988) for the Melanesian context proved productive

1   This work, produced under the auspices of the Ethnographic Horizons project at the Centre for Pacific Studies, University of St Andrews, was supported by the International Balzan Foundation.

for a finer understanding of the Amazonian person, especially its relational dynamics. Similarly, the analogical relations developed by Roy Wagner, and particularly his analysis of indigenous invention processes (Wagner 1975), have offered new tools for the analysis of the phenomena of interethnic contact and cultural transformations in Amazonia (Kelly 2005, 2011; Leite 2013, 2016; Vilaça 2011, 2013, 2016; Viveiros de Castro 2002, 2004, 2014). In the opposite direction, the concepts of perspectivism and multinaturalism developed by Viveiros de Castro (1998) from an Amerindian context have stimulated new analyses by Melanesianists (see Strathern 1999).

Christianity

An important avenue of rapprochement between the two regions, however, has its origins in a concrete ethnographic situation: the Christianization of Indigenous peoples, which – although dating back to the first contacts with whites and their temporalities – has intensified in recent decades in both regions. The works of Barker (1992, 1993, 2010), Cannell (2006), Handman (2015), Hirsch (1994, 2008), Mosko (2010) and, especially, the ethnography of Robbins (2004) on the Christian experience of the Urapmin of Papua New Guinea, inspired by the works of Dumont and Sahlins on cultural transformations, offered new analytical perspectives for understanding the coexistence of traditional and Christian views which, as in the Amazonian case, do not fit into the notion of hybridism usually used as an explanatory tool (Leite 2016; Valentino 2019; Vilaça 2016).

The chapter in this volume by Santos da Costa deals precisely with the centrality of Christianity in Papua New Guinea, through the analysis of politics as experienced in the national parliament in Port Moresby, more specifically in the face of the innovations brought by the Unity Team. This group of politicians and religious personages fastened on the gift of a Bible, aiming to turn it into a political symbol, and associating it with a future project marked by progress and enrichment. Differently from other Pentecostal appropriations of the Bible, the Unity Team does not propose a temporal rupture between past (backward, sinful, immoral) and present-future, but emphasizes the notion of continuity, not within local history, but in a narrative that unites Christian countries, such as Britain and the United States. The future of one country is associated with the past and present of the others, with the Bible being the connecting bridge.

Amazonia and the peoples who inhabit it remain part of the Brazilian state, whose constitution is secular, unlike Papua New Guinea. This same constitution, which dates from 1988 and marks the end of a twenty-year dictatorship, establishes the cultural autonomy of these peoples, as well as guaranteeing possession of their original lands. Thus, although in the past relations between the government and Christian agents were close, Christianization today takes place in a way that is disconnected from the state, almost always through the direct action of Catholic and Evangelical religious missions among specific Indigenous peoples, who in no way conceive themselves as constituting a single nation.

Amaral deals with the effects of Christianity on the Ingarikó of the Amazonian north. In this case, contact with English-speaking religious people in the nineteenth century did not lead to conversion per se, but to the adoption of Christian symbols and ideas by messianic movements that aimed to overcome an imminent cataclysm, which would destroy the earth and its inhabitants. In other words, these symbols and ideas used in an innovative way in a moment of crisis, in order to produce an image of a future in which the riches of the whites change hands, also providing Indigenous people with exclusive access to the exuberant posthumous Christian world. It is known that this type of movement, generally led by Indigenous prophets, has been common in Amazonia since at least the seventeenth century, and is reported for peoples as distinct as the Tupi of the coast, the Baniwa and Tukano of the Upper Rio Negro, the Jê-Timbira of central Brazil, the Jê of southern Brazil, the Kaingang and the Xokleng. In her book (forthcoming), Amaral approaches messianism from the notion of counter-anthropology, developed precisely by Wagner (1975) when he analysed the messianic movements in the Pacific, which were later given ethnographic detail by Lattas (1998).

A little further south in Brazil, the Canela-Ramkokamekra of Maranhão, neighbours of the Canela-Apanjekra and speakers of the same language, as studied by Guimarães, became known in the literature for an intense messianic movement that occurred in 1963, here disconnected from Christian symbols (Carneiro da Cunha 2009). A prophetess, pregnant with a baby, and while it was still in the womb, claimed she was a sister of the mythical hero Aukê, the one who gave rise to the whites. She announced the subversion of power relations: on the day scheduled for the birth, 'the Indians would take over the cities, would fly planes and buses, while the "civilized" ones would be driven to the forest' (Carneiro da Cunha 2009:17). The projected future did not materialize, not only because the baby, a girl and not a boy as announced, was born dead, but also because neighbouring farmers angered by the appropriation of their cattle encouraged by the prophetess, decided to attack the Ramkokamekra, forcing the transfer of the entire group to another region to avoid a massacre.

Although a messianic movement has not been described for their neighbours, the Canela-Apanjekra, it seems interesting to me to relate this movement to their symbolic appropriation of government monetary aid, the family allowance, as a means of overcoming the profound material inequality between Indians and whites. In a kind of 'weakened' re-actualization of messianism, the goods of the whites do not reach them through their own agency, under the guidance of the prophets, but as an initiative of the whites themselves. Having finally realized the need to relate to the Indigenous people, and given that these relations are founded on commercial exchanges by means of payment in money, the whites have resolved to offer the Canela-Apanjekra monthly sums, so that they have the means to effect relations. It is interesting to note that the same type of 'weakening' seems to have occurred among the Ingarikó studied by Amaral, considering that what started as a foreign-inspired messianic movement was re-elaborated over time. Not only has it come to be conceived as fully Indigenous in its origins, but the idea of cataclysm has been re-signified: no longer a future event, but now associated with the social and environmental problems that are part of their current experience.

The expected future of equality between Indigenous and white people, however, is never achieved. Just as the messianic movements were frustrated, because the desired goods that were supposed to arrive in large quantities did not arrive, the family allowance is not sufficient to provide the Indigenous people with the desired goods. On the contrary, a good part of the money is spent in travelling, by river or road, to the cities where the banks are located. In an attempt to overcome these and other difficulties, Apanjekra often give their bank cards into the hands of mediators, non-Indigenous inhabitants of the city, who charge high interest rates to help them buy products. In the end, they find themselves in constant debt to the whites, in a manner analogous to what happened in the nineteenth century with the rubber bosses, who kept Indigenous people in a situation akin to slavery due to their perpetual debts. What strikes us in Guimarães' analysis is that this perception of unilateral exploitation is restricted to non-indigenous agents, among them often anthropologists. For the Apanjekra, the 'card bosses' are important mediators in the relationship with the city and bureaucratic processes; they are people who 'think about them, take care of them [Apanjekra]', precisely because they received an initial 'gift', the bank card, that moves them in that direction.

Unlike the messianic movements that had a sudden end (sometimes involving the assassination of the prophet), frustration deriving from the expectation of a future rich in exogenous material goods occurs, in the case of family allowance, in a gradual way, and leads to a search for other means of accessing money, such as departure from the village for paid work. In the case of messianism, in general the prophet is punished for the same frustrations and he/she in turn blames the failure on the moral problems of the Indigenous people. The moral failures causing the issues with the family allowances are attributed to the whites, but not to the card bosses as one might expect, rather to those in the 'government' who are never willing to provide adequately for the needs of the indigenous people.

Although in a completely different political and social context, the so-called Bougainville Crisis, analysed by Kenema, also refers to dissatisfaction with relations with whites and their organizations. Suffering from the environmental and social damage caused by the activities of the Panguna copper mine and dissatisfied with the maldistribution of profits, the local population initiated a revolt that lasted nine years (1988–97). During this period, they suffered violent repression from the relatively recently independent Papua New Guinea government, leading to police control of all local activities, including daily travel, which had to be reported to patrols. The uprising revived regional rivalries, separating village members and kin with devastating effects on social relations. According to Kenema, this was not in fact a single and continuous crisis, but rather a series of consecutive crises, whose temporalities were experienced differently by the different collectives involved. The resolution involved a referendum that reinforced Bougainville's status as an autonomous region, with its own leaders and symbols, and the prospect of becoming a new nation in the near future.

Consider what happened in the Port Moresby parliament, according to Santos da Costa's analysis, when a crisis associated with corruption and moral failure was translated into and embraced by the language of nationalism. In Bougainville, by comparison, although in its general scope 'the Crisis' was focused on 'national' issues, within Nagovisi social life its effects and the attempts at resolution were based on kinship relations. It was the fear of an irreversible rupture of close kinship ties (*mono*) – as relatives found themselves divided by belonging to rival groups – that animated the search for an end to conflict. Thus, we see the possibility of a totally different constitution of the social in the same ethnographic region, originating from different ethnographic horizons. Kenema participated directly in the armed struggle. From the horizon determined by him, attentive to what the Nagovisi thought was most important, Papua New Guinea is much closer to the Amazon, where the notion of an Indigenous nation is non-existent and actions are determined by local kinship relations.

The notion of crisis as a spectrum is the subject of Crook's chapter. His analysis, focused on Al Gore's work on the climate crisis, examines a projection of a future that becomes ever closer, shortening the present, and inaugurates a relation of continuity between two central notions of Western cosmology: time and nature. It is foreseen that we will have less and less nature and, consequently, less time. It is interesting to note that Al Gore's discourse is full of references to biblical events, which are updated in everyday actions and crises, allowing us to associate his narratives with those of the Unity

Team in the Port Moresby parliament analysed by Santos da Costa. This unusual correlation between the avant-garde discourse of a former American vice-president, focused on environmental issues, and that of members of a conservative Christian collective in Papua New Guinea seems to me to reveal, above all, the strength and plasticity of Christian symbols, evident to all those who have conducted field research among peoples converted to Christianity (as was my case).

It is striking that in these different chapters – with the exception of the Introduction, which puts these same issues into another perspective – what is understood as a crisis always seems to be the result of non-Indigenous action in the form of a disruptive external stimulus, as in the case of the cataclysm predicted by the Ingarikó in the past, the perception of material poverty by the Apanjekra, the action of the mining company in Bougainville and what we could call Western-derived notions of corruption in the Unity Team's case. Regarding the global climate crisis, the deleterious effects of white actions fall not only on Indigenous people, but on all inhabitants of the planet. In this case, Indigenous people are generally exempted from responsibility, because it is known that they are not the ones causing the environmental damage. Could this perception of a crisis of external origin be the result of the ethnographic horizon of the researchers, who, as could only be expected, arrived only after relations with whites had been established? Were there experiences of crisis before the contact events? How do and did the Indigenous people in these two regions perceive the passage of time and of life cycles?

Strathern, in the Introduction to this volume, explores a possible meaning that whites give to the notion of crisis: that it involves separations and ruptures. However, she wishes to use 'rupture' to specific effect, to cover the various daily incisions of life. Drawing analogies between cultivation activities and the passing of generations, the author shows us that in Mt. Hagen renewal is only possible with the active introduction of rupture. Thus, for example, the tubers that constitute the basis of their agriculture, when harvested, must be cut into two parts: what will be eaten and what will remain as the basis for the new crop. In the same way, reproduction requires active separation between the genitors and the children, so that these can develop and one day replace them. The hypothesis is that an immanent approach to events allows new times to erupt without any of the sense of crisis that the notion of time flowing forwards produces.

Futures

In Amazonia, with conversion also comes a new idea of the future. Previously, amidst a regenerative concept of time related to subsistence activities and the replacement of one generation by the next, Indigenous peoples directed their daily efforts towards staying alive alongside their relatives, that is, remaining fully human. The future was to be built every day through care in relations with each other and with animals. With the adoption of Christianity this concept is completely transformed. I observe that the Wari', like other Amazonian peoples, do not have the notion of an absolute beginning to a world, of creation *ex nihilo*, but of successive transformations of pre-existing worlds (which could also be seen in Melanesian mythology in general). Consequently, nor did they conceive of an end of the world in the sense attributed to it by Christianity, as something sudden, complete, to take place at a moment known to God but kept secret. As in the proverb, 'the future belongs to God', the Wari' now say that only God knows the day of the Last Judgement, when Jesus will return to earth and take Christians with him to heaven, leaving sinners on earth to be eaten by gigantic carnivorous animals. An indeterminate extension of time has taken place, an idea of a distant and definitive future that was previously completely foreign to them.

There are evidently other conceptions of the future in Amazonia that, even if originating from Christian principles, reveal another temporality and other notions of agency. Amaral shows us the active production of a future of technological and material abundance among the Ingarikó through millenarianism. Guimarães shows monetary benefits to be a bridge between a past of exploitation by whites and a present of redemption and compensation, thereby producing an image of a future of more egalitarian relations. As we have also seen, Santos da Costa situates the Bible in Papua New Guinea, as appropriated by the Unity Team, as an instrument of mediation between a backwards past and an abundant future.

These contexts of the active production of a desired but uncertain future contrast with the idea of the future projected by dreams, common to several Amazonian Indigenous peoples. In these cases, dreams reveal possible futures that could be actualized through the dreamer's agency. Thus, among the Guarani, for example, it is common for an intimate circle of relatives to gather in the early hours of the morning to tell each other their dreams, so that together they may seek to understand the possible implications for the dreamer's future. Choices of daily activities are made on the basis of understandings of dreams, in order to avoid tragic events and so as to choose paths that lead to well-being (Mendes Jr. 2021; Pissolato 2007; Silva 2010). In an analogous way to the presence of the past in the present, through the immanence of mythical times, everything happens as if the future already existed, and may or may not be actualized by human action.

Another type of conception of the future is revealed in Carneiro da Cunha and Viveiros de Castro's (2009) analysis of the war among the Tupinambá people of the Brazilian coast in the sixteenth century, as already mentioned in Amaral's chapter. According to the authors, war, or more specifically the death of a captive enemy, was a mechanism for the production of time, that is the projection of a future that – in the absence of other means of perpetuating the collectives (such as lineage groups, gift-type exchange cycles) – allowed a notion of continuity. The main evidence of the operation of this mechanism occurs in the ritual dialogue between the killer and the victim at the moment of the murder, as reported by different chroniclers. In it, the enemy who had lived for some time in the village of his captors, sometimes married to a local woman, responds to the insults of his tormentor with bravado, saying that his own have already killed many and will kill even more in the future to avenge his own death. In the words of the authors:

> Tupinambá vengeance speaks only, but it speaks in an essential way, of the
> past and the future. It is it, and only it, that connects those who have lived
> (and died) and those who will live, that makes explicit a continuity that
> is not given in any other instance. The fluidity of this society which does
> not count, apart from revenge, on any strong institution, neither lineages
> properly so called, nor ceremonial groups, nor positive rules of marriage,
> underscores the singularity of the institution of revenge.
>
> It is not about having revenge because people die and need to be
> rescued from the destructive flow of time; it is about dying in order to have
> revenge, and thus to have a future.
>
> But in both, the aspects, and for both groups, revenge is the thread
> that links past and future, and in this sense, revenge, memory and time are
> confused.
>
> (Carneiro da Cunha and Viveiros de Castro 2009:90, 93 and 94,
> my translation)

Long-term research and its horizons

Like me, Strathern has conducted her field research in sojourns scattered over a large expanse of time. In her case, in Hagen, Papua New Guinea, between 1964 and 2015; in mine, among the Wari' of the Amazonian south-west from 1986 to the present. In a recent unpublished paper, Strathern (2019) dramatizes her 'bewilderment' at the changes in farming techniques: gardens replaced by extensive fields, pigs having once moved freely now being locked in cement pens. Expressing her 'surprise', Strathern heard from her interlocutor: 'Now is a new time.' This very common Melanesian trope is especially so among several peoples who have joined Pentecostal evangelical religions, as in the case of the Urapmin studied by Robbins (2004), who see conversion as a moment of radical rupture with the past.

In my case, I once heard the same type of statement from an Indigenous person of the Cabixi people, who was living among the Wari', when I commented to him on the lack of interest of the Wari' youth in themes that guided their lives in the past: 'The people you met when you arrived were bush people. Now they are different people.' In truth, I was, like Strathern, struck by the transformations that had occurred in such a short space of time: in fifteen years they had stopped holding their parties, started selling products among themselves, hoarding manufactured goods at home and aiming for jobs that would give them access to money. The change can be attributed to conversion to evangelical Christianity, but also to coexistence with the most diverse types of whites, leading, among other things, to the arrival of new foods, the imposition of exogenous forms of housing and work organization, and the introduction of salaried positions within the villages, such as those of teacher and nursing assistant. The Christian ideology propagated by the missionaries offered them the moral and cosmological bases for the new socio-economic relations, initially with the whites and then internally.

How can I situate my perception of the Wari' – of their meanings of crisis, rupture and temporality – from my specific ethnographic horizon, that is, from long-term research? In 1986, when I met them, they had been in peaceful contact with whites for a little over 20 years. The experience of contact itself had been traumatic, for between the armed massacres by rubber tappers interested in their land and the diseases brought by the so-called pacification teams, they had lost two thirds of their population. Without having a specific term for crisis, they use expressions related to death, illness and sadness (which brings us close to the Greek concept that relates crisis to illness, see Lloyd 2003). The Wari' think of this period as a kind of 'turning point' in their lives, when they finally decided to accept the call of the whites and let them live among them. Like several Indigenous peoples of the Amazon (such as the Kanamari and the Panoan-speaking peoples) and other regions, the event of contact and coexistence with the whites led them to review the past and to think of a division of time into epochs. The Wari' began to refer to the past as 'the time of the bush' and to the present as 'when we left in the direction of the whites'.

The radical discontinuity that might characterize these two different periods, if seen from an evolutionary concept of time, has no precedent in the case of the Wari' and many other Indigenous peoples. Like several Amazonian peoples, the Wari' refer to the events of the myths as those experienced by the 'ancients from long ago', and as possibly happening again in the present. Unexpected tracks found in the forest can be associated with a mythical people, for example. Furthermore, as is also widespread in the Amazon, shamans may revisit mythical events, associating with the beings who inhabited them. In other words, the past emerges again and again in the present, not as a memory, as among whites, but as a fact, as if the events and the people involved in them remained in a virtual state and can be updated at any moment. This is not just the case in Amazonia, as we've learnt from the chapters dedicated to Papua New Guinea. For the people of Hagen, as Strathern makes clear, the past is not just 'part' of the present, it is essential to it. As with crops, if there were no ruptures there will be no present times. Partition is crucial. From that perspective the concept of crisis, as we understand it, makes no sense, as change and rupture are not just part of everyday life, they are the necessary fuel to ongoing sociability.

Although the re-emergence of the distant past is the source of shamanic power and also the foundation of ritual life as a whole, it must be controlled or it will cause harm, including illness and death. For the Wari' the immanent humanity of the animals, given in the myth, is the cause of most illnesses. The hunt always puts the hunter and his family members at risk. If the rules of cooking and food distribution are not respected, then the animals may want to take revenge, and they do so as humans, striking victims with their arrows and taking the victims to live with them. The Wari' say that animals are always looking for people of their own, and some of them even kidnap children (usually those mistreated by their parents). When captured by animals, the victims are given an animal body and start living with them, as another member of their species. In short, humanity is for them a position (of the predator) to be occupied sometimes by the animal, sometimes by the Wari'.

Death produces a radical rupture between the individual (who will join the community of the dead) and the world of the living (which must forget her or him completely after the mourning period is over). As we know, among Amazonian peoples there is no ancestor cult and the rupture between the living and the dead with specific identities must be definitive, under the risk of death for the living. It is necessary not to look back, not to think about dead relatives, in order to avoid sadness, a source of sickness. Among the Wari', in particular, the living must keep their foot firmly planted in the present. It is worth noting that, although the rapid oblivion of the dead is also common in Melanesia, there the effect is not the radical separation of the living and the dead as distinct collectivities, but the transformation of the dead into ancestors, who can only then be remembered through sacrifices.

It seems to me that the possibility of associating the Wari' conception of illness with a specific notion of humanity as an unstable position rests in the ethnographic horizon of my research. Meeting them before they experienced the radical transformations that only later became visible allowed me to have access, among other things, to aetiological conceptions that are no longer present today. As the Cabixi man said, I met 'bush people', that is, adults and old people who had lived most of their lives in the forest without any contact with white people except through war. Although when I met them they had been in contact with the missionaries for twenty years and had defined themselves as Christians for a period, they had abandoned the new religion, resuming their rituals and the telling of myths to children at nightfall. From 2001, however, they experienced a Christian revival, which continues today. Many of the old people and adults I met have died. The younger ones are no longer interested in the myths, but in Bible stories and television programmes, which occupy their evenings. The rituals were suspended on the recommendation of the pastors because they involved drunkenness and sexual innuendo.

By adopting biblical stories as 'true', to the detriment of myths considered the 'lies' of the ancients, the Wari' have experienced a radical change in their aetiological principles. The teachings of Genesis, the first biblical book to be translated into their language by the fundamentalist evangelicals of the New Tribes Mission, implied a desubjectification of animals, created by God as submissive beings for the exclusive use of humans. Today, in their cults or in everyday conversations, they affirm that animals are simple prey, with no capacity to cause them disease or other harm. Diseases are now attributed to pathological agents introduced by white people, to be treated with Western pharmacological medicines, although some cases are diagnosed as witchcraft. Shamans no longer exist, or, as they say, in order to follow God the Wari' no longer accompany animals. The possibility of turning animal ceased to exist, and humanity settled at the Wari' pole. As my adoptive father, Paletó, said, 'now people are people and animals are animals'.

What would happen to a newly arrived ethnographer if no works were available on the Wari' of the past? How could she associate their enormous interest in the Christian Genesis with the possibility it offered them of bypassing the personal instability that permeated their daily lives by removing agency from the animals? When questioned today, Wari' usually reply that they converted so as not to go to hell or because Christianity allowed them to become numerous and live longer. One very potent connection between past and present is lost amidst the transformations.

Extinctions

To conclude, as an Amazonianist I would like offer my particular ethnographic horizon on the planetary environmental crisis, a theme that runs through almost every chapter of this book, but which is at the heart of Crook's contribution. I am particularly interested in ideas about the extinctions of animal and plant species signalling the gradual arrival of that 'zero' point, of complete destruction, as conceived by Western observers. Let us begin with the following question: would there have been among the Amazonian peoples a reflection on the possibility of extinction of entire collectives prior to the current experience of the environmental crisis brought on by the actions of whites?

Several Amazonian myths deal with this issue, describing mass extinctions of a previous humanity – which includes animals – either by a flood or another catastrophe. The causes are multiple, but they all concern moral infractions in a specific context of relations with a demiurge, or spirits or other beings. The catastrophe is not gradual, but immediate and total, and is produced by those who feel affected, displeased or disrespected. After the destruction a new humanity is established: either created by the unsatisfied demiurge or from a small group of people who escaped the destruction, as is the case of the Yanomami and the Wari'. As Danowski and Viveiros de Castro (2017) have observed, and as already mentioned by Amaral, Amazonian peoples conceive of several endings of the world, possibly consecutive; but in all of them humanity, although transformed, is re-instated. There is not, the authors note, a world without people.

I am interested in a specific problem concerning extinction. For scholars studying the environmental crisis, the drastic reduction in numbers or even the extinction of animal and plant species – measured in the temporal form of a 'counting down' (Muelhmann 2012) – are important signs of the catastrophe in progress, which is heading to hit human populations with equal intensity. In her Introduction, Strathern mentions the Euro-American climate watchers' 'scales and degrees of termination' as instances of their progressive sense of time, which do not seem to fit well among peoples for whom time is episodic and reversible. What do Amerindian peoples think about this? In the myths I referred to above about the extinction of humanity, the disappearance of animals does not pose a problem and is generally not even mentioned. It is understood that they disappeared together with humans, if only because in several cases humans and animals were not yet different from each other, but still constituted a common humanity whose forms were unstable and alternating.

Wari' mythology offers us an interesting perspective on the possibility of animal extinction that does not involve the disappearance of humans. One of the myths takes as its starting point the culinary treatment of a deer that, contrary to the rules of food preparation, was roasted instead of boiled. The next day, when the people woke up, they no longer heard any sounds of animals, even in the forest. All the animals had disappeared. After a while of missing meat, the Wari' heard the characteristic sounds of a different animal species coming from the bottom of a lake. They decided to invite the animals to drink fermented maize beer. These animals then rose to the surface and, when they were drunk, were killed by the Wari'. Although the myth does not mention if those specific animals regenerated, as happens in recent times when they were hunted and eaten, it does say that the animals have subsequently returned to the forest.

Still on the theme of the extinction of what we understand as 'natural resources', another Wari' myth talks about the disappearance of water. A man who felt offended by his brother left, taking all the water from the river with him. Without water, people despaired, especially menstruating women and women who had recently given birth, who could not wash themselves to get rid of the blood and therefore risked being eaten by jaguars attracted by the smell. In the end the offending brother goes after his sibling and offers him his wife, who had been the reason for the quarrel. In return he receives back the water, which arrives with a great storm.

The extinctions are all sudden and caused by relational failures, as is to be expected for peoples where there is no idea of 'nature'. As they arise from relational problems, whether with animals endowed with agency and thought or between humans themselves, extinctions are likely to be reversed through acts that restore the broken relationships.

The lack of interest in any kind of totalization is striking in these narratives. The events are narrated as if they had happened in specific places and there is no mention of their extension or effects in other regions. In the case of the disappearance of the water, the parents of the quarrelling pair received a vat of water from the offended son the day before the event, with an indication that they should take good care of it because the next day no one would have any more. They were also warned by their son that they should not give the water to anyone, not even their grandchildren. Thus, although the suffering of people without water or without animals to hunt is conceived, these disappearances are not the central plot of the narratives, which revolve around moral issues and attempts at resolution.

But what happens nowadays, with actual experience of the scarcity of animals and even water? Is there a possible translation through myth? Evidently, the presence of white people and their destructive potential comes into play and is often incorporated into mythical logic (Lévi-Strauss 1970–81), as in the elaborate interpretation of the Yanomami shaman Davi Kopenawa (Kopenawa and Albert 2013). Moral deficiency is attributed to the whites, exempting the Indigenous people from responsibility. Concomitant with this mode of apprehension of current events, however, a type of apprehension seems to me to persist that is more directly related to the myths I've mentioned. The Wari' say, for example, that the animals no longer come near the villages because, with the conversion to Christianity and the end of shamanism, people are no longer able to relate socially to them. As a consequence, the animals have simply become uninterested in them and no longer approach the villages. I also suppose, although I have not heard this from anyone, that the fact that the dead now go to heaven and remain there, instead of being transformed into animals as happened before, has some relation to the scarcity of game; after all, once the dead longingly approached the living and, as mere game, were killed and eaten by them. An important point is that for the Wari' animals were immortal. Once preyed upon and properly prepared, they revived and returned home to the bosom of their family without any memory of the predation. Until they were hunted and eaten again.

The temporal existence of different non-human collectives is inseparable from a specific notion of humanity and personhood. When interviewing an indigenous leader from another ethnic group, who had witnessed the destruction of aquatic life due to illegal mining waste in his territory, I asked him if the disappearing fish were dead from poisons. This indigenous activist, who is also a shaman, surprised me with his answer: the absence of fish in the rivers was due to the fact that they were turning into mammals and birds and going up to the land. Apparently, they follow the instructions of the mother of the fish, who lives in a waterfall that is affected by mining, and acts with the intention of protecting her children.

Thus, if these Indigenous peoples are clearly capable, from their current experience, of projecting a horizon that is very similar to that projected by whites – that is, of scarcity and extinction – they are also capable of accessing different causalities in a concomitant and alternate manner, without interest in a single explanation. At one moment the focus turns to the destructive agency of white people themselves, beings that various peoples do not consider to be properly human; and at another moment to the direct agency of animals – or their masters and mistresses – dissatisfied with their relations with humans. Given that they derive from relational problems, catastrophes are potentially reversible; all that is required is an agreement between the parties involved. Considering that the disappearance of beings does not occur through definitive death, but through geographical and relational distance, their return does not occur gradually, through repopulation, but rather suddenly and in its entirety.

To conclude, there is one last question to be asked, which is whether there would be a possible approximation between this Indigenous conception of what we would call 'environmental disasters' and the Euro-American environmentalist conceptions of human misdeeds as the main cause of environmental changes, objectified in the notions of the Anthropocene or Capitalocene. Instead of conceiving extinction as arising from the death of passive and submissive beings, for these environmentalists the causes could be situated in the sphere of morality, as they are attributed to people with 'environmental indifference'. There seems to me to be, however, an important difference between these different attributions of morality: among Indigenous peoples what we call nature is composed of social collectives with their own agency, with which inter-human relations are established. These collectives are not passive support for the bad actions of Indigenous people, as they consciously react with retaliation – as is the case of the animals that hid in the water, among the Wari'; or the mother of the fish that sent them to live on the land, among the Munduruku. Among urban Euro-Americans, however, nature appears as a properly biological and to some extent passive support of moral misdeeds. Environmental transformations, in the form of extinctions, are not seen as revenge carried out by collectives with a social and moral life, but as more or less complex biological processes (as in the 'Gaia' concept used by contemporary philosophers, among them Latour). This is exactly what the Yanomami shaman Davi Kopenawa says about these different conceptions: white people think they are destroying what they call the 'environment', but it is in fact the *hutukara*, the 'forest', which is made up of beings with which one can interact in a properly social way. What disappears here is the idea of the domination of man over nature, sedimented in the biblical Genesis, which is replaced by relationships where the agentive capacities are equivalent

As shown by the various authors who have collaborated in this collection, what becomes evident here is that the apprehensions of the same context of crisis and rupture may be very diverse, and that the ethnographic horizon of the researcher is significant for the type of understanding to which the researcher has access.

Acknowledgements

The author would like to thank the editors Marilyn Strathern and Tony Crook for their careful reading of the text, and the other authors and participants in the Balzan project for their lively discussions. Field research among the Wari' was funded by CNPq, Faperj, the Wenner-Gren Foundation and the Guggenheim Foundation, with the support of the Museu Nacional of the Universidade Federal do Rio de Janeiro.

References

Amaral, V. Forthcoming. *Areruya and Indigenous Prophetism in Northern Amazonia.* London: Bloomsbury.

Barker, J. 1992. 'Christianity in western Melanesian ethnography'. In J. Carrier (ed.), *History and Tradition in Melanesian Anthropology*, pp. 145–73. Berkeley: University of California Press.

——— 1993. 'We are Ekelesia': conversion in Uiaku, Papua New Guinea'. In R. Hefner (ed.), *Conversion to Christianity. Historical and Anthropological Perspectives on a Great Transformation*, pp. 199–230. Berkeley: University of California Press.

———— 2010. 'The varieties of Melanesian Christian experience: a comment on
    Mosko's "partible penitents"', *Journal of the Royal Anthropological Institute*
    (NS) 16:247–9.

Cannell, F. (ed.) 2006. *The Anthropology of Christianity*. Durham: Duke University
    Press.

Carneiro da Cunha, M. 2009. 'Lógica do mito e da ação: o movimento messiânico
    canela de 1963'. In M. Carneiro da Cunha (ed.), *Cultura com Aspas*, pp.
    15–49. São Paulo: Cosac Naify.

Carneiro da Cunha, M. and Viveiros de Castro, E. 2009. 'Vingança e temporalidade:
    os Tupinambás'. In M. Carneiro da Cunha (ed.), *Cultura com Aspas*, pp.
    77–99. São Paulo: Cosac Naify.

Danowski, D. and Viveiros de Castro, E. 2017. *Há Mundo por Vir? Ensaios Sobre os
    Medos e os Fins*. São Paulo: ISA

Gregor, T. and Tuzin, D. (eds) 2001. *Gender in Amazonia and Melanesia: An
    Exploration of the Comparative Method*. Berkeley: University of California
    Press.

Handman, C. 2015. *Critical Christianity. Translation and Denominational Conflict in
    Papua New Guinea*. Berkeley: University of California Press.

Hirsch, E. 1994. 'Between mission and market: events and images in a Melanesian
    society', *Man* (NS) 29:689–711.

———— 2008. 'God or *Tidibe*? Melanesian Christianity and the problem of wholes',
    Ethnos 73(2):141–62.

Kelly, J.A. 2005. 'Fracticality and the exchange of perspectives'. In M. Mosko and F.
    Damon (eds), *On the Order of Chaos: Social Anthropology and the Science
    of Chaos*, pp. 108–35. New York: Berghahn.

———— 2011. *State Healthcare and Yanomami Transformations: A Symmetrical
    Ethnography*. Tucson: The University of Arizona Press.

Kopenawa, D. and Albert, B. 2013. *The Falling Sky. Words of a Yanomani Shaman* (tr.
    N. Elliott and A. Dundy). Cambridge, MA: Harvard University Press.

Lattas, A. 1998. *Cultures of Secrecy. Reinventing Race in Bush Kaliai Cargo Cults*.
    Wisconsin: The University of Wisconsin Press.

Leite, T. 2013. 'Imagens da humanidade: metamorfose e moralidade na mitologia
    Yanomami', *Mana. Estudos de Antropologia Social* 19(1):69–97.

———— 2016. 'Ninam (Yanomami) e missionários cristãos no alto Mucajaí (RR):
    modos de alteração', PhD Thesis. Rio de Janeiro: Programa de Pós-
    Graduação em Antropologia Social, Museu Nacional, Universidade Federal
    do Rio de Janeiro.

Lévi-Strauss, C. 1970–81. *Introduction to the Science of Mythology* (4 vols.; tr. J. and D.
    Weightman). London: Jonathan Cape.

Lloyd, G.E.R. 2003. *In the Grip of Disease: Studies in the Greek Imagination*. Oxford:
    Oxford University Press.

Mendes Jr., R. 2021. *A Terra Sem Mal. Uma Saga Guarani.* Rio de Janeiro: Editora UFRJ.

Mosko, M. 2010. 'Partible penitents: dividual personhood and Christian practice in Melanesia and the West', *Journal of the Royal Anthropological Institute* (NS) 16:215–40.

Muehlmann, S. 2012. 'Rhizomes and other uncountables: the malaise of enumeration in Mexico's Colorado River delta', *American Ethnologist* 39(2):339–53.

Pissolato, E. 2007. *A Duração da Pessoa. Mobilidade, Parentesco e Xamanismo Mbya (Guarani).* São Paulo: Instituto Socioambiental, Editora Unesp, NuTI.

Robbins, J. 2004. *Becoming Sinners. Christianity and Moral Torment in a Papua New Guinea Society.* Berkeley: University of California Press.

Silva, E. 2010. *Folhas ao Vento: A Micromobilidade de Grupos Mbya e Nhandéva (Guarani) na Tríplice Fronteira.* Cascavel: Edunioeste.

Strathern, M. 1988. *The Gender of the Gift: Problems with Women and Problems with Society in Melanesia.* Berkeley: University of California Press.

———— 1999. *Property, Substance and Effect: Anthropological Essays on Persons and Things.* London: The Athlone Press.

——— 2019. 'Regeneration and its hazards: a commentary on our times'. Paper presented at the workshop 'Time and the ethnographic horizon in moments of crisis', St Andrews, 26–29 November 2019.

Valentino, L. 2019. 'As transformações da pessoa entre os Katwena e os Tunayana dos rios Mapuera e Trombetas', PhD Thesis. Rio de Janeiro: Programa de Pós-Graduação em Antropologia Social, Museu Nacional, Universidade Federal do Rio de Janeiro.

Vilaça, A. 2011. 'Dividuality in Amazonia: God, the devil and the constitution of personhood in Wari' Christianity', *Journal of the Royal Anthropological Institute* (NS) 17(2):243–62.

——— 2013. 'Reconfiguring humanity in Amazonia: Christianity and change'. In J. Boddy and M. Lambek (eds), *A Companion to the Anthropology of Religion*, 363–86. London: Wiley Blackwell.

——— 2016. *Praying and Preying: Christianity in Indigenous Amazonia.* Berkeley: University of California Press.

Viveiros de Castro, E. 1998. 'Cosmological deixis and Amerindian perspectivism', *Journal of the Royal Anthropological Institute* (NS) 4(3):469–88.

——— 2002. 'Atualização e contra-efetuação do virtual: o processo do parentesco'. In *A Inconstância da Alma Selvagem e Outros Ensaios de Antropologia,* pp. 401–56. São Paulo: Cosac Naify.

——— 2004. 'Perspectival anthropology and the method of controlled equivocation', *Tipití* 2(1):3–22.

——— 2014. *Cannibal Metaphysics* (tr. P. Skafish). Minneapolis: Univocal Publishing.

Wagner, R. 1975. *The Invention of Culture.* New Jersey: Prentice-Hall.

Epilogue

Sisters on doom and gloom

A dialogue about horizons

ANDREW MOUTU

✺

Kandara: Are you hungry? Have you had dinner?

Chapara: You look weak and frail.

Kandara: I know. I have been thinking a lot, since the news came out
of that little girl who died because she was refused access to medical
treatment at the hospital because of Covid-19.

Kandara: It's just so spiteful and depressing under the current circumstances.

Chapara: I don't want to turn the Blackswan guards at the entrance to the
hospital into the objects of my spite.

Kandara: When insanity and inanity combine, what is their combined effect?

Chapara: The looming fear and uncertainty of Covid-19 becomes darkened
with gloom and doom.

Kandara: Yes, indeed, but that is to give too much of a consolation to
pessimism.

Chapara: It mortifies our thoughts and expectations of a future.

Kandara: It is a future that is to be lived for and lived with the doom and
gloom of Covid-19 in our midst.

Chapara: Sounds like you are in cynical and lyrical mood simultaneously!

Kandara: You get the drift of the looming gloom and doom.

Chapara: The lyrical rhyme! What counts for their difference?

Kandara: With doom ahead of us, it means things will not be good, but
eventually it will come to an end.

Chapara: So doom is a horizon our fatality is drawn towards?

Kandara: Yes, it's like a moment when our humanity drifts towards what it is
not!

Chapara: And the gloom?

Kandara: Gloom is like the atmosphere, the weather patterns that precipitate into doom, if you like.

Chapara: You make me think of the recent overcasts of Port Moresby in the last two weeks.

Kandara. I know. If you were up early in the morning, you will have seen the haze and the mist that were hovering over Moresby.

Chapara: That's what I meant. Gloom is climatological. It is hazy, blocked by an overcast with misty and lethargic fogs that are too lazy to lift off for a clearer view of the skies, especially after dawn has lifted the curtains of the night.

Chapara: Gloom evaporates slowly.

Kandara: Gloom and doom are mirror inversions of each other's thought patterns.

Chapara: How so?

Kandara: Gloom is futile and doom is fatal.

Chapara: The rhyme comes up again in a lyrical chiasma.

Kandara: Yes, doom is marked with a temporality that draws to an end. Gloom is a drag marked with austere silence and stillness. Imagine the thoughts that preoccupy those moments!

Chapara: So doom is to death as gloom is to the horror of stasis and civil strife?

Kandara: Yes, if we can approach life in the new normal with the pessimism of doom and gloom!

Chapara: Sure, but your metaphors of climatology make the doom and gloom of pessimism appear as a matter of observation.

Kandara: That's true too but it is also a matter of predilection. Sometimes one is contained in the other!

I had been thinking about ideas on the horizon, especially the kind of colour or texture that comes to such ideas. This short dialogue was written in June 2021 at the height of Covid-19.

Contributors

Virgínia Amaral obtained her Ph.D. (2019) in Social Anthropology at the Museu Nacional of Universidade Federal do Rio de Janeiro (Brazil). She currently works at the same institution (at LARMe and LInA research centres) as a postdoctoral researcher, with funding from the National Council for Scientific and Technological Development (CNPq - Brazil). Between 2019 and 2022, she was a Balzan Postdoctoral Research Fellow at the Centre for Pacific Studies at the University of St Andrews. Since 2012, she has been studying prophetisms and conceptions of crisis and temporality of the Ingarikó Indigenous people of northern Amazonia.

Tony Crook directs the Centre for Pacific Studies at the University of St Andrews. He began fieldwork in the Min area of Papua New Guinea in 1990, completing his Ph.D. at Cambridge in 1997, and publishing his monograph, *Exchanging Skin* in 2007. Alongside analysing the epistemological problems anthropology created for itself in the 'Min problem', the practical problems created by Euro-Australian mis-readings of Pacific life-worlds have featured in writings and policy work on mining and resource extraction; on gender violence in 'Understanding Gender Inequality Actions in the Pacific' (2016); and on the climate crisis in *Pacific Climate Cultures* (2018).

Bruno Nogueira Guimarães obtained his Ph.D. in Social Anthropology in 2017 at the Museu Nacional (UFRJ, Brazil). In his ethnographic research among the Apanjekra people in Brazil, he studied the Indigenous people's relations with settler colonialists, focusing on the effects of cash-transfer policies (such as the Bolsa Família Programme). Since then, Guimarães has taken part in different efforts to investigate the design of public policies on Indigenous peoples in Brazil, also observing their application on a national scale, having published articles on the production of Indigenous demographic statistics that inform these policies. As a Balzan Fellow, he was interested in exploring how Apanjekra notions of crisis, agency and change shape their experience with cash-transfer programmes.

Simon Kenema is a Papua New Guinean anthropologist. He obtained his Master of Research (MRes) qualification in 2009 followed by a Ph.D. in Social Anthropology from the University of St Andrews in 2015. His academic and research interests include political conflict and politics of landownership in the context of natural-resource development. He has over 15 years of practical work and academic research experience in natural-resource development in

PNG. In addition, Simon has undertaken various consulting roles – United Nations Population Fund (PNG Office); University of Queensland's Centre for Social Responsibility in Mining – and is currently employed by the World Bank as a Social Development Specialist.

Andrew Moutu (Ph.D. Cambridge 2003) began working at the Papua New Guinea National Museum and Art Gallery in 1996, and returned as Curator in 2003 following his studies in Cambridge. From 2004–10 he held postdoctoral fellowships from the British Academy and the Royal Anthropological Institute, followed by a Lectureship at the University of Adelaide. His monograph *Names Are Thicker Than Blood* was published in 2013. He served as Director of the PNG National Museum for two terms, from 2012–16 and 2018–22. He oversaw its regeneration and expansion through exhibitions, outreach and international partnerships.

Priscila Santos da Costa is a former Balzan Fellow and Assistant Professor at the IT University of Copenhagen. She is a social scientist with a Ph.D. in Social Anthropology from the University of St. Andrews. Priscila has conducted fieldwork in the Parliament of Papua New Guinea in Port Moresby, where her research focused on the state, bureaucracy, and Christianity. Since then, Santos da Costa has been undertaking an ethnographic project on the sociocultural dimensions of new technologies in efforts to develop the Brazilian Amazon.

Marilyn Strathern (Ph.D. Cambridge 1968) had the good fortune to begin her research career in Papua New Guinea, working on law, kinship and gender relations. She subsequently became involved with anthropological approaches to the new reproductive technologies, intellectual property and audit cultures. Her best known comparativist forays are *The Gender of the Gift* (1988) and *Partial Connections* (1991). Her latest book is *Relations: An Anthropological Account* (2020). She is Emeritus Professor of Social Anthropology at Cambridge and Life Fellow of Girton College.

Aparecida Vilaça (Ph.D. 1996) is Professor at the Graduate Program in Social Anthropology at the Museu Nacional of the Universidade Federal do Rio de Janeiro. For nearly forty years she has been working with the Wari', an Indigenous people from Rondônia, Brazil. She is the author of *Strange Enemies: Indigenous Agency and Scenes of Encounter in Amazonia* (2010), *Praying and Preying: Christianity in Indigenous Amazonia* (2016) and *Paletó and Me: Memories of my Indigenous Father* (2021).

INDEX

www.ingramcontent.com/pod-product-compliance
Lightning Source LLC
Chambersburg PA
CBHW052008270326
41929CB00015B/2839